HOLLYWOOD AT WAR

OTHER BOOKS BY THE AUTHORS

Dr. McClure is the author of *The Truman Administration and the Problems of Postwar Labor* and *The Versatiles,* with Alfred E. Twomey; Dr. McClure is the editor of the anthology *The Movies: An American Idiom.*

Mr. Jones and Dr. McClure, together with Mr. Twomey, are the authors of *The Films of James Stewart.*

Mr. Jones and Dr. McClure are the authors of *Heroes, Heavies and Sage-brush.*

HOLLYWOOD AT WAR

The American Motion Picture and World War II

Ken D. Jones and Arthur F. McClure

SOUTH BRUNSWICK AND NEW YORK: A. S. BARNES AND COMPANY
LONDON: THOMAS YOSELOFF LTD

A. S. Barnes and Co., Inc.
Cranbury, New Jersey 08512

Thomas Yoseloff Ltd
108 New Bond Street
London W1Y OQX, England

Library of Congress Cataloging in Publication Data

Jones, Ken D.
    Hollywood at war.

    Bibliography: p.
    1. Moving-pictures—United States—History.
2. Moving-pictures—Plots, themes, etc—War.
I. McClure, Arthur F., joint author. II. Title.
    PN1993.5.U6J6   791.43'7   70–37828
    ISBN 0-498-01107-0

The Introductory Essay originally appeared in
abridged form in *The Journal of Popular Film,*
volume I, number 2.

Printed in the United States of America

For

Mr. and Mrs. Cliff G. Jones
who made it possible for
their son to see the films herein

and

Jim McClure

A young boy who joined John Wayne and Errol
Flynn in the final destruction of the Axis tyranny—
and all the while loyally assisted by his little
brother.

CONTENTS

FOREWORD

Motion pictures made prior to and during World War II each had their own meaning and usefulness to audiences. Their comic, tragic, educational, and informational aspects all contributed to an understanding of the war. From the first, strange as it may seem, there were many comic elements in the war. The comedy was inherent not only on the battlefront and in the training camps, but at home as well. We were all a part of the war, young and old alike, and we grew to appreciate our common goal of final victory. The movies were an important part of this communion. The reason may well be because as Americans we had a side to our makeup that could see something funny in a tragic period. This, perhaps, was unique to America and Americans.

The tragic needs no explanation. We all felt it and went on.

As far as the educational value of movies during the war, I might have better used the word informational. We were widely separated from our families, neighbors, and even our nationality groups. From these motion pictures we sometimes learned, as the saying goes, "how the other half lives." We also learned about the traditions, problems, joys, and bitter disappointments of a wartime effort.

I'm proud of the motion picture industry for the job it did, although it sometimes exaggerated, overplayed, or underplayed real-life situations. But every film had a small part in forming our attitude and incentive toward accomplishing victory. Not all of the fighting was done with guns. The fantasies of film were an important morale factor. I happened to have been lucky enough to have been in my life both an actor and a military man. Therefore, I appreciate this history of the war movie written in the popular culture vein. Hopefully it will make its contribution not only to the history of the American motion picture, but to the history of American life.

TIM HOLT
Harrah, Oklahoma
June 1972

PREFACE

This volume makes a special effort to describe the unique qualities of American motion pictures and how they were affected by World War II. On the one hand, these films shared the common characteristic of the war itself, but on the other hand, each film represents a selective facet of the war experience. In that spirit, we have attempted to choose a representative sampling of films to show the relative importance of different aspects of Hollywood's war experience in feature films. The more than 400 films chosen are not meant to be all-inclusive, but more to provide a sort of multi-faceted synthesis. We are, then, because of boyhood movie memories, more the informed participants than mere observers. We are students sharing with other students the results of our investigations of a crucial phase of American motion picture history. As we see it, these movies left a lasting imprint—some of it good and some of it bad—upon the very fabric of American cultural life.

This book would never have come about without the encouraging help of many people. Charles Smith generously extended his help in the search for photographic material.

But while we are very grateful to many people, we are most grateful to our wives, Nancy Jones and Judy McClure, who know all of the reasons why.

HOLLYWOOD AT WAR

INTRODUCTORY ESSAY

The American war movie was probably more important as an historical phenomenon than as an artistic achievement. The films of the period revealed a great deal about American culture not only during the war years but in the years that followed. War movies revealed not only a rather desperate affirmation of the war but an excellent view of the societal tensions of the day. Because it was fought far from American shores, World War II resolved itself into the military effort abroad and the war effort at home. And movies had an importance that was twofold; to give unity of purpose for the war itself, and to give strength of purpose to the people on the home front. Films that dealt with the war tried in their own way to define the objectives of the war and the way in which these objectives were to be achieved. They also sought to show somehow why it was necessary to make such sacrifices. Many feature films ended with appeals for audiences to enlist in the armed forces, and many Hollywood stars made an even more personal appeal by criss-crossing the country on countless bond tours.

Viewing these films today can be a source of consolation amidst the cruelness of the contemporary world. Staughton Lynd, a noted historian, maintains that the first duty of his profession "is the sensitive chronicling in depth of the important events of his own lifetime." American war films, at least the ardent viewing of them, both the good and the bad ones, represent an important facet in the lives of many of those who were regular movie-goers during the turbulence of the late 1930s and 1940s. Despite their distortions, these films represent all kinds of good things in what has been termed "the history of the inarticulate." Obviously, most people are not professional historians; nor do most people leave much of a written record of any sort.

The popularity of the war films is enduring. People flocked to the theaters to see them when they first appeared, and today they gather around their TV sets to enjoy them again. In the confusion over the war in Vietnam, these old movies represent a neater historical period in which the forces of good always prevailed over the dark shadows of evil. Historians have always been fascinated with the role of leaders. The war movies and their audiences, however, are a part of the social development of 1940s America in that they represent a restructuring of its history from the standpoint of the lives and aspirations of the people "at the bottom." These movies are thus an important part of the American history of the inarticulate.

Jesse Lemisch, one of the leading young historians of the inarticulate, accepts the importance of the "accidental and the irrational in human affairs" as well as the importance of the character and condition of the "dumb masses." If John Wayne was vastly popular during World War II, why then is he still such a hero to all generations of Americans, considering that our society has become more sophisticated in every sense in the quarter century since the close of the war?

Part of the answer is the sentimental nature of nostalgia. Cultural traditions do have an ambivalence, but everyone would like to know where he came from because when one does "it's less lonely" to face life in the present. The nostalgia of World War II can have a lulling effect. It can distort images and reinforce prejudices. But it can also recall an individualism which seems no longer to exist in today's complexities. Most scientific studies indicate that movies do not change fundamental ideas but that they do encourage audiences to think. When an individual, temporarily isolated from society, sits in a darkened theater and questions his preconceptions, this is in many instances a very productive activity—even though it is seldom a distinct one to historians and other observers.

Historian Charles Alexander has written of the war films that "absorbed and diffused the experience of war, but received little inspiration from it. Just as Hollywood had eluded most of the realities of Depression America, so it refused to deal honestly with the realities of America at war." Not unexpectedly then, although some of the war pictures were of a high quality many of them were poor—of the "hiss-and-boo" variety. The latter were justly criticized for their lack of realism and plausibility.

Approximately one-third of all Hollywood feature films produced between 1942 and 1945 (approximately 500 of 1700) could be termed "war movies." War movies provided a stimulation that was peculiar to them alone: First, they quenched the tremendous public thirst for information about the war; second, they improved the morale of home front audiences by depicting their husbands and sons in action. This fact can explain why, early in the war, the government offered to cooperate with Hollywood in the production of war films. Various governmental agencies including the War Department, Navy Department and Office of War Information gave the studios technical advice as well as more tangible forms of help. Military personnel and equipment were often used in Hollywood war films, which accounts for the unprecedented scope of many of them. Early in the war the United States government became very interested in the political and social significance of the contents of feature motion pictures. The Media Division, Bureau of Intelligence, Office of War Information was created and began issuing weekly summaries and analyses of feature films in October 1942. Judgments were made concerning the favorable portrayal of life in the United States, its ideals and institutions; the portrayal of Latin American customs and cultural life; the

treatment of the war, the issues, the enemy, our allies, the prospects for victory, and the character of our armed forces.

After the 1940 presidential election, Joseph P. Kennedy, the Boston millionaire businessman and our nation's ambassador to Great Britain, continued to warn the American public against entering the war. In November he visited Hollywood and at a private dinner meeting lectured leaders of the motion picture industry. He insisted that the production of anti-Nazi films must stop because we would have to make peace with Hitler since the fall of England was inevitable. Kennedy noted that many industry leaders were Jewish and allegedly suggested that their fate might eventually be as tragic as that of European Jews if they were not more careful in their pro-Allied film treatments. Despite the controversy that raged over Kennedy's statements, there is some historical evidence that points to a strong interventionist sentiment among movie makers. Producer Walter Wanger, a Jew, who believed strongly in the informational value of movies for the public, was a strong advocate for the cause of intervention and served as a speaker and fund-raiser with the industry. In June 1938, Wanger had produced *Blockade,* a picture that dealt with the Spanish Civil War although the film did not identify the opposing forces. Though it was a mild film, plainly sympathetic to the Loyalists, it created a furor. Picketed in some cities and banned in others, it was not a box office success.

Amidst the public debate upon the effects of Hollywood pro-Allied movies there were various congressional figures involved in investigations of the industry. Among the most prominent were Senators Gerald T. Nye and Burton K. Wheeler. Charges and counter charges were leveled that the Roosevelt administration brought pressure upon moviemakers to produce anti-Fascist, anti-pacifist, and interventionist motion pictures.

In the spring of 1939 appeared *Confessions of a Nazi Spy.* This film was made by Warner Brothers in an effort to throw terror into the life of Americans by its look at Nazi sabotage and propaganda activity within the United States. The film was based on an actual German spy ring that was exposed by Leon G. Turron, a former FBI investigator, in New York in 1938. To make the film more effective, newsreel shots of Hitler were interspersed with the spy story. The thesis was that the

German-American Bund was a disloyal organization, run by the Nazis to overthrow the American government, and thus the group should be wiped out. Even though this film was made before the actual involvement of the United States in the shooting war, the American public was made to feel in many respects that this country was already at war. Many criticized the film for its propaganda techniques as an anti-isolationist challenge.

In 1939 Charlie Chaplin made a powerful plea for peace and unity against the fascists through his film *The Great Dictator,* which he wrote, produced, directed, and starred in. It was a satirical look at fascism, which took place in the fictitious country of Ptomania. Chaplin used this film as part of his personal campaign to illustrate the mistreatment of German Jews.

The first motion picture to actually name Hitler was a depressing one about a German community, *Mortal Storm.* The film opens with a scene set in 1933 showing the good things which Americans love and respect in Germans—industriousness, honor, and close family ties. When two sons join the National Socialist Party, the forces of evil begin to grow stronger. The father goes to a concentration camp and the good things of German life cease. This film, however, was one of the few which said that not all Germans were Nazis and therefore bad. There was a tone of hopefulness for Germany offered to audiences when one character relates that "the real Germany will rise again."

Another film made in 1944 with a similar theme was the *Seventh Cross,* which starred Spencer Tracy. Seven men, having escaped from a concentration camp near Mainz, Germany, in 1936, are all eventually captured except one. George Heisler, portrayed by Tracy, is bitter, tortured, in low spirits, and trusts no one. He becomes a desperate man after his former girl friend throws him out for fear of going to prison herself. The other six are captured and hanged from six trees which have been stripped, and thus give the viewer a feeling of the Crucifixion of Christ. Only the seventh tree remains empty waiting for its victim. As the seventh man flees, he meets anti-Nazis who try to convince him that not all Germans are like the Nazis and that there is a God-given decency in men that eventually will emerge.

With the actual participation of the United States in the war the movies produced in Hollywood became less subtle. Many films were conceived in praise of a branch of the armed forces, such as *The Story of G. I. Joe, Dive Bomber, So Proudly We Hail,* and *Flying Tigers.* Others were half-fictional accounts of actual battles, such as *Thirty Seconds Over Tokyo, Destination Tokyo, Guadalcanal Diary,* and *Wake Island.* Still others attempted to show the resistance of the native populations in Europe to the Nazi conquerors. Examples of this type of film were *Paris Underground* and *North Star.* Representing another approach were films depicting the home front, which also had to make sacrifices. Foremost among this type were *Since You Went Away* and *Joe Smith, American.*

It did not matter what branch of the armed forces the film industry was interested in, the group was the center of interest. The crew, the company, the squadron were all acting together to emphasize oneness against the enemy, whether the Japanese or the Germans. One of the first films to glorify a particular branch of the Armed Forces was *Dive Bomber* (1941), a tribute to the United States Navy air section and the flight surgeons. Errol Flynn, as the surgeon, whose job is to keep pilots in the air, invents a flying suit and dies trying to perfect it. The film shows the research on fliers' blackout and high-altitude sickness with Fred MacMurray as the flight instructor teaching the surgeon the intricacies of flying.

Another group of men, the "Flying Tigers," received recognition in a movie of that title. John Wayne starred in this tribute to the American volunteer airmen who fought the Japanese in the air over China before Pearl Harbor. In this film there is the hero who is the squadron commander, the nurse, the rookie who gets killed, the old-timer who is grounded, the drunk, and the individualist who learns what the fight is about but not until he has destroyed the squad's morale, materials, and even human life. Wayne played the role of the commander who is the type of man that has the competence men expect in their leaders. The destruction and cruelty of the Japanese was shown by their bombing of an orphanage and wounding innocent children; however, there were no scenes that depicted the Flying Tigers bombing anything.

So Proudly, We Hail was the story of the army nurses escaping from the Philippines to Australia.

The lead, played by Claudette Colbert, shows the sacrifices of the women as well as the men in the armed forces. The film itself is a flashback of the nurses' harrowing escape from the Japanese invasion of the Philippine Islands. Another nurse, played by Veronica Lake, becomes embittered because her fiance is killed by the Japanese, and therefore devotes the rest of her life to killing the enemy. Sacrificing her life in order for the other nurses to get away, she takes a grenade and destroys herself among the Japanese. The Japanese are portrayed as ruthless killers, for which the Americans were unprepared, but both the Americans and the Filipinos show their bravery.

The Merchant Marine, though not usually thought of as a branch of the armed forces, but just as important to the war effort, received recognition in the film *Action in the North Atlantic,* which starred Humphrey Bogart and Raymond Massey. Not only did this film emphasize the heroic nature of the Merchant Marine, but also the importance of the Allies, and in particular the Soviet Union, desperately in need of supplies. In *Air Force,* to make sure that the audience saw the war in an "historical perspective," the film opens with the Gettysburg address followed by scenes or narration of Honolulu, Guam, Wake Island, Manila, General Douglas MacArthur, and President Roosevelt's "day that will live in infamy" speech with a view of Pearl Harbor in flames. The story is about the crew of a Boeing B-17 Flying Fortress with the good American name of "Mary Ann." As in *Action in the North Atlantic* and *Flying Tigers* the plot revolves around the group.

One of the best American films of World War II was *The Story of G. I. Joe,* based on the correspondence of writer Ernie Pyle, whose column appeared in more than three hundred newspapers. He was portrayed by Burgess Meredith. There were no other big stars in this film which depicted the boredom, weariness, fear, and hunger of ordinary fighting men. Less realistic was *The Fighting Seabees* starring John Wayne as a construction engineer named "Wedge" Donovan. This was the first film on this branch of the Navy and its purpose was to show the Seabees at work under combat conditions. The idea of the group came up again and again in such films as *Sahara, Bataan,* and *Purple Heart. Bataan* was a classic example of the company with cross-section personality types all banded together to fight the enemy to the last man. Robert Taylor played the sergeant whose platoon, comprised of inexperienced but willing troops, must cover the retreat by making sure that a bridge remains demolished. In this film the group included a conscientious objector as the medic, an adolescent "hepcat," a Filipino corporal, and a Negro who is studying for the ministry.

In *Sahara,* again the group as a whole was the center of interest. A small group of Americans, separated from their unit after the fall of Tobruk in June 1942, take off across the desert of Libya in a tank. They hold off and capture a battalion of Germans, meet some British stragglers, are joined by a Sudanese corporal and his Italian prisoner, and shoot down a Messerschmitt and capture the pilot. Humphrey Bogart played the American sergeant and J. Carrol Naish the Italian prisoner. The U.S. Army thought the picture worthy enough to allow soldiers training at Camp Young, California, to be used as extras.

The first film to be specially concerned with the treatment of American prisoners of war by the Japanese was *Purple Heart.* After the Doolittle raid on Japan, eight American fliers are forced to bail out and land in occupied China. Betrayed by a Chinese collaborator the fliers are put on trial for bombing hospitals and machine-gunning civilians. The trial is to show that the Japanese are terrified of the prospect of future raids and are thus using this as a way to calm their population and to throw fear into future raiders. The atrocities of the Japanese are not shown, but the effects are: mutilated hands in black gloves or destroyed vocal cords. The United States government in the early years of the war usually desired to have the atrocities of the enemy soft-pedalled, but in 1943 it urged Darryl Zanuck, producer of *The Purple Heart,* to finish his film as soon as possible.

There were many films that were concerned with the Doolittle raid over Japan. Two other films, which were more or less based on this actual happening, were *Destination Tokyo* and *Thirty Seconds Over Tokyo. Destination Tokyo* deals with the life of the submarine *USS Copperfin* and the men aboard it from Christmas Eve of 1942 until months later when the sub is dragged into San Francisco Bay. *Thirty Seconds Over Tokyo* was more of a documentary in tone. The film was taken from Ted Lawson's book of the same title and who was portrayed in the film by Van Johnson. The preparation, the tension, and the agony of the fliers was to show the home front an idealized view of what these fighting men went through in combat.

In *The Sullivans,* the film was not so much concerned with the action of the war as with the lives of the five Sullivan brothers before they enlisted in the U.S. Navy. The film focused on the feeling of family relationship, and the ties that bind the Sullivans to church, state, and each other. Like other films that saluted the various branches of the armed forces, this film was really a tribute to American parenthood.

Many films took their titles from scenes of battle. *Wake Island* and *Guadalcanal Diary* are of such a kind. Coming close to a factual account was *Wake Island* as it portrayed the defense of the island by the Marines between December 8 and 22, 1941. There was little humor in this picture as it showed the continual battering of the island by the Japanese. Even more emotional than *Wake Island* was *Guadalcanal · Diary.* A narrator describes the circumstances and the setting for the amphibious landing, and as with other films there was the usual group of men: Lloyd Nolan as the sergeant, William Bendix as the former taxi driver from Brooklyn, Richard Conte as the captain, Anthony Quinn as the courageous Arizona Indian, and Preston Foster as the Catholic priest who was loved by all of the men.

Few films dealt with the resistance of the native populations in Asia, but there were numerous ones on those in Europe. The heroic stand of the Russian peasants and their government was the theme of *Mission to Moscow, Song of Russia,* and *North Star.*

Mission to Moscow, based on former Ambassador Joseph E. Davies's book, stresses the importance of unity among the Allies, that there must be mutual understanding and confidence. This film caused more than the usual criticism given to a movie. Since Davies was representing the American government it was thought to have at least semi-official sanction. The film begins with a foreword delivered by former Ambassador Davies himself. The text of his statement indicates the lengths to which Hollywood went in order to present our Russian allies in a favorable light.

When I was your Ambassador in Russia, I little expected to write "Mission to Moscow," much less see it projected on the screen, but, when Germany attacked Russia, the Soviet Union became one of the Nations fighting Hitler, and it was a desperate hour.

If Hitler were to destroy the Red Armies and smash the Soviet Union, the three aggressor nations would dominate Europe, Asia, and Africa. The riches of these three continents and the enslaved labor of three quarters of the population of the World would be harnessed to conquer the rest of the earth.

The Americans would be next. Us! Unity among the forces fighting Hitler was vital; nothing as I saw it was more important than the fighting nations should understand and trust each other. There was so much prejudice and misunderstanding of the Soviet Union in which I partly shared, that I felt it was my duty to tell the truth about the Soviet Union, as I saw it, for such value as it might have.

If I were down there in the audience with you, there are certain things that I would want to know about the man who is telling the story, so that I could assess the reliability of his judgment and his bias, or his lack of bias. Those things about me you are entitled to know. I would want to know them if I were you. Well, they are very simple. My people were pioneers. They came to New Orleans in a sailing ship. I was born in Wisconsin, educated in the public schools, graduated from University of Wisconsin, and went to Washington as one of Woodrow Wilson's young men, and practiced law successfully in New York and Washington. My religious convictions are basic. My sainted mother was an ordained Minister of the gospel. I think that I am peculiarly the product of our great country, and its free institutions and opportunities in a competitive society of free enterprise, that is not only free but is fair and regulated.

I came up the hard way, and I am glad of it. I had a deep conviction and firm faith that that system and our form of Government is the best the world has yet produced for the common man, such as you and me.

I went to Russia with that conviction, and I returned from Russia with that conviction. But while I was in Russia, I came to have a very high respect for the honesty of the Soviet leaders. They respected the honesty of my conviction, and I respected theirs. I also came back with a firm conviction that these people were sincerely devoted to peace, and that what they and their leaders most desired was to live as good neighbors in a world at peace. That peace has not yet been won. If unity, mutual understanding, confidence in each other is necessary to win the War, it is still more necessary to win the Peace. For there can be no durable peace without an agreement among those nations that have won the war, that they will project that peace and maintain that peace and protect that peace. Without understanding, mutual understanding, confidence in each other, there will be no durable or secure peace, and if that should happen, then the dead in Flanders Fields, Guadalcanal, China, Dunkirk, Africa, the Ukraine, would not sleep, for we again would have broken faith with the dead, and the hope of humanity, dead and living, would once again be betrayed. That is why I wrote "Mission to Moscow." That is why I am deeply grateful to those patriotic citizens, the Warner Brothers, and to their great organization of dramatists, artists and technicians, who have projected this book upon the screen for you, my fellow citizens of the Americas, and for you, my fellow free men of the world. I thank you.

The film itself begins with Davies's assignment to Russia by President Roosevelt. Davies undertakes it with an open mind as to the Soviet Union. Ambassador Davies (Walter Huston), his wife (Ann Harding) and daughter, Emlen (Eleanor Parker), arrive in Moscow after a brief visit enroute to Berlin. In Moscow, Davies presents his credentials to President Kalinin (Vladimir Sokoloff). The latter expressed Russia's earnest desire for peace and urges the American ambassador to see all he can before arriving at any conclusions about Russia. Davies listens to all in Russia and visits much of its territory. Then come the historic purge trials where Davies is an interested spectator. Because of his long career as a trial lawyer, Davies believes each man told the truth.

In an effort to learn as much as possible about world events, Davies talks with diplomats, politicians and bankers in many European nations. At the close of his mission, Davies calls on President Kalinin and is startled when Joseph Stalin (Manart Kippen) strides into the room, asking for a personal talk with him. Stalin had never previously met an ambassador from any nation and the two men have a long frank talk, exchanging views and opinions. In America, Davies, who is convinced that Russia sincerely wants peace, tours the country pleading that Russia is the world's last rampart against fascism and, with U.S. help, Russia will hold that rampart.

After World War II, *Mission to Moscow* became one of the early targets of McCarthyistic charges that the film was the work of communists not only in the government but in the movie industry. It was true that the film gave a distorted view of Russian life as well as whitewashing its leaders. Indeed, historical facts were inaccurate in several instances. However, within the context of World War II tensions and as a rather crude attempt to sell Russia as an alley to the suspicious American public, the charge that the film was communist inspired was certainly overstated.

Another film that did not deal accurately with the common Russian people, except to show that they like music and are good fighters, was *Song of Russia*. After falling in love and marrying, the American composer, played by Robert Taylor, and his wife, Nadya, played by Susan Peters, learn of the Nazi menace. Nadya returns to her village, while John follows when he hears that the Germans are approaching Taschekouskoe. After helping with the scorched earth policy, the newlyweds learn that it is their duty to go to America. A film that dealt more with the people of the Soviet Union rather than the privileged was *North Star*. Using the life of one village, the film concentrated on those who are doing the fighting by defending their own homes.

One of the last films made about the resistance movement in 1945 was *Paris Underground*. *Paris Underground* was the story of two women who helped to smuggle three hundred Allied fliers out of Occupied France. The women are captured by the Germans, and are finally released from their prison camp in the summer of 1944, proving the bravery of the underground movement in Europe, and especially in France.

One of the best films of the war years was *Mrs. Miniver* with the unforgettable acting of Greer Garson and Walter Pidgeon. This film examined the social structure of middle-class England with its feeling for equality despite its past history of caste. *This Above All* also treated the problem of social class in England. The hero, Tyrone Power, is a young, disillusioned, lower-middle-class Englishman who wants to know why he should risk his life for the upper classes. England was a popular setting for other Hollywood movies such as *White Cliffs of Dover* and *Journey for Margaret.* Many had the plot of an American helping the English in their fight. This was especially true before the United States was directly involved in the war. *A Yank in the R.A.F.,* made in 1941, was frankly pro-British.

A number of films portrayed the frustration of life on the home front. One of the best was *Since You Went Away* with Claudette Colbert and Joseph Cotton. As a sort of panorama of the home front, this film covered everything from gas rationing to the sorrow of death, and portrayed all of it well and in good taste. While *Since You Went Away* was concerned with the life of a "typical" American family during war time, *Joe Smith, American* dealt with an important part of American war production, the production of armaments. Joe Smith, a typical American name, played by Robert Young, is an ordinary mechanic working for the Atlas Aircraft Corporation, when he is asked to install a new bombsight. At this point he becomes of interest to enemy agents, who kidnap and torture him, in the hopes of getting information on this new weapon. Warning Americans of the activities of the fifth Columnists who appear as ordinary law-abiding citizens, was the subject of *Saboteur.* Another spy thriller was *House on 92nd Street,* but this time with the spy working for the Federal Bureau of Investigation.

An earlier film with more of an emotional impact was *Watch on the Rhine,* starring Bette Davis and Paul Lukas as Sara and Kurt Muller, who after seventeen years return to the United States. Kurt, who is wanted in Germany for being an underground agent, cannot understand America's luxury of freedom and isolation. This film was made in 1943 and was an attempt to clarify the meaning of fascism and why the United States must fight it.

Some films like *Casablanca* and *Foreign Correspondent* were spy thrillers with the war used as a setting. *Lifeboat* dealt with the survivors of a ship torpedoed by a German submarine. *Casablanca,* filmed in 1942 before that city was made famous by the meeting of Roosevelt and Churchill with the Free French General Charles deGaulle and General Henri Giraud, High Commissioner of French Africa, was the story of refugees trying to reach Lisbon. The suspense is heightened because of the mixture of the refugees, the Vichy French,

the Free French, and the Nazi hunters.

Two excellent films that were made during World War II had their setting in World War I, *Sergeant York* with Gary Cooper in 1941 and *Wilson* in 1944. *Sergeant York* may have been set in 1917, but the message was for the people of the wartorn 1940s. Alvin York, a man from the Tennessee hills, is pictured with honesty and simplicity. He is a hard working man who wants to own his own land, but is swindled. As he sets out to kill the man who cheated him, he is struck by lightning and miraculously becomes religious. When he is drafted, he does not wish to go because he now feels it is wrong to kill. He goes up into the mountains with his Bible and an American history book to evaluate his feelings and comes to the conclusion that American heritage must be protected. He decides that there are times when a man has no choice but to fight for his country, if only to prevent more killing. This film was termed by *Time* magazine as "Hollywood's first solid contribution to national defense."

In *Wilson,* Woodrow Wilson, one of our most complex presidents, is pictured as a man of dignity and sincerity. This film preached for world understanding and peace as Wilson did in an earlier time. Although little is said about the struggle in the United States over the League of Nations, the point is made that if this country had joined such an organization in 1919 there might not have been a World War II. The film completed the wartime process of reversing Wilson's unfavorable historical image. It was, according to Charles Alexander, "an interesting example of Hollywood's power to destroy one set of myths, only to replace them with another."

Not all of the war films during World War II were of a serious nature. There were numerous musicals and comedies. Abbott and Costello performed their antics in such films as *Buck Privates* and *In the Navy.* In the latter film, Dick Powell, a singing sensation, enlists in the Navy to get away from all his women admirers and meets, of course, Abbott and Costello. Another film, *See Here, Private Hargrove,* was a satirical look at army life. It starred Robert Walker as Hargrove and Keenan Wynn as his buddy Mulvehill. Hargrove is the naive farm boy, while Mulvehill is the chiseler and parasite that can be found in any army camp. Both finally land easy jobs in the army as public relations men. When the order comes for their old unit to be shipped overseas, they decide to go too. The point of the film was that even the most misfitted of men become good soldiers through the leveling influence of the Army.

Seldom did war films clarify any of the fundamental issues of the war or display our basic differences from the enemy in terms of ideals and philosophy. References to issues usually were generalities such as "the fight for freedom" or a "free world."

Some films presented aspects of the Nazi system and culture that pointed up the character of the Nazi regime. *Hitler's Children* was one of the first extended treatments of the Nazis produced by the movie industry. Dealing with the education of the German children, it showed the Nazis as glorifying war and militarism, distorting history, exacting obedience from Germans by force, and as brutal in their treatment of those opposed to them. They were pictured as completely anti-Christian. The civilian population was shown to be in terror of the secret police and as spying on each other and being spied upon. Education of German children was pictured as preparation for military service. Various forms of coercion were shown, the forced labor camps, the sterilization clinics for women of suspected political opinions, and barbarous forms of punishment for misdemeanors against the state. Though there was no treatment of the reasons for Nazism or the forces which brought about this movement, various aspects of Nazi practices and ideals were portrayed in a highly melodramatic form and as background to incidents in a love story.

In other films the stereotyped characterizations of the Nazis continued. In the "cop and agent" thrillers, the Nazis were shown as brutal killers. The usual pattern prevailed: A German headed the gang and his stooges were Italians and Japanese. The whole group bickered and fought among themselves and the mysterious female spy usually appeared.

In films representing the Nazis and the German Army, the usual representations held. Army officers were shown as impeccable aristocrats, cold, aloof, and efficient. The Gestapo men were clever and merciless but were outwitted in the end, frequently in some ludicrously impossible fashion. German civilians were shown as kindly, fat and

pleasant but dominated by the Nazis. German officers' wives swarmed through conquered Paris in search of French dresses for their dowdy and formless figures.

In war films, the Americans who worked for the Axis powers did so for money. There were usually two types, the petty gangster and the intelligent, upper class businessman. The gangsters were the typical "lugs" of the gangster and racketeer pictures of the 1930s. They did not hesitate to slug or shoot if necessary but they did not exhibit the cold ruthlessness with which the German and especially the Japanese spies were endowed. The upper class businessman who sold out bore some resemblance to the ostensibly honest "front" who ran the gang in the gangster pictures. He was usually an executive, known throughout the town and well-liked.

In a number of early war films the agents were not explicitly characterized as being of a given country. Their nationality was indefinite. In *Panama Hattie, Ship Ahoy, My Favorite Spy, Danger in the Pacific* and *Drums on the Congo* the foreign agents were Oriental or Germanic. The spies in *Panama Hattie* served as a final episode for the comedians. In the others the espionage theme was dominant in the plot but there was no effort at a development of the character of the spies. The leader of the enemy in *Danger in the Pacific* was fairly typical. He showed scorn for the American and British agents who tracked him down but the actual dirty work was done for the agent by a native. This film was similar in this respect to *Journey into Fear* and *Cairo*. The agent was motivated by patriotism, the native only by greed. In *Eyes in the Night* the plot development makes it almost impossible for the enemy to be anything but German, but they are never called German. In *Riders of the Northland* a U-boat commander is introduced in a nondescript uniform of no particular nation. In *Eyes in the Night* the coldly efficient woman who sacrifices all for her cause was again present. She was very similar to the German woman agent in *Adventures of Smilin' Jack* and *Madame Spy*. The U-boat commander in *Riders of the Northland* was cruel with the usual taut expression around his mouth, characteristic of so many German agents in the films. The typical picture that concerned Nazi espionage and sabotage inside the United States showed a group of foreign agents who worked under the direction of a skillful and brilliant leader. He planned their activities, directed their work and they in turn carried out his orders with military precision.

There was usually a clear distinction between the leader and his men. He commanded and they followed without question, blindly obedient. They differed in appearance also. The head agent was typically middle-aged, tall, well-dressed, "smooth" in manner and cultivated in speech. The woman agents, who in some films were the head agents of the organization, were generally cold and beautiful. They were definitely upper class and moved easily in social circles. In *Cairo* the woman agent was attractive, well-dressed and intelligent. The woman spy in *Madame Spy* was much the same. The leader, in addition, was often depicted as an intellectual, articulate in presenting his cause and obviously well above the average person in education and intelligence. Dr. Lorentz in *Across the Pacific*, was a professor of sociology and Haller, in *Journey into Fear*, was an archaeologist. The German agent in *Madame Spy* was introduced as he was studying butterflies and was later shown playing chess. In other pictures where there was no explicit evidence of the leader's intelligence, from his excellent diction and perfect English one could only conclude that he was a person of breeding and education. The men in almost any group of agents were, in some instances, Germanic in appearance: blond, heavy-set, and with rather expressionless features. Their representation differed from film to film.

The distinction between the leader and his men did not mirror clearly the distinction between the Prussians and the traditional south Germans, nor the distinction between the Nazi party and the German "people." But films of this genre did not appear to spring from such considerations. They resulted instead from the effect of modelling this type of picture on the older theme of the skilled, ostensibly honest private citizen, and the ruthless underworld gang which he secretly guides. The Nazi agent was shown as extremely clever in his plots, fanatically devoted to his country and its "philosophy" and absolutely ruthless in executing his plans. His men were also fanatically patriotic and ruthless in carrying out his orders.

In almost every picture showing Nazi agents working in this country, they had succeeded in setting up an elaborate organization within the United States for either the collection of information or the perpetration of sabotage, or both. This was especially noticeable in such films as *Counter Espionage, Enemy Agents Meet Ellery Queen, Cairo,* several Sherlock Holmes films, and *Careful, Soft Shoulders.* This organization was usually very elaborate and when the films opened it was working apparently without opposition. In some cases, some of the members of the spy organization turned out to be individuals in highly responsible positions. In two films, *The Great Impersonation* and *Sherlock Holmes and the Voice of Terror*, the heads of the Nazi rings were revealed as men in high posts in the British Government. The American government seldom suffered from such treason in high quarters. The only comparable incident was in *Pacific Rendezvous* in which a naval commander was shown as having a mistress who is a Nazi spy who is using him as a means of securing information.

The German soldiers were generally pictured as efficient, disciplined, and unswervingly patriotic. Morally, they were not depicted as delighting in cruelty. They did their work as soldiers very efficiently, as in *Eagle Squadron.* In *Eagle Squadron* the German military forces were not personalized. Only one incident gave them some distinction as human beings. After they shoot down a pilot they drop the wrist band and mascot kitten in a parachute over the British field. With these was a note which says they are sorry for the death of the Allied pilot and that the English are brave but foolish. In *Mrs. Miniver* the captured Nazi flyer delivers a short speech. He boasts of the bombings of Rotterdam, and Warsaw and warns the English woman that the same thing will happen to England. This young German is extremely unbending in his determination to escape, and refuses any aid, though he is faint from wounds and hunger.

Some pictures showed the German army and Gestapo concerned with the activities of our agents in Germany itself. These films included *Berlin Correspondent, Desperate Journey* and *Invisible Agent.* The general picture of German efficiency was not a favorable one. In two of them the Germans fail completely to stop the Americans and British in their sabotage and flight from Germany. In the third, *The Invisible Agent,* they fail too but with more plausibility. The German Gestapo is pictured as determined but competent. The heads are cruel and vain, but ineffectual. In *Berlin Correspondent* the newspaper reporter has no difficulty in outwitting the Gestapo in Berlin. The woman operator who is assigned the job of getting evidence on the American falls in love with him, the Gestapo captain who is handling the case is tricked by a change of clothing and a jealous ex-mistress. The captain is cruel, vain and apparently ruthless, but unsuccessful. The whole film shows Germans as bunglers and fools. They allow the American, for example, to get into an insane asylum for an interview with an inmate. The definite impression was given that a clever American could run around Germany impersonating high Nazi officials and accomplishing all sorts of feats. In *Desperate Journey,* with the same basic plot as the former film, five British airmen romp through Germany from one end to another, knocking out guards and officers and escaping in a plane.

The Japanese spy and saboteur usually had much the same general character as the Nazi. He was intensely patriotic and carried out orders in the performance of his duty with an implacable exactness. The leader of the gang displayed the same characteristics as do the Germans in his willingness to sacrifice his own men in carrying out a mission. In the serial *Junior G-Men of the Air* the leader of the Japanese acts in this way with no more compunction about the lives of his men than for the lives of the Americans. Their ruthlessness was clearly motivated by their patriotism. They usually sacrifice themselves as well as their men for the cause. This also occurred in *Let's Get Tough* and *Prisoner of Japan.*

In several films which showed the American defeated by Japanese soldiers and sailors, the Japanese methods of combat were given a distinctly dishonorable color. In *Manila Calling,* the Japanese were shown at their worst. The fighting was done in the jungle and the Japanese sniped from trees and bushes. They mutilated and tortured the Filipinos and poisoned drinking wells. In *Wake Island* the Japanese were seen shooting wounded men and bayoneting men who were prone and defenseless. In *Submarine Raider* there was a scene of a Japanese pilot attacking the lifeboat of a torpedoed ship, and the pilot was shown as laughing while he attacks the helpless crew. In a few films the policy and activities of the Japanese government were brought in and shown to be corrupt

and untrustworthy. There were numerous mentions of the treacherous attack at Pearl Harbor. In *Wake Island* the envoy, Kurusu, was shown as he pledges peace and toasts President Roosevelt while stopping at Wake Island on his way to Washington. The peace talk was contrasted with the violent attack shortly after. When the Japanese failed, he was often shown committing harikari. The films often treated this act as one for which the Japanese should be given credit, for when an individual fails to carry it out he is ridiculed, as in Lorenz in *Across the Pacific,* who cannot stomach this form of suicide.

There was one element in the pictures about Japanese espionage which was not present in those showing Nazis. This was the recognition of the presence of the Nisei—American-born Japanese who remained in this country for their education. They entered into the picture *Little Tokyo U.S.A.* The leader of the saboteurs here is an American-born Japanese who goes to Tokyo and pledges his allegiance to the Emperor, accepting responsibility for directing the subversive activities in his town. Also in this same film a Nisei tries to help the United States but is killed by his fellow Nisei for his efforts. Incidentally, an American-born German works with them but is not essential to their operations. In *Across the Pacific* the American-born Japanese turns traitor and sides with the enemy.

In appearance the Japanese agents were stereotyped: short, sly, thin, and often with spectacles. The underlings, given very little character delineation, were merely a group of sinister-appearing individuals, expressionless and wooden throughout the pictures. In appearance the Japanese soldier was nearly always well-dressed, short and strong. He behaved in a briskly military fashion and with discipline. He appeared to be much superior physically to the Japanese agents. The Japanese agents were more implacable and sterner than their Nazi counterparts, and were extremely scornful of the United States. This was quite pointed in *Little Tokyo U.S.A.* and *Junior G-Men of the Air.*

In the days before the "Good Neighbor" policy of the 1930s there were many distortions in our feature films as they depicted life in South America. The long-prevailing conception of this hemisphere, built up and carried on in the films, was that of South America as a land of amorous idleness where "romance" throve to strains of exotic music. Novelists, playwrights and movie producers pictured the men as playboys and gigolos, slight of build, indolent, delicate. Mexican men became the "heavies" of the melodramas. In the Westerns the stock villain was the Mexican cattle rustler. Needless to say, the picture of Latin America thus presented did little to inform American audiences of the institutions and culture of these countries.

But with the advent of the "Good Neighbor" policy in the 1930s there was a decided effort, initiated by the government, to have the film producers eliminate material from films that might cause offense to audiences of the southern hemisphere. A number of changes were made which were quickly apparent. The villains of the Westerns were no longer Mexicans from over the border. Play-boys were no longer Latins and the South American gigolo disappeared. There was a decrease in references to South America as a world solely concerned with amorous affairs. During World War II, when material which was clearly objectionable was eliminated by governmental agencies, the producer was faced with the alternative of either introducing authentic representations of South American life or of eliminating all references from the films. The latter course appears to have been taken as the simpler solution. There were extremely few films throughout the war years which dealt at all extensively with South American themes.

In the final analysis, American films concerned with the war changed as the war itself changed. It was the vividness of feeling that these films brought to the audiences that was probably their greatest accomplishment. The image of the war that these films presented to the American public was not always starkly realistic, but they did convey some sense of the complexities of global war to civilians even if it was done in such an uneven manner. No other literary or cultural form was as able to provide the immediate communication of these realities of war as well as the movies.

It is obvious that there were many developments in our culture during World War II which produced feelings of marked anxiety, tension, fear, and apprehension. There were many uncertainties. The war movies assuaged many of the uncertainties because they provided a means of escaping from the feelings of insecurity connected with the war effort. Wartime anxiety was a family problem of no mean proportions. Many historians and sociologists have pointed to the war as a serious inroad into the strength of American family life. The movies, however, represented culturally a reverse side to all this. The war curtailed many activities which had tended to be disruptive of family life. For example, less gasoline and fewer cars meant *more* family life in many homes—and with it an increased attendance at movies as a form of family entertainment. This means that movies represented in many ways a chance for a protraction of cultural activities rather than a curtailment.

Film historian Lewis Jacobs probably sums up best the value of the American motion picture during World War II. He concludes:

Energized by the demands of war, the motion picture during these war years gained point, purpose and direction. They provided entertainment to those hammering out the weapons of war as well as to those fighting the battles. They furthered the military effort by conveying information about war and increased the public's awareness of what was going on. Their real opportunity came in emotionalizing the war situation. This led to an exposure of the nature of the enemy and his assaulting ideology, a more realistic treatment of Allied efforts, and a more dignified portrayal of the fighting men. In dramatizing the stories of conquered countries and attempting to tell what Americans and their allies were fighting for, the screen psychologically and materially met the crisis persuasively and with an urgent sense of its obligations.*

---

* Lewis Jacobs, "World War II and the American Film," *Cinema Journal*, Volume VII, Winter, 1967–68, p. 21.

FOR FURTHER READING

Books

Alexander, Charles C. *Nationalism in American Thought, 1930–1945*. Chicago: Rand McNally & Company, 1969. See Chapter VIII, "For a Better World?", pp. 190–229.

Higham, Charles, and Greenberg, Joel. *Hollywood in the Forties*. New York: A. S. Barnes and Co. Inc., 1968.

Lingeman, Richard R. *Don't You Know There's a War On?: The American Home Front, 1941–1945*. New York: G. D. Putnam's Sons, 1970. See Chapter VI, "Will This Picture Help Win the War?", pp. 168–233.

Articles

Farber, Manny. "Movies in Wartime." *New Republic*, January 3, 1944, pp. 16–20.

Jones, Dorothy B. "Hollywood Goes to War." *Nation*, January 27, 1945, pp. 93–95.

Jacobs, Lewis. "World War II and the American Film," *Cinema Journal*, VII (Winter, 1967–68), 1–21.

Wanger, William. "Movies With a Message." *Saturday Review of Literature*, March 7, 1942, p. 12.

FILMOGRAPHY

BLOCKADE

Norma	Madeleine Carroll
Marco	Henry Fonda
Luis	Leo Carrillo
Andre Gallinet	John Halliday
Basil, Norma's Father	Vladimir Sokoloff
General Vallejo	Robert Warwick
Edward Grant	Reginald Denny
Magician	Peter Godfrey
Cabaret Girl	Katherine de Mille
Commandant	William B. Davidson
Pietro	Fred Kohler
Major del Rio	Carlos de Valdez
Beppo	Nick Thompson
Singer	George Houston
Palm Reader	Lupita Tovar
Waitress	Rosina Galli

Distributor: United Artists
Director: William Dieterle
Released: June 17, 1938

CONFESSIONS OF A NAZI SPY

Ed Renard	Edward G. Robinson
Schneider	Francis Lederer
Schlager	George Sanders
Dr. Kassel	Paul Lukas
D. A. Kellogg	Henry O'Neill
Erika Wolff	Lya Lys
Mrs. Schneider	Grace Stafford
Scotland Yard Man	James Stephenson
Krogman	Sig Rumann
Phillips	Fred Tozere
Hilda	Dorothy Tree
Mrs. Kassel	Celia Sibelius
Renz	Joe Sawyer
Hintze	Lionel Royce
Wildebrandt	Hans von Twardowsky
Helldorf	Henry Victor
Captain Richter	Frederick Vogeding
Klauber	George Rosener
Straubel	Robert Davis
Westphal	John Voight
Gruetzwald	Willy Kaufman
Captain von Eichen	William Vaughn
McDonald	Jack Mower
Harrison	Robert Emmett Keane
Mrs. Maclaughlin	Eily Malyon
Staunton	Frank Mayo
Postman	Alec Craig
Kassel's Nurse	Jean Brook
Kranz	Lucien Prival
A Man	Niccolai Yoshkin
Anna	Bodil Rosing
Young	Charles Sherlock
U. S. District Court Judge	Frederick Burton
Narrator	John Deering
American Legionnaire	Ward Bond
Goebbels	Martin Kosleck

Distributor: Warner Brothers
Director: Anatole Litvak
Released: April 28, 1939

TORPEDOED!

H. B. Warner, Robert Douglas, Richard Crom-

Henry Fonda and Madeleine Carroll in **Blockade** (United Artists).

well, Hazel Terry, Noah Beery, Esme Percy, Frederick Culley, Binky Stuart, Henry Victor.

Distributor: Film Alliance of the U.S.
Director: Norman Walker
Released: September 28, 1939

BEASTS OF BERLIN

Hans	Roland Drew
Elsa	Steffi Duna
Anna	Greta Granstedt
Karl	Alan Ladd
Sachs	Lucien Prival
Lustig	Vernon Dent
Schulz	John Ellis
Wunderlich	George Rosener
Frau Kohler	Bodil Rosing
Albert	Hans von Twardowski
Herr Kohler	Willie Kaufman
Lippert	Hans Joby
Pommer	Frederick Giermann
Klee	Clen Wilenchick
Erlich	Henry von Zynda
Kleswig	John Voight
Schaefer	Hans Schumm
Kruger	John Peters
Braun	Hans von Morehart
Colonel Hess	Walter Stahl
Berkley	Josef Forte
Jouvet	Francisco Moran
Ratig	Fred Mellinger
Buchman	Dick Wessel

Ruchtbien	A. Palasthy	Dorothy	Maris Wrixon
Kalmeit	Walter Thiele	Frank Bennett	Bruce Lester
Brahm	Paul Panzer	James Yeats	Leonard Mudie
Wolff	Fred Vogeding	Arthur Bennett	Holmes Herbert
Kopke	Abe Dinovitch	Mrs. Bennett	Winifred Harris
Romholtz	Bob Stevenson	Thompson	Lester Matthews
Bertha	Anna Lisa	Crichton	John Graham Spacy
		George Bennett	Austin Fairman
Distributor: PRC		Milkman	Clarence Derwent
Director: Sherman Scott		Miss Risdon	Louise Brien
Released: November 22, 1939		Kuglar	Frederick Vogeding
		Von Ritter	Carlos de Valdez
BRITISH INTELLIGENCE		Kurtz	Frederick Giermann
		Corporal	Willy Kaufman
Valdar	Boris Karloff	Brixton	Frank Mayo
Helene Von Lobeer	Margaret Lindsay	Luchow	Stuart Holmes
		Crowder	Sidney Bracy

George Sanders with Francis Lederer in **Confessions of a Nazi Spy** (Warner Bros.).

29

John Ellis, player, Roland Drew, Steffi Duna, Greta Granstedt, Alan Ladd, Henry von Zynda and player in **Beasts of Berlin** (PRC).

Hazel Terry and Richard Cromwell, center, in **Torpedoed!** (Film Alliance of the U.S.).

Margaret Lindsay, Holmes Herbert, Boris Karloff and Leonard Mudie in **British Intelligence** (Warner Bros.).

Morton .... Jack Mower

Distributor: Warner Bros.
Director: Terry Morse
Released: February 14, 1940

HIDDEN ENEMY

Bill .... Warren Hull
Sonia .... Kay Linaker
Werner .... William von Brinken
McGregor .... George Cleveland
Bowman .... William Costello
Aunt Mary .... Fern Emmett
Editor .... Ed Keane

Distributor: Monogram
Director: Howard Bretherton
Released: March 23, 1940

ENEMY AGENT

Jimmy Saunders .... Richard Cromwell
Irene Hunter .... Helen Vinson
Gordon .... Robert Armstrong
Peggy O'Reilly .... Marjorie Reynolds
Lester Taylor .... Jack Arnold
Lyman Scott .... Russell Hicks
Dr. Jeffrey Arnold .... Philip Dorn
Alex .... Jack Larue

Distributor: Universal
Director: Lew Landers
Released: April 26, 1940

WATERLOO BRIDGE

Myra .... Vivien Leigh
Roy Cronin .... Robert Taylor
Lady Margaret Cronin .... Lucile Watson
Kitty .... Virginia Field
Madame Olga Kirowa .... Maria Ouspenskaya
The Duke .... C. Aubrey Smith
Maureen .... Janet Shaw
Elsa .... Janet Waldo
Lydia .... Steffi Duna
Sylvia .... Virginia Carroll
Marie .... Leda Nicova
Beatrice .... Florence Baker

Mary .... Marjorie Manning
Violet .... Frances MacInerney
Grace .... Eleanor Stewart
Mrs. Bassett .... Clara Reid
Policeman .... Leo G. Carroll

Distributor: M-G-M

Kay Linaker with Warren Hull in **Hidden Enemy**
(Universal).

Director: Mervyn Leroy
Released: May 16, 1940

WOMEN IN WAR

O'Neil .... Elsie Janis
Pamela .... Wendy Barrie
Larry .... Patric Knowles
Gail .... Mae Clarke
Ginger .... Dennie Moore
Frances .... Dorothy Peterson
Pierre .... Billy Gilbert
Capt. Tedford .... Colin Tapley
Col. Starr .... Stanley Logan
Millie .... Barbara Pepper
Phyllis .... Pamela Randell
Gordon .... Lawrence Grant
King's Counsel .... Lester Matthews

Distributor: Republic
Director: John H. Auer
Released: May 27, 1940

A NEW UNIVERSAL PICTURE

Richard Cromwell, Russell Hicks, Robert Armstrong
and Milburn Stone in **Enemy Agent** (Universal).

Robert Taylor with Vivien Leigh in **Waterloo Bridge**
(M-G-M).

Elsie Janis in **Women in War** (Republic).

Frank Morgan, Robert Young, Margaret Sullavan, James Stewart, Irene Rich, Robert Stack, Gene Reynolds and William T. Orr in **The Mortal Storm** (M-G-M).

THE MORTAL STORM

Freya Roth	Margaret Sullavan
Martin Brietner	James Stewart
Fritz Marberg	Robert Young
Professor Roth	Frank Morgan
Otto von Rohn	Robert Stack
Elsa	Bonita Granville
Mrs. Roth	Irene Rich
Erich von Rohn	William T. Orr
Mrs. Brietner	Maria Ouspenskaya
Rudi	Gene Reynolds
Rector	Russell Hicks
Lehman	William Edmunds
Marta	Esther Dale
Holl	Dan Dailey Jr.
Berg	Granville Bates
Professor Werner	Thomas Ross
Franz	Ward Bond
Theresa	Sue Moore
Second Colleague	Harry Depp
Third Colleague	Julius Tannen
Fourth Colleague	Gus Glassmire
Guard	Dick Rich
Guard	Ted Oliver
Man	Howard Lang
Woman	Bodil Rosing
Passport Officials	Lucien Prival
	Dick Elliott
Gestapo Official	Henry Victor
Waiter	William Irving
Fat Man In Cafe	Bert Roach

Gestapo Guard	Bob Stevenson
Old Man	Max Davidson
Gestapo Official	John Stark
Oppenheim	Fritz Leiber
Hartman	Robert O. Davis

Distributor: M-G-M
Director: Frank Borzage
Released: June 11, 1940

FOUR SONS

Chris	Don Ameche
Frau Bernie	Eugenie Leontovich

George Ernest, Alan Curtis, Eugenie Leontovich, Don Ameche and Robert Lowery in **Four Sons** (20th Century-Fox).

Anna	Mary Beth Hughes
Karl	Alan Curtis
Fritz	George Ernest
Joseph	Robert Lowery
Max Sturm	Lionel Royce
Newmann	Sig Rumann
Pastor	Ludwig Stossel
Kapek	Christian Rub
Gustav	Torben Meyer
Richter	Egon Brecher

Distributor: 20th Century-Fox
Director: Archie Mayo
Released: June 14, 1940

SAILOR'S LADY

Sally Gilroy	Nancy Kelly
Danny Malone	Jon Hall
Myrtle	Joan Davis
Scrappy Wilson	Dana Andrews
Miss Purvis	Mary Nash
Rodney	Larry Crabbe
Georgine	Katharine Aldridge
Father McGann	Harry Shannon
Goofer	Wally Vernon
'Skipper'	Bruce Hampton
Captain Roscoe	Charles D. Brown

Distributor: 20th Century-Fox
Director: Allan Dwan
Released: July 3, 1940

THE MAN I MARRIED

Carol	Joan Bennett
Eric Hoffman	Francis Lederer
Kenneth Delane	Lloyd Nolan
Freda Heinkel	Anna Sten
Henrich Hoffman	Otto Kruger
Frau Gerhardt	Maria Ouspenskaya
Dr. Hugo Gerhardt	Ludwig Stossel
Ricky	Johnny Russell
Herr Deckart	Lionel Royce
Traveler	Fredrik Vogeding

Dana Andrews and Wally Vernon in **Sailor's Lady** (20th Century-Fox).

Johnnie Russell, Joan Bennett and Francis Lederer
in **The Man I Married** (20th Century-Fox).

Otto	Ernst Deutsch	Blake, 3rd Mate	Wallace Rairden
Czech	Egon Brecher	Sven	Sven-Hugo Borg
Conductor	William Kaufman	Commander Bulow	Henry Victor
Friehoff	Frank Reicher	Lieutenant Schmidt	Roland Varno
		Lerner	Louis Adlon

Distributor: 20th Century-Fox
Director: Irving Pichel
Released: July 16, 1940

Lieutenant Felder .... Will Kaufman
Capt. Norberg .... Monte Blue
Capt. Howard .... Matthew Boulton
Capt. van Wyck .... Gohr Van Vleck
Capt. Benoit .... Jean Del Val
Flossie La Mare .... Kay Linaker
Hughes, Carl's Chauffeur .... Reed Howes
Sparks, Radio Operator .... Philip Warren

MYSTERY SEA RAIDER

June McCarthy .... Carole Landis
Capt. Jimmy Madden .... Henry Wilcoxon
Carl Cutler .... Onslow Stevens
Maggie Clancy .... Kathleen Howard

Distributor: Paramount
Director: Edward Dmytryk
Released: August 5, 1940

Onslow Stevens and Henry Victor in **Mystery Sea Raider** (Paramount).

FOREIGN CORRESPONDENT

Johnny Jones	Joel McCrea
Carol Fisher	Laraine Day
Stephen Fisher	Herbert Marshall
Scott Ffolliott	George Sanders
Van Meer	Albert Basserman
Stebbins	Robert Benchley
Rowley	Edmund Gwenn
Krug	Eduardo Ciannelli
Tramp	Martin Kosleck
Mr. Powers	Harry Davenport
Doreen	Barbara Pepper
Latvian Diplomat	Eddie Conrad
Assassin	Charles Wagenheim
Toastmaster	Crauford Kent
Mrs. Sprague	Frances Carson
Valet	Alexander Granach
Jones' Mother	Dorothy Vaughan
Donald	Jack Rice
Sophie (Becky)	Rebecca Bohannen
Clipper Captain	Marten Lamont
Miss Pimm	Hilda Plowright
Mrs. Benson	Gertrude Hoffman
Miss Benson	Jane Novak
Mr. Brood	Roy Gordon
Inspector McKenna	Leonard Mudie
Commissioner Ffolliott	Holmes Herbert
John Martin	Emory Parnell
Dutch Peasant	James Finlayson
Bradley	Charles Halton
Jones' Sister	Joan Brodel

George Sanders, Laraine Day, Herbert Marshall and Joel McCrea in **Foreign Correspondent** (United Artists).

Henry Daniell, Charles Chaplin and Jack Oakie in **The Great Dictator** (United Artists).

Dr. Williamson	Paul Irving
Jones' Father	Ferris Taylor
Clark	John T. Murray
Stiles, the Butler	Ian Wolfe
Captain Lanson	Louis Borrell
Italian Waiter	Gino Corrado
English Cashier	Eily Malyon
English Radio Announcer	John Burton
Mr. Naismith	E. E. Clive
Man With Newspaper	Alfred Hitchcock

Distributor: United Artists
Director: Alfred Hitchcock
Released: August 29, 1940

THE GREAT DICTATOR

Hynkel (Dictator of Tomania), A Jewish Barber	Charles Chaplin
Hannah	Paulette Goddard
Napaloni (Dictator of Bacteria)	Jack Oakie
Schultz	Reginald Gardiner
Garbitsch	Henry Daniell
Herring	Billy Gilbert
Mr. Jaeckel	Maurice Moscovich
Mrs. Jaeckel	Emma Dunn
Madame Napaloni	Grace Hayle
Bacterian Ambassador	Carter de Haven
Mr. Mann	Bernard Gorcey
Mr. Agar	Paul Weigel

Also: Chester Conklin, Hank Mann, Ester Michel-son, Florence Wright, Eddie Gribbon, Robert O. Davis, Eddie Dunn, Nita Pike, Peter Lynn.

Distributor: United Artists
Director: Charles Chaplin
Released: October 16, 1940

Philip Dorn, Blanche Yurka and Nazimova in **Escape** (M-G-M).

ARISE, MY LOVE

Augusta Nash	Claudette Colbert
Tom Martin	Ray Milland
Shep	Dennis O'Keefe
Mr. Phillips	Walter Abel
Pink	Dick Purcell
Governor	George Zucco
Father Jacinto	Frank Puglia
Botzelberg	Cliff Nazarro
Botzelberg's Asst.	Michael Mark
Guard	Jesus Topete
Uniformed Clerk	Nestor Paiva
Mechanic	Fred Malatesta

Distributor: Paramount
Director: Mitchell Leisen
Released: October 17, 1940

Ray Milland and Claudette Colbert in **Arise My Love** (Paramount).

ESCAPE

Countess Von Treck	Norma Shearer

Melville Cooper, Stanley Logan, Francis Pierlot,
Pat O'Brien, John Halliday, Frank Sully and Edgar
Buchanan in **Escape to Glory** (Columbia).

Mark Preysing	Robert Taylor
General Kurt Von Kolb	Conrad Veidt
Emmy Ritter	Nazimova
Fritz Keller	Felix Bressart
Dr. Arthur Henning	Albert Basserman
Dr. Ditten	Philip Dorn
Ursula	Bonita Granville
Commissioner	Edgar Barrier
Mrs. Henning	Elsa Basserman
Nurse	Blanche Yurka
Anna	Lisa Golm

Distributor: M-G-M
Director: Mervyn Leroy
Released: October 31, 1940

ESCAPE TO GLORY

Mike Farrough	Pat O'Brien

Christine Blaine	Constance Bennett
John Morgan	John Halliday
Penny	Melville Cooper
Larry Perrin	Alan Baxter
Charles Atterbee	Edgar Buchanan
Mrs. Winslow	Marjorie Gateson
Professor Mudge	Francis Pierlot
Mrs. Mudge	Jessie Busley
Capt. Hollister	Stanley Logan
Tommy Malone	Frank Sully
Dr. Behrens	Erwin Kalser
Chief Engineer	Don Beddoe
First Mate	Leslie Denison

Distributor: Columbia
Director: John Brahm
Released: November 18, 1940

FLIGHT COMMAND

Ensign Alan Drake	Robert Taylor

Lorna Gary	Ruth Hussey
Squadron Comdr. Bill Gary	Walter Pidgeon
Lieut. Comdr. 'Dusty' Rhodes	Paul Kelly
Lieut. Jerry Banning	Shepperd Strudwick
Lieut. 'Mugger' Martin	Red Skelton
C.P.O. 'Spike' Knowles	Nat Pendleton
Lieut. 'Stitcy' Payne	Dick Purcell
Lieut. Freddy Townsend	William Tannen
Lieut. Bush	William Stelling

Shepperd Strudwick in **Flight Command** (M-G-M).

Lieut. Frost	Stanley Smith
Vice-Admiral	Addison Richards
First Duty Officer	Donald Douglas
Second Duty Officer	Pat Flaherty
Captain	Forbes Murray
Claire	Marsha Hunt

Distributor: M-G-M
Director: Frank Borzage
Released: December 23, 1940

SO ENDS OUR NIGHT

Josef Steiner	Fredric March
Ruth Holland	Margaret Sullavan
Marie Steiner	Frances Dee
Ludwig Kern	Glenn Ford
Lilo	Anna Sten
Brenner	Erich von Stroheim
Merrill	Allan Brett
Potzloch	Joseph Cawthorn

The Chicken	Leonid Kinskey
The Pole	Alexander Granach
Mr. Kern	Roman Bohnen
Ammers	Sig Rumann
Professor Meyer	William Stack
Barnekrogg	Lionel Royce
Dr. Behr	Ernst Deutsch
Swiss Policeman	Spencer Charters
Kobel	Hans Schumm
Police Captain	Walter Stahl
Bachman	Philip Van Zandt
Gestapo Colonel	Fredrik Vogeding
The Bird	Joe Marks
Elvira	Greta Rozan
Herbert	James Bush
Weiss	Emory Parnell
Mrs. Ammers	Kate MacKenna
Ammers's Sister-In-Law	Edith Angold
Durant	Edward Fielding
German Official	William von Brincken
The Harpy	Gisela Werbiseck
The Pale Woman	Lisa Golm
Black Pig Proprietor	Adolf Milar

Distributor: United Artists
Director: John Cromwell
Released: January 27, 1941

Anna Sten and Fredric March in **So Ends Our Night** (United Artists).

BUCK PRIVATES

Randolph Parker III	Lee Bowman

Bob Martin	....	Alan Curtis
Slicker Smith	....	Bud Abbott
Herbit Brown	....	Lou Costello
The Andrews Sisters	....	Themselves
Judy Gray	....	Jane Frazee
Sgt. Michael Collins	....	Nat Pendleton
Major General Emerson	....	Samuel S. Hinds
Sgt. Callahan	....	Harry Strang
Mrs. Parker II	....	Nella Walker
Henry	....	Leonard Elliott
Chef	....	Shemp Howard
Announcer	....	Mike Frankovitch
Miss Durling	....	Dora Clemant
Camp Hostesses	....	Jeanne Kelly
		Elaine Morey
		Kay Leslie

Nina Orla
Dorothy Darrell

Distributor: Universal
Director: Arthur Lubin
Released: February 3, 1941

THE PHANTOM SUBMARINE

Madeleine	....	Anita Louise
Sinclair	....	Bruce Bennett
Valsar	....	Oscar O'Shea
Dreux	....	John Tyrell
Jerome	....	Pedro de Cordoba
Ming	....	Victor Wong

Lou Costello, Bud Abbott, Lee Bowman and Jane
Frazee in **Buck Privates** (Universal).

James Millican, Charles McMurphy, Oscar O'Shea, Harry Strang and Pedro de Cordoba in **The Phantom Submarine** (Columbia).

Second Mate	Charles McMurphy		President of the Court	Edward Fielding
Engineer	Harry Strang		Judge Advocate	Willard Robertson
			Flight Commander	Richard Lane
Distributor: Columbia			Flight Surgeon	Addison Richards
Director: Lionel Banks			Mickey	Hobart Cavanaugh
Released: February 13, 1941			Lieut. Hopkins	Douglas Aylesworth
			Lieut. Ronson	John Trent
			Lieut. Clankton	Archie Twitchell
I WANTED WINGS			Cadet Captain	Richard Webb
			Radio Announcer	John Hiestand
Jeff Young	Ray Milland		Montgomery	Harlan Warde
Al Ludlow	William Holden		Ranger	Lane Chandler
Tom Cassidy	Wayne Morris		Cadet	Charles Drake
Capt. Mercer	Brian Donlevy		Cadet	Alan Hale, Jr.
Carolyn Bartlett	Constance Moore		Cadet	Renny McEvoy
Sally Vaughn	Veronica Lake		Detective	Ed Peil, Sr.
'Sandbags' Riley	Harry Davenport		Detective	Frank O'Connor
Jimmy Masters	Phil Brown		Corporal	James Millican

Ray Milland, Constance Moore and William Holden in **I Wanted Wings** (Paramount).

Sergeant .... Emory Johnson
Supply Sergeant .... Russ Clark
Private .... George Turner
Private .... Hal Brazeale

Cadet Adjutant .... Warren Ashe
Meteorology Instructor .... Charles A. Hughes
Buzzer Class Instructor .... George Lollier
Mrs. Young .... Hedda Hopper
Mr. Young .... Herbert Rawlinson

Distributor: Paramount
Director: Mitchell Leisen
Released: March 27, 1941

ROOKIES ON PARADE

Duke Wilson .... Bob Crosby
Lois Rogers .... Ruth Terry
Marilyn Fenton .... Gertrude Niesen
Cliff Dugan .... Eddie Foy, Jr.
Kitty Mulloy .... Marie Wilson
Joe Martin .... Cliff Nazarro
Mike Brady .... William Demarest
Augustus Moody .... Sidney Blackmer

William Wright, William Demarest and Bob Crosby in **Rookies On Parade** (Republic).

Tiger Brannigan	Horace MacMahon
Bob Madison	William Wright
Tommy	Jimmy Alexander
Harry Haxom	Louis DaPron
Bill	Bill Shirley

Distributor: Republic
Director: Joseph Santley
Released: April 28, 1941

Fred MacMurray with Madeleine Carroll in **One Night in Lisbon** (Paramount).

ONE NIGHT IN LISBON

Dwight Houston	Fred MacMurray
Leonora Perrycoste	Madeleine Carroll
Gerry Houston	Patricia Morison
Catherine Enfilden	Billie Burke
Commander Peter Walmsley	John Loder
Florence	Dame May Whitty
Lord Fitzleigh	Edmund Gwenn
Erich Strasser	Reginald Denny
Popopopoulos	Billy Gilbert
Concierge	Marcel Dalio
Strasser's Aide	Bruce Wyndham
Waiter	Jerry Mandy

Distributor: Paramount
Director: Edward H. Griffith
Released: May 14, 1941

THEY DARE NOT LOVE

Prince Kurt von Rotenberg	George Brent

Marta Keller	Martha Scott
Baron von Helsing	Paul Lukas
Professor Keller	Egon Brecher
Baron Shafter	Roman Bohnen
Captain Wilhelm Ehrhardt	Edgar Barrier
Barbara Murdock	Kay Linaker
Captain	Frank Reicher

Distributor: Columbia
Director: James Whale
Released: May 16, 1941

CAUGHT IN THE DRAFT

Don Gilbert	Bob Hope
Tony Fairbanks	Dorothy Lamour
Steve	Lynne Overman
Bert	Eddie Bracken
Colonel Peter Fairbanks	Clarence Kolb
Sergeant Burns	Paul Hurst
Yetta	Ferike Boros
Margie	Phyllis Ruth
Cogswell	Irving Bacon
Director	Arthur Loft
Recruiting Sergeant	Edgar Dearing
Make-up Man	Murray Alper
Colonel's Orderly	Dave Willock
Twitchell	Frank Marlowe
Sign Hanger	Heinie Conklin
Susan	Phyllis Kennedy
Medical Examiner	Edwin Stanley
Fat Girl	June Bryde

Martha Scott and George Brent in **They Dare Not Love** (Columbia).

Bob Hope and Eddie Bracken in **Caught In the Draft**
(Paramount).

Bud Abbott, Dick Foran, Lou Costello and Ralph Dunn in **In the Navy** (Universal).

Sgt. at Examining Depot	Weldon Heyburn	Dorothy Roberts	Claire Dodd
Quartermaster Sergeant	George McKay	The Andrew Sisters	Themselves
Pilot	Peter Lynn	Dynamite Dugan	Dick Foran
Justice of the Peace	Andrew Tombes	Butch	Billy Lenhardt
Operation Manager	Edward Hearn	Buddy	Kenneth Brown
		Dizzy	Shemp Howard

Distributor: Paramount
Director: David Butler
Released: May 29, 1941

Distributor: Universal
Director: Arthur Lubin
Released: June 2, 1941

IN THE NAVY

Smokey Adams	Bud Abbott
Pomeroy Watson	Lou Costello
Tommy Halstead	Dick Powell

POWER DIVE

Brad Farrell	Richard Arlen
Carol Blake	Jean Parker

Don Castle, Jean Parker and Richard Arlen in **Power Dive** (Paramount).

Mrs. Coles	Helen Mack
Dan McMasters	Roger Pryor
Doug Farrell	Don Castle
Squid Watkins	Cliff Edwards
Brad Coles, Jr.	Billy Lee
Prof. Blake	Thomas Ross
Johnny Coles	Louis Jean Heydt

Distributor: Paramount
Director: James P. Hogan
Released: June 4, 1941

MAN HUNT

Captain Thorndike	Walter Pidgeon

Joan Bennett and Walter Pidgeon in **Man Hunt** (20th Century-Fox).

Jerry	Joan Bennett
Quive-Smith	George Sanders
Mr. Jones	John Carradine
Vaner	Roddy McDowall
Doctor	Ludwig Stossel
Lady Risborough	Heather Thatcher
Lord Risborough	Frederick Worlock
Captain Jensen	Roger Imhof
Whiskers	Egon Brecher
Major	Lester Matthews
Farnsworthy	Holmes Herbert
Postmistress	Eily Malyon
Police Lieutenant	Arno Frey
Ambassador	Fredrik Vogeding
Umbrella Man	Lucien Prival

Jeffrey Lynn, Lisa Golm, Ilka Gruning, Erwin Kalser and Philip Dorn in **Underground** (Warner Bros.).

Reeves	Herbert Evans
Bobby	Keith Hitchcock

Distributor: 20th Century-Fox
Director: Fritz Lang
Released: June 13, 1941

UNDERGROUND

Kurt Franken	Jeffrey Lynn
Eric Franken	Philip Dorn
Sylvia Helmuth	Kaaren Verne
Fraulein Gessner	Mona Maris
Alex	Peter Whitney

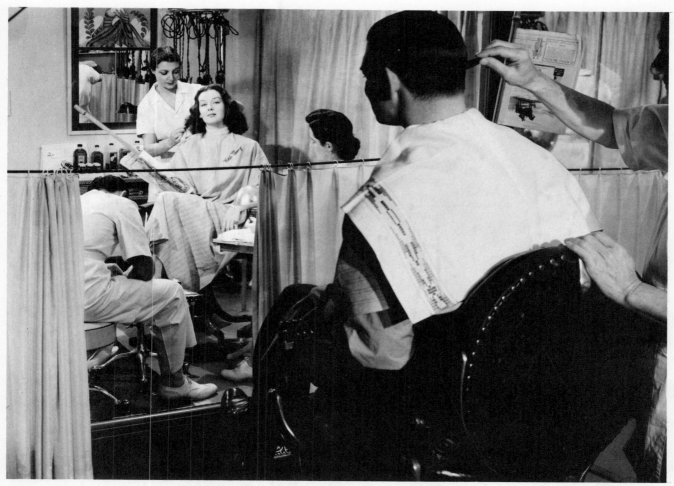

Rosalind Russell and Clark Gable in **They Met In Bombay** (M-G-M).

Heller	Martin Kosleck		

Heller .... Martin Kosleck
Dr. Franken .... Edwin Kalser
Frau Kranken .... Ilka Gruning
Prof. Baumer .... Frank Reicher
Herr Director .... Egon Brecher
Herr Muller .... Ludwig Stossel
Heller's Aide .... Hans Schumm
Hoffman .... Wolfgang Zilzer
Ernst Demmler .... Roland Varno
Rolf .... Henry Brandon
Greta Rolf .... Lotte Palfi
Ella .... Lisa Golm
Otto .... Louis Arco
Gestapo .... Roland Drew

Distributor: Warner Bros.
Director: Vincent Sherman
Released: June 18, 1941

THEY MET IN BOMBAY

Gerald Meldrick .... Clark Gable
Anya von Duren .... Rosalind Russell
Captain Chang .... Peter Lorre
Duchess of Beltravers .... Jessie Ralph
The General .... Reginald Owen
Inspector .... Matthew Boulton
Hotel Manager .... Eduardo Ciannelli
Maitre D'Hotel .... Luis Alberni
Carmencita .... Rosina Galli
Bolo .... Jay Novello

Distributor: M-G-M
Director: Clarence Brown
Released: June 24, 1941

PARACHUTE BATTALION

Donald Morse	Robert Preston
Kit Richards	Nancy Kelly
Bill Burke	Edmond O'Brien
Bill Richards	Harry Carey
Jeff Hollis	Buddy Ebsen
Tex	Paul Kelly
Spence	Richard Cromwell
Colonel Burke	Robert Barrat
Pa Hollis	Erville Alderson
Chief of Infantry	Edward Fielding
Thomas Morse	Selmer Jackson
Captain	Grant Withers
Private	Jack Briggs
Medical Officer	Walter Sande
Ma Hollis	Kathryn Sheldon
Private	Lee Bonnell
Private	Robert Smith
Staff Officer	Gayne Whitman
Radio Announcer	Douglas Evans
Recruiting Sergeant	Eddie Dunn

Distributor: RKO
Director: Leslie Goodwins
Released: July 15, 1941

HOLD BACK THE DAWN

George Iscovesco	Charles Boyer
Emmy Brown	Olivia De Havilland
Anita Dixon	Paulette Goddard
Professor Van Den Luecken	Victor Francen
Hammock	Walter Abel
Anatole Bonbois	Curt Bois

Edmond O'Brien, Buddy Ebsen, Robert Preston, Paul Kelly and soldiers in **Parachute Battalion** (RKO).

Flores	Nestor Paiva
Lupita	Eva Puig
Joseph Kurz	Eric Feldary

Olivia de Havilland, Charles Boyer and Paulette Goddard in **Hold Back the Dawn** (Paramount).

Christine Van Den Luecken	Michelaine Cheirel
Anie Van Den Luecken	Madeleine Le Beau
Tony	Billy Lee
Berta Kurz	Rosemary De Camp
Mechanic	Mikhail Rasumny
Sam	Sonny Boy Williams
American Consul	Edward Fielding
Young Woman (Climax Bar)	Gertrude Astor
Joe	Don Douglas
Man	Chester Clute
Second Mechanic	Jesus Topete
Third Mechanic	Tony Roux
Mexican Doctor	Francisco Maran
Mexican Judge	Carlos Villarias
Hollander	Arthur Loft
Mr. MacAdams	John Holland

Distributor: Paramount
Director: Mitchell Leisen
Released: July 31, 1941

INTERNATIONAL SQUADRON

Jimmy Grant	Ronald Reagan
Jeanette	Olympe Bradna

Squadron Leader	James Stephenson
Lt. Rog Wilkins	William Lundigan
Connie	Joan Perry
Wing Commander	Reginald Denny
'Omaha' McGrath	Cliff Edwards
Mary	Julie Bishop
Michele Edme	Michael Ames
Bill Torrence	John Ridgely
Biddle	Charles Irwin
Chief Engineer	Addison Richards
Sounders	Selmer Jackson
Sir Basil Wryxton	Holmes Herbert
Major Fresney	Crauford Kent

Distributor: Warner Bros.
Director: Lewis Seiler
Released: August 13, 1941

NAVY BLUES

Margie Jordan	Ann Sheridan
Cake O'Hara	Jack Oakie
Lilibelle Bolton	Martha Raye
Powerhouse Bolton	Jack Haley
Homer Matthews	Herbert Anderson
'Buttons' Johnson	Jack Carson
Tubby	Jackie C. Gleason

Michael Ames, Ronald Reagan and James Stephenson in **International Squadron** (Warner Bros.).

'Rocky' Anderson	Richard Lane
Mac	William T. Orr
Jersey	John Ridgely

Jack Oakie and the Island beauties from **Navy Blues**
(Warner Bros.).

Officer	Frank Wilcox	Tim Griffin	Regis Toomey
Jonesy	William Justice	Art Lyons	Robert Armstrong
Lucky	Ray Cook	Lucky Dice	Allen Jenkins
Captain Willard	Selmer Jackson	John Thomas Anthony	Craig Stevens

Also: Navy Blues Sextet, Peggy Diggins, Georgia
Carroll, Loraine Gettman, Marguerite Chapman,
Katharine Aldridge, Claire James

Chubby	Herbert Anderson
Senior Flight Surgeon	Moroni Olsen
Swede	Louis Jean Heydt
Mrs. James	Dennie Moore
Corps Man	Cliff Nazarro
Helen	Ann Doran
Senior Flight Surgeon	Addison Richards
Admiral	Russell Hicks
Admiral	Howard Hickman

Distributor: Warner Bros.
Director: Lloyd Bacon
Released: August 13, 1941

DIVE BOMBER

Doug Lee	Errol Flynn
Joe Blake	Fred MacMurray
Dr. Lance Rogers	Ralph Bellamy
Linda Fisher	Alexis Smith

Pilot	Dewolfe Hopper
Pilot	Charles Drake
Pilot	Byron Barr
Squadron Commander	Alexander Lockwood
Commander	George Meeker
General	Wedgewood Nowell

Ralph Bellamy, Robert Armstrong and Errol Flynn in **Dive Bomber** (Warner Bros.).

Hospital Attendant	Creighton Hale
Hostess	Charlotte Wynters
Singer	Jane Randolph
Cigarette Girl	Juanita Stark
Girl At Newsstand	Alice Talton
Squadron C.O.	Max Hoffman, Jr.
Pilot	Alan Hale, Jr.
Pilot	Sol Gorss
Blue Jacket	Walter Sande
Telephone Man	Michael Ames
Flag Man	Harry Lewis

Distributor: Warner Bros.
Director: Michael Curtiz
Released: August 15, 1941

MYSTERY SHIP

Allan Harper	Paul Kelly
Patricia Marshall	Lola Lane
Tommy Baker	Larry Parks
Ernst Madek	Trevor Bardette
Condor	Cy Kendall
Captain Randall	Roger Imhof
Turillo	Eddie Laughton
Sam	John Tyrell
Wasserman	Byron Foulger
Van Brock	Dick Curtis
Rader	Dwight Frye
Gorman	Kenneth MacDonald

Distributor: Columbia
Director: Lew Landers
Released: August 18, 1941

WORLD PREMIERE

Duncan DeGrasse	John Barrymore
Kitty Carr	Frances Farmer
Gregory Martin	Eugene Pallette
Lee Morrison	Virginia Dale
Mark Saunders	Ricardo Cortez
Franz von Bushmaster	Sig Rumann
Joe Bemis	Don Castle
Luther Skinkley	William Wright
Muller	Fritz Feld
Signor Scaletti	Luis Alberni
Peters	Cliff Nazarro
Nixon	Andrew Tombes

Distributor: Paramount
Director: Ted Tetzlaff
Released: August 21, 1941

A YANK IN THE R. A. F.

Tom Baker	Tyrone Power
Carol Brown	Betty Grable
Wing Commander Morley	John Sutton
Roger Pillby	Reginald Gardiner
Corporal Harry Baker	Donald Stuart
Squadron Leader	Morton Lowry
Al	Ralph Byrd

Trevor Bardette, Cy Kendall, Paul Kelly and Lola Lane in **Mystery Ship** (Columbia).

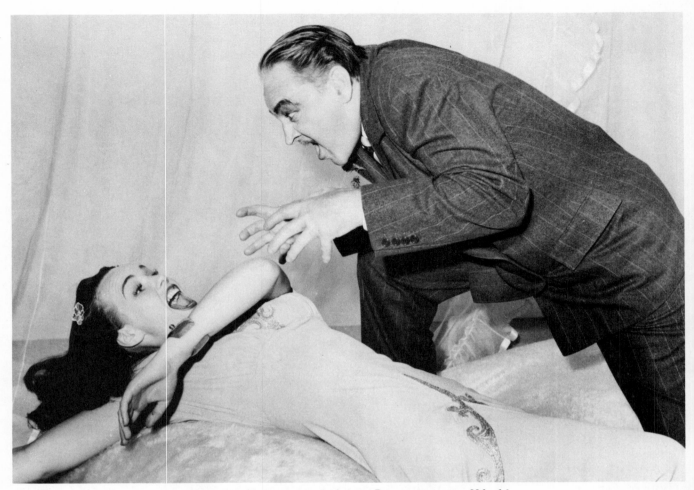

Frances Farmer and John Barrymore in **World Premiere** (Paramount).

Tyrone Power in **A Yank In the R.A.F.** (20th Century-Fox).

Brian Aherne and Ian Hunter in **Smilin' Through**
(M-G-M).

Thorndyke	Richard Fraser
Flight Lieutenant Redmond	Denis Green
Flight Lieutenant Richardson	Bruce Lester
Wales	Gilchrist Stuart
Group Captain	Lester Matthews
Canadian Major	Frederick Worlock
Mrs. Fitzhugh	Ethel Griffies
Headwaiter	Fortunio Bonanova
Instructor	James Craven
Radio Operator	G. P. Huntley
Intelligence Officers	Stuart Robertson
	Dennis Hoey

Distributor: 20th Century-Fox
Director: Henry King
Released: September 9, 1941

SMILIN' THROUGH

Kathleen	Jeannette MacDonald
Sir John Carteret	Brian Aherne
Kenneth Wayne	Gene Raymond
Reverend Owen Harding	Ian Hunter
Ellen	Frances Robinson
Willie	Patrick O'Moore
Charles (Batman)	Eric Lonsdale
Kathleen (As a child)	Jackie Horner
Sexton	David Clyde
Dowager	Frances Carson
Woman	Ruth Rickaby

Distributor: M-G-M
Director: Frank Borzage
Released: September 12, 1941

William Tracy, James Gleason and Elyse Knox in
Tanks a Million (United Artists).

Charlie .... Noah Beery, Jr.
Sergeant Ames .... Joe Sawyer
Jeanne .... Elyse Knox
Campain Rossmead .... Douglas Fowley
Radio Announcer .... Knox Manning
Skivic .... Frank Faylen
Monkman .... Dick Wessel
Cleary .... Frank Melton
Lieutenant Caldwell .... Harold Goodwin
Major Green .... William Gould
Major .... Norman Kerry

Distributor: United Artists
Director: Fred Guiol
Released: September 12, 1941

TANKS A MILLION

Dodo .... William Tracy
Barkley .... James Gleason

YOU'LL NEVER GET RICH

Robert Curtis .... Fred Astaire

Rita Hayworth, Frank Ferguson and Fred Astaire in
You'll Never Get Rich (Columbia).

Sheila Winthrop .... Rita Hayworth
Tom Barton .... John Hubbard
Martin Cortland .... Robert Benchley
Sonya .... Osa Massen
Mrs. Cortland .... Frieda Inescourt
Kewpie Blain .... Guinn Williams
Top Sergeant .... Donald MacBride
Swivel Tongue .... Cliff Nazarro
Aunt Louise .... Marjorie Gateson
Mrs. Barton .... Ann Shoemaker
Colonel Shiller .... Boyd Davis

Distributor: Columbia
Director: Sidney Lanfield
Released: September 25, 1941

Chick Chandler, Earl Hodgins and Cliff Nazarro in **Sailors on Leave** (Republic).

Frank Marlowe, George Tobias, Gary Cooper and Joe Sawyer in **Sergeant York** (Warner Bros.).

Zeb Andrews .... Robert Porterfield
Lem .... Howard da Silva
Zeke .... Clem Bevans
Sergeant Early .... Joseph Sawyer
Sergeant .... Frank Wilcox
Captain Tillman .... Donald Douglas
Sergeant Harry Parsons .... Pat Flaherty
Corporal Savage .... Lane Chandler
Beardsley .... Frank Marlowe
Corporal Cutting .... Jack Pennick
Eb .... James Anderson
Tom .... Guy Wilkerson
Rosie York .... June Lockhart
Uncle Lige .... Tully Marshall
Luke (Target Keeper) .... Lee "Lasses" White
Nate Tompkins .... Erville Alderson

SERGEANT YORK

Alvin York .... Gary Cooper
Pastor Rosier Pile .... Walter Brennan
Gracie Williams .... Joan Leslie
Pusher (Michael T. Ross) .... George Tobias
Bert Thomas .... David Bruce
Major Buxton .... Stanley Ridges
Ma York .... Margaret Wycherly
George York .... Dickie Moore
Ike Botkin .... Ward Bond
Buck Lipscomb .... Noah Beery, Jr.
Captain Danforth .... Harvey Stephens
Cordell Hull .... Charles Trowbridge
German Major (Carl) .... Charles Esmond

George Brent and Ilona Massey in **International Lady** (United Artists).

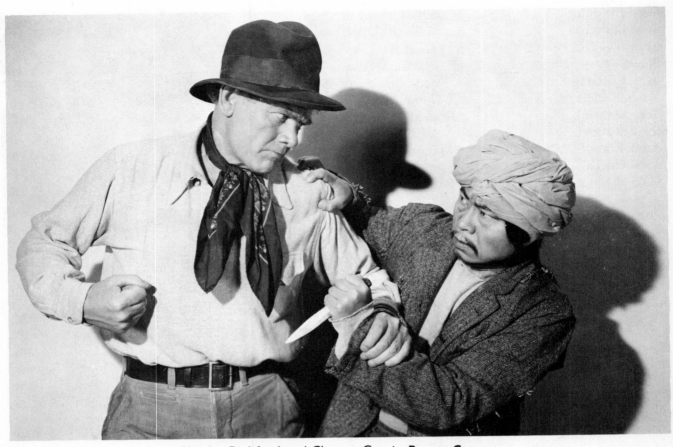

Charles Bickford and Chester Gan in **Burma Convoy** (Universal).

Mountaineer	Charles Middleton	Linda Hall	Shirley Ross
Andrews	Victor Kilian	Swifty	Chick Chandler
Prison Camp Commander	Theodore von Eltz	Aunt Navy	Ruth Donnelly
Gracie's Sister	Jane Isbell	Gwen	Mae Clarke
Drummer	Frank Orth	Mike	Cliff Nazarro
Marter, Bartender	Arthur Aylesworth	Dugan	Tom Kennedy
Piano Player	Elisha Cook, Jr.	Sadie	Mary Ainslee
Card Player	William Haade	Bill Carstairs	Bill Shirley
General Pershing	Joseph Girard	Thompson	Gary Owen
Marshal Foch	Jean Del Val	Sawyer	William Haade
Mayor Hylan	Douglas Wood	Sunshine	Jane Kean
Oscar Of The Waldorf	Ed Keane		

Distributor: Warner Bros.
Director: Howard Hawks
Released: September 27, 1941

Distributor: Republic
Director: Albert S. Rogell
Released: October 3, 1941

SAILORS ON LEAVE

Chuck Stepherns .... William Lundigan

INTERNATIONAL LADY

Tim Hanley .... George Brent
Carla Nillson .... Ilona Massey

Reggie Oliver	Basil Rathbone	Anne McBrogal	Evelyn Ankers
Sidney Grenner	Gene Lockhart	Mike Weldon	Frank Albertson
Webster	George Zucco	Lloyd McBrogal	Cecil Kellaway
Dr. Rowan	Francis Pierlot	Victor Harrison	Truman Bradley
Bruner	Martin Kosleck	Smitty	Willie Fung
Tetlow	Charles D. Brown	Maisie	Viola Vaughn
Mrs. Grenner	Marjorie Gateson	Lin Tai Yen	Keye Luke
Moulton	Leyland Hodgson		
Sewell	Clayton Moore		
Denby	Gordon De Main		
Sir Henry	Frederic Worlock		

Also: Turhan Bey, Ken Christy, C. Montague Shaw, Harry Stubbs, Chester Gan.

Distributor: United Artists
Director: Tim Whelan
Released: October 16, 1941

Distributor: Universal
Director: Noel Smith
Released: October 17, 1941

BURMA CONVOY

SUNDOWN

		Zia	Gene Tierney
		Crawford	Bruce Cabot
Cliff Weldon	Charles Bickford	Major Coombes	George Sanders

George Sanders, Harry Carey and Reginald Gardiner
in **Sundown** (United Artists).

Bishop	Sir Cedric Hardwicke
Dewey	Harry Carey
Pallini	Joseph Calleia
Lieutenant Turner	Reginald Gardiner
Kuypens	Carl Esmond
Hammud	Marc Lawrence
Miriami	Jeni Le Gon
Kipsang	Emmett Smith
Kipsang's Bride	Dorothy Dandridge
Asburton	Gilbert Emery

Also: Horace Walker, Edward Das, Prince Madupe, Hassan Said, Wesley Gale, Jester Hairston, Curtis Nero, Al Duval, Kenny Washington, Woodrow Strode, Walter Knox, William Broadus, Ivan Browning, William Dunn, Tetsu Komai, Frederick Clark, Darby Jones, Blue Washington, Lawrence Lamarr, Frank Clark, George Lincoln.

Distributor: United Artists
Director: Henry Hathaway
Released: October 20, 1941

SWING IT SOLDIER

Jerry	Ken Murray
Patricia	Frances Langford
Brad	Don Wilson
Brenda	Blanche Stewart

Skinnay Ennis and Frances Langford in **Swing It Soldier** (Universal).

Cobina	Elvia Allman
Maxwellton	Hanley Stafford

Clementine	Susan Miller
Senor Lee	Senor Lee
Dena	Iris Adrian
Bill	Lewis Howard
Oscar Simms	Thurston Hall
Mrs. Simms	Kitty O'Neil
Dr. Browning	Lew Valentine

Tris Coffin, Charles Hall, Nat Pendleton and Frank Faylen in **Top Sergeant Mulligan** (Monogram).

Elevator Boy	Peter Sullivan
Sergeant	Tom Dugan

Also: Skinnay Ennis and his Orchestra, Kenny Stevens, Louis Da Pron, Stop, Look and Listen, Three Cheers.

Distributor: Universal
Director: Harold Young
Released: October 24, 1941

TOP SERGEANT MULLIGAN

Mulligan	Nat Pendleton
Avis	Carol Hughes
Snark	Sterling Holloway
Gail	Marjorie Reynolds
Dolan	Frank Faylen
Doolittle	Charles Hall
Don	Tom Neal
Mrs. Lewis	Betty Blythe
Mr. Lewis	Dick Elliott
Briggs	Maynard Holmes
Wonderful Smith	Himself

Joan Bennett and Don Ameche in **Confirm or Deny**
(20th Century-Fox).

Distributor: Monogram
Director: Jean Yarbrough
Released: November 14, 1941

CONFIRM OR DENY

Mitch .... Don Ameche
Jennifer Carson .... Joan Bennett
Albert Perkins .... Roddy McDowall
Captain Channing .... John Loder
H. Cyrus Sturtevant .... Raymond Walburn
Jeff .... Arthur Shields
Mr. Hobbs .... Eric Blore

Distributor: 20th Century-Fox
Director: Archie Mayo
Released: November 19, 1941

YOU'RE IN THE ARMY NOW

Jeeper Smith .... Jimmy Durante
Bliss Dobson .... Jane Wyman
Breezy Jones .... Phil Silvers
Captain Radcliffe .... Regis Toomey
Colonel Dobson .... Donald MacBride
Captain Austin .... George Meeker
Sergeant Madden .... Joseph Sawyer
Sergeant Thorpe .... William Haade
General Winthrop .... Clarence Kolb
General Philpot .... Paul Harvey
Lt. Col. Rogers .... Paul Stanton
Army Doctor .... John Maxwell
Della .... Etta McDaniel

Distributor: Warner Bros.
Director: Lewis Seiler

Phil Silvers, Joe Sawyer and Jimmy Durante in **You're in the Army Now** (Warner Bros.)

Lee J. Cobb, Charles Wagenheim and William Yetter in **Paris Calling** (Universal).

Wallace Beery and William Lundigan in **The Bugle Sounds** (M-G-M).

Released: December 3, 1941

PARIS CALLING

Marianne	Elizabeth Bergner
Nick	Randolph Scott
Benoit	Basil Rathbone
Colette	Gale Sondergaard
Lance	Charles Arnt
Mouche	Eduardo Ciannelli
Mme. Jannetier	Elizabeth Risdon

Distributor: Universal
Director: Edwin L. Marin
Released: December 4, 1941

THE BUGLE SOUNDS

'Hap' Doan	Wallace Beery
Susie	Marjorie Main
Colonel Lawton	Lewis Stone
Russell	George Bancroft
Lieut. Col. Seton	Henry O'Neill
Sally Hanson	Donna Reed
Dillon	Chill Wills
Joe Hanson	William Lundigan
Sergeant Strong	Tom Dugan
Krims	Guinn Williams
Cartaret	Ernest Whitman
Leech	Roman Bohnen
Nichols	Jerome Cowan
Hank	Arthur Space
Brigadier-General	Jonathan Hale

Frank Reicher, John Ridgely, player, Raymond Massey, Nancy Coleman, Moroni Olsen and John Garfield in **Dangerously They Live** (Warner Bros.).

Distributor: M-G-M
Director: S. Sylvan Simon
Released: December 17, 1941

DANGEROUSLY THEY LIVE

Dr. Michael Lewis	John Garfield
Jane	Nancy Coleman
Dr. Ingersoll	Raymond Massey
Mr. Goodwin	Moroni Olsen
Dawson	Esther Dale

Joe Sawyer, William Tracy and Arthur Hunnicutt in **Hay Foot** (United Artists—Hal Roach).

Nurse Johnson	Lee Patrick
John	John Ridgely
Steiner	Christian Rub
Jarvis	Frank Reicher
Eddie	Ben Welden
John Dill	Cliff Clark
Dr. Murdock	Roland Drew
Gate Keeper	Arthur Aylsworth
George, Taxi Driver	John Harmon
Capt. Hunter	Matthew Boulton
Capt. Strong	Gavin Muir
Mrs. Steiner	Ilka Gruning
Ralph Bryan	Frank M. Thomas
Carl	James Seay

Distributor: Warner Bros.
Director: Robert Florey
Released: December 24, 1941

HAY FOOT

William Tracy, Joe Sawyer, James Gleason, Noah Beery, Jr., Elyse Knox, Douglas Fowley, Harold Goodwin.

Distributor: United Artists—Hal Roach
Director: Fred Guiol
Released: January 2, 1942

JOE SMITH, AMERICAN

Joe Smith	Robert Young
Mary Smith	Marsha Hunt
Freddie Dunhill	Harvey Stephens
Johnny Smith	Darryl Hickman
Blake McKettrick	Jonathan Hale
Schricker	Noel Madison
Mead	Don Costello
Conway	Joseph Anthony
Gus	William Forrest
Mr. Edgerton	Russell Hicks
Pete	Mark Daniels
Eddie	William Tannen

Distributor: M-G-M
Director: Jack Chertok
Released: January 7, 1942

JOAN OF PARIS

Paul Lavallier	Paul Henreid

Marsha Hunt with Robert Young in **Joe Smith, American** (M-G-M).

Michele Morgan with Laird Cregar in **Joan of Paris**
(RKO-Radio).

William Holden, Dorothy Lamour and Eddie Bracken in **The Fleet's In** (Paramount).

The Countess .... Dorothy Lamour
Casey Kirby .... William Holden
Barney Waters .... Eddie Bracken
Bessie Day .... Betty Hutton
Cissie .... Cass Daley
Spike .... Gil Lamb
Jake .... Leif Erickson
Diana Golden .... Betty Jane Rhodes
Dance Team .... Lorraine and Rognan
Kellogg .... Jack Norton
Also: Jimmy Dorsey and his Band with Helen O'Connell and Bob Eberly

Joan .... Michele Morgan
Father Antoine .... Thomas Mitchell
Herr Funk .... Laird Cregar
Mlle. Rosay .... May Robson
Baby .... Alan Ladd
Splinter .... Jimmy Monks
Robin .... Jack Briggs
Geoffrey .... Richard Fraser
Gestapo Agent .... Alex Granach

Distributor: RKO-Radio
Director: Robert Stevenson
Released: January 9, 1942

Truman Bradley and Maria Montez in **Bombay Clipper** (Universal).

Distributor: Paramount
Director: Victor Schertzinger
Released: January 19, 1942

A YANK ON THE BURMA ROAD

Gail Farwood .... Laraine Day
Joe Tracey .... Barry Nelson
Tom Farwood .... Stuart Crawford
Kim How .... Keye Luke
Wing .... Sen Yung
Dr. Franklin .... Philip Ahn
Radio Announcer .... Knox Manning
Rangoon Aide De Camp .... Matthew Boulton

Distributor: M-G-M

Barry Nelson, Laraine Day and Stuart Crawford in **A Yank on the Burma Road** (M-G-M).

Dennis Morgan, James Cagney and James Bush in
Captains of the Clouds (Warner Bros.).

Director: George B. Seitz
Released: January 19, 1942

BOMBAY CLIPPER

Jim .... William Gargan
Frankie .... Irene Hervey
Tex .... Charles Lang
Mrs. Landers .... Maria Montez
Lewis .... Lloyd Corrigan
Abigail .... Mary Gordon
Dr. Landers .... Truman Bradley
Hare .... Philip Trent
Chundra .... Turhan Bey
Paul .... John Bagni
Steward .... Roy Harris
Bland .... Peter Lynn

Ruggles .... Wade Boteler
Lamb .... Billy Wayne
Photographer .... Paul Dubov

Distributor: Universal
Director: John Rawlins
Released: January 19, 1942

CAPTAINS OF THE CLOUDS

Brian MacLean .... James Cagney
Johnny Dutton .... Dennis Morgan
Emily Foster .... Brenda Marshall
Tiny Murphy .... Alan Hale
Blimp Lebec .... George Tobias
Scrounger Harris .... Reginald Gardiner
Commanding Officer .... Reginald Denny

Roland Young, Paulette Goddard and Albert Dekker in **The Lady Has Plans** (Paramount).

Prentiss	Russell Arms
Group Captain	Paul Cavanagh
Store-Teeth Morrison	Clem Bevans
Foster	J. M. Kerrigan

Dr. Neville	J. Farrell MacDonald
Fyffo	Patrick O'Moore
Carmichael	Morton Lowry
Chief Instructor	S. L. Cathcart-Jones
President of Court Martial	Frederic Worlock
Officer	Roland Drew
Blondo	Lucia Carroll
Playboy	George Meeker
Popcorn Kearns	Benny Baker
Kingsley	Hardie Albright
Mason	Ray Walker
Nolan	Charles Halton
Provost Marshall	Louis Jean Heydt

Distributor: Warner Bros.
Director: Michael Curtiz
Released: January 20, 1942

THE LADY HAS PLANS

Sidney Royce	Paulette Goddard

Conrad Veidt in a dual role with Ann Ayars in **Nazi Agent** (M-G-M).

Humphrey Bogart with Martin Kosleck in **All Through the Night** (Warner Bros.—First National).

Kenneth Harper	Ray Milland	Baron Hugo von Detner	Conrad Veidt
Ronald Dean	Roland Young	Kaaren De Relle	Ann Ayars
Baron von Kemp	Albert Dekker	Fritz	Frank Reicher
Rita Lenox	Margaret Hayes	Miss Harper	Dorothy Tree
Peter Miles	Cecil Kellaway	Professor Sterling	Ivan Simpson
Paul Baker	Addison Richards	Ludwig	William Tannen
Joe Scalsi	Gerald Mohr	Kurt Richten	Martin Kosleck
Frank Richards	Edward Norris	Joe Aiello	Marc Lawrence
Abner Spencer	Thomas W. Ross	Arnold Milbar	Sidney Blackmer
Weston	Arthur Loft		

Distributor: Paramount
Director: Sidney Lanfield
Released: January 20, 1942

Distributor: M-G-M
Director: Jules Dassin
Released: January 21, 1942

NAZI AGENT

Otto Becker .... Conrad Veidt

ALL THROUGH THE NIGHT

Gloves Donahue .... Humphrey Bogart
Hall Ebbing .... Conrad Veidt

Charles Brinley, Edgar Kennedy, Bud Duncan and Frank Austin in **Snuffy Smith, Yard Bird** (Monogram).

Leda Hamilton	Kaaren Verne
Ma Donahue	Jane Darwell
Barney	Frank McHugh
Pepi	Peter Lorre
Madame	Judith Anderson
Sunshine	William Demarest
Starchie	Jackie Gleason
Waiter	Phil Silvers
Spats Hunter	Wallace Ford
Marty Callahan	Barton MacLane
Joe Denning	Edward Brophy
Steindorff	Martin Kosleck
Annabelle	Jean Ames
Mr. Miller	Ludwig Stossel
Mrs. Miller	Irene Seidner
Forbes	James Burke
Smitty	Ben Welden
Anton	Hans Schumm
Spence	Charles Cane
Sage	Frank Sully
Deacon	Sam McDaniel

Distributor: Warner Bros—First National
Director: Vincent Sherman
Released: January 28, 1942

SNUFFY SMITH, YARD BIRD

Snuffy Smith	Bud Duncan
Sergeant Cooper	Edgar Kennedy
Lowizie	Sarah Padden
Cindy	Doris Linden
Janie	Andria Palmer
General	J. Farrell MacDonald
Lloyd	Pat McVeigh
Saul	Frank Austin
Don	Jimmie Dodd

Distributor: Monogram
Director: Edward Cline
Released: January 28, 1942

TO BE OR NOT TO BE

Maria Tura	Carole Lombard
Joseph Tura	Jack Benny
Lieut. Stanislav Sobinski	Robert Stack
Greenberg	Felix Bressart
Rawitch	Lionel Atwill
Professor Siletsky	Stanley Ridges
Col. Ehrhardt	Sig Rumann
Bronski	Tom Dugan
Producer Dobosh	Charles Halton
Actor-Adjutant	George Lynn
Capt. Schultz	Henry Victor
Anna	Maude Eburne
Makeup Man	Armand Wright
Stage Manager	Erno Verebes
General Armstrong	Halliwell Hobbes
Major Cunningham	Miles Mander
Captain	Leslie Denison

Robert Stack with Carole Lombard in **To Be or Not to Be** (United Artists).

Polish Official	Frank Reicher
William Kunze	Peter Caldwell
Man In Bookstore	Wolfgang Zilzer
Polonius In Warsaw	Olaf Hytten
Reporter	Charles Irwin
Second Reporter	Leyland Hodgson
Scottish Farmer	Alec Craig
Second Farmer	James Finlayson

Bud Abbott, John Carroll, Lou Costello and Peter Whitney in **Rio Rita** (M-G-M).

Prompter	Edgar Licho
Gestapo Sergeant	Robert O. Davis
Pilot	Roland Varno
Co-Pilot	Helmut Dantine
Co-Pilot	Otto Reichow
Polish R.A.F. Flyers	Maurice Murphy
	Gene Rizzi
	Paul Barrett
	John Kellogg

Distributor: United Artists
Director: Ernest Lubitsch
Released: February 19, 1942

RIO RITA

'Doc'	Bud Abbott
'Wishy'	Lou Costello
Rita Winslow	Kathryn Grayson
Ricardo Montera	John Carroll
Lucette Brunswick	Patricia Dane

Maurice Craindall	Tom Conway
Jake	Peter Whitney
Harry Gantley	Barry Nelson

Distributor: M-G-M
Director: S. Sylvan Simon
Released: March 11, 1942

TO THE SHORES OF TRIPOLI

Chris Winters	John Payne
2nd Lt. Mary Carter	Maureen O'Hara
Dixie Smith	Randolph Scott
Helene	Nancy Kelly
Johnny	William Tracy
Okay	Maxie Rosenbloom
Mouthy	Henry Morgan
Butch	Edmund MacDonald

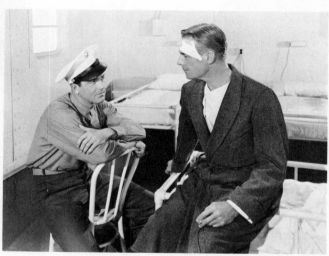

John Payne and Randolph Scott in **To the Shores of Tripoli** (20th Century-Fox).

Major Wilson	Russell Hicks
Captain Winter	Minor Watson
Bill Grady	Ted North
Barber	Frank Orth
Blonde	Iris Adrian
Tom Hall	Alan Hale, Jr.
Joe	Basil Walker
Swifty	Charles Tannen
Doctor	Stanley Andrews
Lieutenant	Richard Lane
Corporal	Gordon Lane

Joan Barclay with Bela Lugosi in **Black Dragons** (Monogram).

Corporal	Gaylord Pendleton	Radio Operator	Pat McVey
Ensign	Robert Conway	Driver	Frank Sully
Dancer Specialty	Elena Verdugo	Officer	Jack Arnold
Bartender	James C. Morton		
Spanish Girl	Esther Estrella		
Spanish Girl	Marissa Flores		
Bellboy	Frank Coghlan, Jr.		
Truck Driver	William Haade		
Pharmacist's Mate	Walter Sande		
Warden	James Flavin		
Orderly	Hugh Beaumont		
Girl	Hillary Brooke		
Captain	Byron Shores		
Newscaster	Knox Manning		
Officer	Charles Brokaw		
C.P.O.	Harry Strang		
Chinaman	Chester Gan		

Distributor: 20th Century-Fox
Director: Bruce Humberstone
Released: March 11, 1942

BLACK DRAGONS

Dr. Melcher	
Colomb	Bela Lugosi
Alice	Joan Barclay
Don Martin	Clayton Moore
Saunders	George Pembroke

Preston Foster with Lynn Bari in **Secret Agent of Japan** (20th Century-Fox).

Hanlin	Robert Frazer	Saito	Noel Madison
The Dragon	Stanford Jolley	Fu Yen	Sen Yung
Kerney	Max Hoffman, Jr.	Doris Poole	Janis Carter
Van Dyke	Irving Mitchell	Alecsandri	Steve Geray
Wallace	Edward Peil	Traeger	Kurt Katch
Ryder	Bob Fiske	Remsen	Addison Richards
Colton	Kenneth Harlan	Captain Larsen	Ian Wolfe
Stevens	Joe Eggenton	Mrs. Alecsandri	Hermine Sterler
		Naval Captain	Selmer Jackson
		Eminescu	Frank Puglia
		English Secret Service	Leyland Hodgson
			Leslie Denison
		Solaire	Jean Del Val

Distributor: Monogram
Director: William Nigh
Released: March 12, 1942

SECRET AGENT OF JAPAN

Roy Bonnell	Preston Foster
Kay Murdock	Lynn Bari

Distributor: 20th Century-Fox
Director: Irving Pichel
Released: March 16, 1942

Bob Hope and Madeleine Carroll in **My Favorite Blonde** (Paramount).

MY FAVORITE BLONDE

Larry Haines	Bob Hope
Karen Bentley	Madeleine Carroll
Madame Stephanie Runick	Gale Sondergaard
Dr. Hugo Streger	George Zucco
Karl	Lionel Royce
Dr. Faber	Walter Kingsford
Miller	Victor Varconi
Lanz	Otto Reichow
Turk O'Flaherty	Charles Cane
Ulrich	Crane Whitley
Sheriff	Erville Alderson
Mrs. Topley	Esther Howard
Mulrooney	Ed Gargan
Union Secretary	James Burke
Porter	Dooley Wilson
Mortician	Milton Parsons
Tom Douglas	Tom Fadden
Sam	Fred Kelsey
Joe	Edgar Dearing
Elvan	Leslie Dennison
Burton	Robert Emmett Keane
Herbert Wilson	Addison Richards

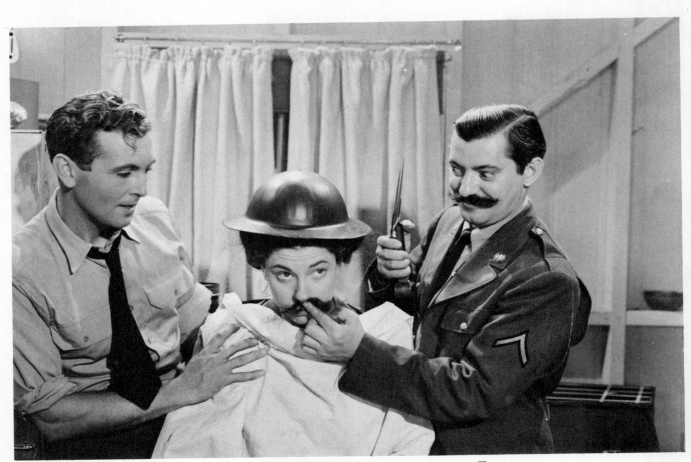

Allan Jones, Judy Canova and Jerry Colonna in **True to the Army** (Paramount).

Veronica Lake with Alan Ladd in **This Gun for Hire** (Paramount).

Colonel Ashmont	Matthew Boulton	Frozen-Faced Woman	Minerva Urecal
Conductor	Wade Boteler	Truck Driver	James Millican
Colonel Raeburn	William Forrest	Yard Man	Edmund Cobb
Frederick	Carl Switzer	Stuttering Boy	Jimmy Dodd
Frederick's Mother	Isabel Randolph	Pilots	Eddie Dew
Train Official	Edward Hearn		George Turner
English Driver	Leyland Hodgson		Kirby Grant
Spectator	Jack Luden		William Cabanne
Cop At Union Hall	Monte Blue		
Backstage Doorman	Dick Elliott		
Male Nurse	Arno Frey		
Apartment Manager	Lloyd Whitlock		
Bartender	Vernon Dent		
Mrs. Weatherwax	Sarah Edwards		
Dr. Higby	Paul Scardon		
Telegraph Operator	Bill Lally		

Distributor: Paramount
Director: Sidney Lanfield
Released: March 18, 1942

TRUE TO THE ARMY

Daisy Hawkins	Judy Canova

Frank Sully, Ken Christy, Pat O'Brien, Roger Clark, Brian Donlevy and Frank Jenks in **Two Yanks in Trinidad** (Columbia).

Private Bill Chandler	Allan Jones
Vicki Marlow	Ann Miller
Private Fothergill	Jerry Colonna
Sergeant Butes	William Demarest
Colonel Marlow	Clarence Kolb
Lieutenant Danvers	William Wright
Junior	Edward Pawley
Ice	Edwin Miller
Ray	Arthur Loft
Private Dugan	Gordon Jones
Private O'Toole	Rod Cameron
Sergeant Riggs	Eddie Acuff
Target Sergeant	Edgar Dearing
Drake	John Miljan
Mae	Mary Treen
Congressman	Selmer Jackson

Distributor: Paramount
Director: Albert S. Rogell
Released: March 18, 1942

THIS GUN FOR HIRE

Ellen Graham	Veronica Lake
Michael Crane	Robert Preston
Willard Gates	Laird Cregar
Raven	Alan Ladd
Alvin Brewster	Tully Marshall
Sluky	Mikhail Rasumny
Tommy	Marc Lawrence
Annie	Pamela Blake
Steve Finnerty	Harry Shannon

Albert Baker	Frank Ferguson
Baker's Secretary	Bernadene Hayes
Blair Fletcher	Olin Howland
Senator Burnett	Roger Imhof
Ruby	Patricia Farr
Night Watchman	James Farley
Crippled Girl	Virita Campbell
Brewster's Secretary	Victor Kilian
Police Captain	Charles C. Wilson
Salesgirl	Mary Davenport
Mr. Collins	Earle Dewey
Gates' Secretary	Lynda Grey
Charlie	Emmett Vogan
Mr. Stewart	Chester Clute
Will Gates	Charles Arnt
Lieutenant Clark	Dick Rush
Scissor Grinder	Clem Bevans
Restaurant Manager	Harry Hayden
Weems, Guard	Tim Ryan
Police Captain	Edwin Stanley
Officer Glennon	Elliott Sullivan
Mrs. Mason	Sarah Padden
Piano Player	Don Barclay
Young Man	Richard Webb
Keever	John Sheehan
Frong	Alan Speer
Waiter	Cyril Ring
Walt	Fred Walburn
Jimmie	Robert Winkler
Special Dancer	Yvonne DeCarlo

Distributor: Paramount
Director: Frank Tuttle
Released: March 23, 1942

TWO YANKS IN TRINIDAD

Tim Reardon	Pat O'Brien
Vince Barrows	Brian Donlevy
Patricia Dare	Janet Blair
James W. Buckingham III	Roger Clark
Sergeant Valentine	Donald MacBride
Chicago Hagen	John Emery
Joe Scavenger	Frank Jenks
Mike Paradise	Frank Sully
Bubbles	Veda Ann Borg
Colonel Powers	Clyde Fillmore
Sea Captain	Dick Curtis
Maitre D'	Sig Arno

Distributor: Columbia
Director: Gregory Ratoff
Released: March 26, 1942

CANAL ZONE

'Hardtack' Hamilton	Chester Morris
Susan Merrill	Harriet Hilliard
Harley Ames	John Hubbard
Kincaid	Larry Parks
Madigan	Forrest Tucker
Hughes	Eddie Laughton
Baldwin	Lloyd Bridges

John Hubbard and Harriet Hilliard in **Canal Zone** (Columbia).

MacNamara	George McKay
Commander Merrill	Stanley Andrews
'Red' Connors	John Tyrrell
Jones	Stanley Brown
Henshaw	John Shay

Distributor: Columbia
Director: Lew Landers
Released: March 28, 1942

UNSEEN ENEMY

Nick	Leo Carrillo
Sam	Andy Devine
Gen	Irene Hervey
Bill	Don Terry

Frederick Giermann, Hector V. Sarno and Turhan Bey in **Unseen Enemy** (Universal).

Roering	Lionel Royce
Ito	Turhan Bey
Muller	Frederick Gierman
Callahan	William Ruhl
Davies	Clancy Cooper
Badger	Eddie Fetherston

Distributor: Universal
Director: John Rawlins
Released: April 1, 1942

TRAMP, TRAMP, TRAMP

Hank	Jackie Gleason

Jack Durant, Jackie Gleason and Mabel Todd in **Tramp, Tramp, Tramp** (Columbia).

Jed	Jack Durant
Pam Martin	Florence Rice
Tommy Lydel	Bruce Bennett
Granny	Hallene Hill
Midget	Billy Curtis
Vivian	Mabel Todd
Blond Bomber	Forrest Tucker
Biggie Waldron	James Seay
Lefty	John Tyrrell
Mousey	John Harmon
Blackie	Eddie Foster
Tim	Al Hill
Borrah Minevitch and	
	Themselves
Harmonica Rascals	

Thurston Hall with Frank Albertson in **Shepherd of the Ozarks** (Republic).

Distributor: Columbia
Director: Charles Barton
Released: April 2, 1942

SHEPHERD OF THE OZARKS

Abner	Leon Weaver
Cicero	Frank Weaver
Elviry	June Weaver
Susanna Weaver	Marilyn Hare
Jimmy Maloney	Frank Albertson
James Maloney	Thurston Hall
Doolittle	Johnny Arthur
Dudd Hitt	William Haade
Kirk	Wade Crosby

William Tracy, Marjorie Lord, Margaret Dumont
and Joe Sawyer in **About Face** (United Artists).

Louie	Joe Devlin	Colonel Gunning	Joe Cunningham
Scully	Fred Sherman	Captain Caldwell	Harold Goodwin
General Tobin	Guy Usher	Jerry	Frank Faylen
		Charley	Dick Wessel
		Garage Manager	Charles Lane

Distributor: Republic
Director: Frank McDonald
Released: April 6, 1942

Distributor: United Artists
Director: Kurt Neumann
Released: April 16, 1942

ABOUT FACE

Sergeant Doubleday	William Tracy
Sergeant Ames	Joe Sawyer
Sally	Jean Porter
Betty Marlow	Marjorie Lord
Mrs. Culpepper	Margaret Dumont
Daisy	Veda Ann Borg

SHIP AHOY

Tallulah Winters	Eleanor Powell
Merton K. Kibble	Red Skelton
'Skip' Owens	Bert Lahr
Fran Evans	Virginia O'Brien

Eleanor Powell and Red Skelton in **Ship Ahoy** (M-G-M).

H. U. Bennet	William Post, Jr.	Tobin	Otto Kruger
'Stump'	James Cross	Miller	Vaughan Glaser
'Stumpy'	Eddie Hartman	Truck Driver	Murray Alper
Art Higgins	Stuart Crawford	Mrs. Mason	Dorothy Peterson
Dr. Farno	John Emery	Mrs. Sutton	Alma Kruger
Pietro Polesi	Bernard Nedell		
Tommy Dorsey and Orchestra	Themselves		

Distributor: Universal
Director: Alfred Hitchcock
Released: April 23, 1942

Distributor: M-G-M
Director: Edward N. Buzzell
Released: April 17, 1942

SABOTEUR

Pat	Priscilla Lane
Barry Kane	Robert Cummings
Fry	Norman Lloyd

THE WIFE TAKES A FLYER

Anita Woverman	Joan Bennett
Christopher Reynolds	Franchot Tone
Major Zellfritz	Allyn Joslyn
Countess Oldenburg	Cecil Cunningham
Keith	Roger Clark

Priscilla Lane, Robert Cummings and Otto Kruger in **Saboteur** (Universal).

Thomas Woverman	Lloyd Corrigan
Muller	Lyle Latell
Mrs. Woverman	Georgia Caine
Maria Woverman	Barbara Brown
Jan	Erskine Sanford
Adolph Bietjelboer	Chester Clute
Hendrik Woverman	Hans Conried
Zanten	Romaine Callender
Chief Justice	Aubrey Mather
Gustav	William Edmunds
Mrs. Brandt	Curtis Railing
Miss Updike	Nora Cecil
Capt. Schmutnick	Kurt Katch
The Twins	Margaret Seddon
	Kate MacKenna
Major Wilson	Gordon Richards

Distributor: Columbia
Director: Richard Wallace
Released: April 28, 1942

MY FAVORITE SPY

Kay	Kay Kyser
Terry	Ellen Drew
Connie	Jane Wyman
Robinson	Robert Armstrong
Aunt Jessie	Helen Westley
Flower Pot Cop	William Demarest
Cora (Maid)	Una O'Connor
Winters	Lionel Royce
Major Allen	Moroni Olsen

Gus	George Cleveland
Col. Moffett	Vaughan Glaser
Jules	Hobart Cavanaugh
Higgenbotham	Chester Clute
Soldier	Teddy Hart

Distributor: RKO
Director: Tay Garnett
Released: May 6, 1942

POWDER TOWN

Jeems O'Shea	Victor McLaglen
Pennant	Edmond O'Brien
Dolly	June Havoc
Sally	Dorothy Lovett
Meeker	Eddie Foy, Jr.
Oliver Lindsay	Damian O'Flynn
Chick Parker	Marten Lamont
Dr. Wayne	Roy Gordon
Sue	Marion Martin
Mrs. Douglas	Mary Gordon
Carol	Frances Neal
Betty	Julie Warren
Helen	Jane Woodworth
Gus	George Cleveland
Harvey Dodge	John Maguire

Distributor: RKO
Director: Rowland V. Lee
Released: May 11, 1942

Joan Bennett with Franchot Tone in **The Wife Takes A Flyer** (Columbia).

Kay Kyser in **My Favorite Spy** (RKO).

REMEMBER PEARL HARBOR

Steve 'Lucky' Smith	Donald M. Barry
Bruce Gordon	Alan Curtis
Marcia Porter	Fay McKenzie
Van Hoorten	Sig Ruman
Capt. Hudson	Ian Keith
Senor Anderson	Rhys Williams
Portly Porter	Maynard Holmes
Doralda	Diana Del Rio
Mr. Littlefield	Robert Emmett Keane
Sergeant Adams	Sammy Stein
Jap Bartender	Paul Fung
Jap Major	James B. Leong

Distributor: Republic
Director: Joseph Santley
Released: May 11, 1942

THIS ABOVE ALL

Clive	Tyrone Power
Prudence	Joan Fontaine
Monty	Thomas Mitchell
General Cathaway	Henry Stephenson
Ramsbottom	Nigel Bruce
Iris	Gladys Cooper

Dorothy Lovett, Victor McLaglen and June Havoc **Powder Town** (RKO).

Fay McKenzie, Donald Barry and John James in **Re-member Pearl Harbor** (Republic).

Roger	Philip Merivale
Waitress in Tea Room	Sara Allgood
Rector	Alexander Knox
Violet	Queenie Leonard
Wilbur	Melville Cooper
Nurse Emily	Jill Esmond
Chaplain	Arthur Shields
Parsons	Dennis Hoey
Major	Miles Mander
Sergeant	Rhys Williams
Joe	John Abbott
Maid	Carol Curtis-Brown
Maid	Mary Field
Rosie	Lilyan Irene
Dr. Mathias	Holmes Herbert
Dr. Ferris	Dennis Green
Vicar	Thomas Louden
Vicar's Wife	Mary Forbes

Joan Fontaine and Philip Merivale in **This Above All** (20th Century-Fox).

Walter Pidgeon in **Mrs. Miniver** (M-G-M).

Paul Cavanagh with Jean Rogers and Lee Bowman in
Pacific Rendezvous (M-G-M).

Proprietor	Forrester Harvey	Clem Miniver	Walter Pidgeon
Conductor	Harold de Becker	Carol Beldon	Teresa Wright
Matron	Jessica Newcombe	Lady Beldon	Dame May Whitty
Farmer	Billy Bevan	Mr. Ballard	Henry Travers
Mae	Brenda Forbes	Foley	Reginald Owen
Sergeant	Doris Lloyd	Vicar	Henry Wilcoxon
Porter	Alan Edmiston	Vin Miniver	Richard Ney
Soldier	Morton Lowry	Toby Miniver	Christopher Severn
Proprietor	Olaf Hytten	Gladys	Brenda Forbes
		Judy Miniver	Clare Sandars
		Horace	Rhys Williams

Distributor: 20th Century-Fox
Director: Anatole Litvak
Released: May 14, 1942

Ada	Marie de Becker
German Flyer	Helmut Dantine
Miss Spriggins	Mary Field
Nobby	Paul Scardon
Ginger	Ben Webster
George	Aubrey Mather
Huggins	Forrester Harvey

MRS. MINIVER

Kay Miniver	Greer Garson

Fred	John Abbott	Bickles	Colin Campbell
Simpson	Connie Leon	Doctor	Herbert Clifton
Conductor	Billy Bevan	Man In Tavern	Walter Byron
Saleslady	Ottola Nesmith	Mr. Verger	Thomas Louden
Car Dealer	Gerald Oliver Smith	Pilot	Peter Lawford
Joe	Alec Craig	German Agent's Voice	Miles Mander
Mrs. Huggins	Clara Reid		
William	Harry Allen		
Halliday	John Burton		

Distributor: M-G-M
Director: William Wyler
Released: May 13, 1942

Beldon's Butler	Leonard Carey
Marston	Eric Lonsdale
Mac	Charles Irwin
Dentist	Ian Wolfe
Sir Henry	Arthur Wimperis
Carruthers	David Clyde

PACIFIC RENDEZVOUS

Lieutenant Bill Gordon .... Lee Bowman

Dennis Morgan, Jerry Mandy, Clancy Cooper, Jack Carson and Ann Sheridan in **Wings for the Eagle** (Warner Bros.).

George Meeker, Stuart Holmes, Irene Manning, player, Peter Whitney and Roland Drew in **Spy Ship** (Warner Bros.).

Elaine Carter	Jean Rogers
Olivia Kerlov	Mona Maris
Andre Leemuth	Carl Esmond
Commander Brennan	Paul Cavanaugh
Mrs. Savarina	Blanche Yurka
John Carter	Russell Hicks
Prof. Harvey Lessmore	Arthur Shields
Lanny	William Post, Jr.
Jasper Dean	William Tannen
Dr. Jackwin	Frederic Worlock
Kestrin	Curt Bois
De Segroff	Felix Basch
Gordon Trisby	Addison Richards
Secretary of Navy	Edward Fielding

Distributor: M-G-M
Director: George Sidney
Released: May 21, 1942

WINGS FOR THE EAGLE

Roma Maple	Ann Sheridan
Corky Jones	Dennis Morgan
Brad Maple	Jack Carson
Jake Hanso	George Tobias
Pete Hanso	Russell Arms
Gil Borden	Don DeFore
Tom 'Cyclone' Shaw	Tom Fadden
Johnson	John Ridgely
Stark	Frank Wilcox

Personnel Man	George Meeker
Miss Baxter	Fay Helm
Midget	Billy Curtis
Policeman	Emory Parnell
Motorcycle Officer	Edgar Dearing

Distributor: Warner Bros.
Director: Lloyd Bacon
Released: June 4, 1942

SPY SHIP

Ward Prescott	Craig Stevens
Pamela Mitchell	Irene Manning
Sue Mitchell	Maris Wrixon
Gordon Morrel	Michael Ames
Zinner	Peter Whitney
Ernie Haskell	John Maxwell
Martin Oster	William Forrest
Nils Thorson	Roland Drew
Paul	George Meeker
Harry Mitchell	George Irving
Burns	Frank Ferguson
Drake	Olaf Hytten
Inspector Bond	Jack Mower
Haru	Keye Luke

Distributor: Warner Bros.
Director: B. Reaves Eason
Released: June 4, 1942

Maxine Andrews, Patti Andrews, LaVerne Andrews and Shemp Howard in **Private Buckaroo** (Universal).

Robert Lowery, Veda Ann Borg and Lyle Talbot in
She's in the Army (Monogram).

PRIVATE BUCKAROO

Andrews Sisters	Themselves
Lon Prentice	Dick Foran
Lancelot Pringle McBiff	Joe E. Lewis
Joyce Mason	Jennifer Holt
Sergeant 'Muggsy' Shavel	Shemp Howard
Lieutenant Mason	Richard Davies
Bonnie-Belle Schlopkiss	Mary Wickes
Colonel Weatherford	Ernest Truex
Donny	Donald O'Connor
Peggy	Peggy Ryan
Corporal Anemic	Huntz Hall
Tagalong	Susan Levine
The Jivin' Jacks and Jills	Themselves
Harry James and his Music Makers	Themselves

Distributor: Universal
Director: Eddie Cline
Released: June 11, 1942

SHE'S IN THE ARMY

Hannah	Lucile Gleason
Diane	Veda Ann Borg
Susie	Marie Wilson
Steve	Lyle Talbot
Jim	Robert Lowrey
Rita	Maxine Leslie
Helen	Charlotte Henry
Lundigan	John Holland
Lewis	Marcella Richards

Joe .... Warren Hymer

Distributor: Monogram
Director: Jean Yarbrough
Released: June 16, 1942

Leif Erickson, Robert Stack and John Loder in **Eagle Squadron** (Universal).

EAGLE SQUADRON

Chuck Brewer	Robert Stack
Anne Partridge	Diana Barrymore
Paddy Carson	John Loder
Leckie	Eddie Albert
McKinnon	Nigel Bruce
Johnny Coe	Leif Erickson
Wadislaw Borowsky	Edgar Barrier
Hank Starr	John Hall
Nancy Mitchell	Evelyn Ankers
Dame Elizabeth Whitby	Esobel Elsom
Olesen	Alan Hale, Jr.
Ramsey	Don Porter
Grenfall	Frederick Worlock
Air Minister	Stanley Ridges
The Kid	Gene Reynolds
Bullock	Robert Warwick
Chandler	Clarence Straight
Meeker	Edmund Glover
Aunt Emmeline	Gladys Cooper
Sergeant Johns	Rhys Williams
Sir John	Paul Cavanagh

Severn	Gavin Muir
Lieutenant Jefferys	Richard Fraser
Griffith	Richard Crane
Barker	Howard Banks
Welch	Harold Landon
Meyers	Todd Karns
Chubby	Charles King, Jr.
Phyllis	Jill Esmond
Sir Charles Porter	Ian Wolfe
Black Watch Officer	Alan Napier
Private Owen	Harold de Becker
Hoskins	Donald Stuart
Lubbock	Carl Harbord
Sir Benjamin Trask	Charles Irwin
Day Controller	Olaf Hytten
R.A.F. Flyer	Stanley Smith
R.A.F. Flyer	Richard Davies
Lankershire Blonde	Queenie Leonard
Simms	Ivan Simpson
Wing Commander	John Burton
King	Bruce Lester
Allison	Tom Stevenson
Blind Patient	James Eagles
Medical Officer	James Seay
Nurse	Audrey Long
Mother	Mary Carr
Pilot	Peter Lawford
German Soldier	Rex Lease
Children	Tarquin Olivier
	William Severn
	Linda Bieber
	Peggy Ann Garner

Shirley Patterson, Kenneth MacDonald, Russell Hayden and Charles Starrett in **Riders of the Northland** (Columbia).

Marguerite Chapman, John Howard, Bruce Bennett and Forrest Tucker in **Submarine Raider** (Columbia).

Distributor: Universal
Director: Arthur Lubin
Released: June 16, 1942

Distributor: Columbia
Director: William Berke
Released: June 18, 1942

RIDERS OF THE NORTHLAND

Steve Bowie .... Charles Starrett
Lucky Laidlaw .... Russell Hayden
Sheila Taylor .... Shirley Patterson
Harmony Bumpas .... Cliff Edwards
Buddy Taylor .... Bobby Larson
Alex .... Lloyd Bridges
Matt Taylor .... Kenneth MacDonald
Chris Larsen .... Paul Sutton
Agent .... Robert O. Davis
Stacy .... Joe McGuinn
Dobie .... Francis Walker
Luke .... George Piltz

SUBMARINE RAIDER

Chris Warren .... John Howard
Sue Curry .... Marguerite Chapman
First Officer Russell .... Bruce Bennett
Bill Warren .... Warren Ashe
Vera Lane .... Eileen O'Hearn
Captain Yamanada .... Nino Pipitone
First Officer Kawakami .... Philip Ahn
Sparksie .... Larry Parks
Steward Seffi .... Rudy Robles
Grant Duncan .... Roger Clark
Pulaski .... Forrest Tucker
Shannon .... Eddie Laughton

Levy	Stanley Brown
Oleson	Jack Shay
Brick Brandon	Gary Breckner

Distributor: Columbia
Director: Lew Landers
Released: June 20, 1942

FRIENDLY ENEMIES

Karl Pfeiffer	Charles Winninger
Henry Block	Charlie Ruggles
William Pfeiffer	James Craig
June Block	Nancy Kelly
Anton Miller	Otto Kruger
Mrs. Pfeiffer	Ilka Gruning

Gretchen	Greta Meyer
Inspector McCarty	Allison Richards
Braun	Charles Lane
Schnitzler	John Piffle
Nora	Ruth Holly

Distributor: United Artists
Director: Allan Dwan
Released: June 24, 1942

FLIGHT LIEUTENANT

Sam Doyle	Pat O'Brien
Danny Doyle	Glenn Ford
Susie Thompson	Evelyn Keyes
Sanford	Jonathan Hale

James Craig, Nancy Kelly, Charles Winninger, Ilka Gruning and Charles Ruggles in **Friendly Enemies** (United Artists).

Pat O'Brien and Douglas Croft in **Flight Lieutenant** (Columbia).

Major Thompson	Minor Watson
Father Carlos	Frank Puglia
Larsen	Edward Pawley

Becker	Gregory Gay
Scanlon	Clancy Cooper
Carey	Trevor Bardette
Faulet	Marcel Dalio
Jackson	John Gallaudet
Sandy Roth	Larry Parks
Bill Robinson	Lloyd Bridges
John McGinnis	Hugh Beaumont
Danny Doyle (As A Boy)	Douglas Croft

Distributor: Columbia
Director: Sidney Salkow
Released: June 29, 1942

ESCAPE FROM HONG KONG

Pancho	Leo Carrillo
Blimp	Andy Devine
Valerie Hale	Marjorie Lord
Rusty	Don Terry

Leyland Hodgson and Gilbert Emery in **Escape from Hong Kong** (Universal).

Dewey Robinson, Rochelle Hudson, John Abbott, Ricardo Cortez and Milburn Stone in **Rubber Racketeers** (Monogram).

Major Crossley	Gilbert Emery	Mary Dale	Barbara Read
Major Reeves	Leyland Hodgson	Angel	Milburn Stone
Kosura	Frank Puglia	Larkin	Dewey Robinson
Yamota	Chester Gan	Dumbo	John Abbott
Sergeant	Frank Kelly	Curley	Pat Gleason
Franz Schuler	Paul Dubov	Mule	Dick Rich
		Red	Alan Hale, Jr.
		Freddy Dale	Sam Edwards
		Tom	Kam Tong
		Bert	Dick Hogan
		Lila	Marjorie Manners
		Butch	Alex Callam

Distributor: Universal
Director: William Nigh
Released: June 30, 1942

RUBBER RACKETEERS

Gilin	Ricardo Cortez
Nikki	Rochelle Hudson
Bill Barry	Bill Henry

Distributor: Monogram
Director: Harold Young
Released: June 30, 1942

Ernest Dorian, Tommy Seidel and Alan Baxter in
Prisoners of Japan (PRC).

<table>
<tr><td colspan="2">

PRISONER OF JAPAN

</td><td colspan="2">

THE PIED PIPER

</td></tr>
<tr><td>David Bowman</td><td>Alan Baxter</td><td>Howard</td><td>Monte Woolley</td></tr>
<tr><td>Toni Chase</td><td>Gertrude Michael</td><td>Ronnie Cavanaugh</td><td>Roddy McDowall</td></tr>
<tr><td>Matsuru</td><td>Ernest Dorian</td><td>Nicole Rougeron</td><td>Anne Baxter</td></tr>
<tr><td>Loti</td><td>Corinna Mura</td><td>Major Diessen</td><td>Otto Preminger</td></tr>
<tr><td>Ensign Bailey</td><td>Tommy Seidel</td><td>Aristide Rougeron</td><td>J. Carrol Naish</td></tr>
<tr><td>Maui</td><td>Billy Boya</td><td>Mr. Cavanaugh</td><td>Lester Matthews</td></tr>
<tr><td>Lieutenant Morgan</td><td>Ray Bennett</td><td>Mrs. Cavanaugh</td><td>Jill Esmond</td></tr>
<tr><td>Marine</td><td>Dave O'Brien</td><td>Madame</td><td>Ferike Boros</td></tr>
<tr><td>Edie</td><td>Ann Staunton</td><td>Sheila Cavanaugh</td><td>Peggy Ann Garner</td></tr>
<tr><td>Jap Operator</td><td>Beal Wong</td><td>Willem</td><td>Merrill Rodin</td></tr>
<tr><td>U.S. Operator</td><td>Gilbert Frye</td><td>Pierre</td><td>Maurice Tauzin</td></tr>
<tr><td>Commander McDonald</td><td>Kent Thurber</td><td>Rose</td><td>Fleurette Zama</td></tr>
<tr><td></td><td></td><td>Frenchman</td><td>William Edmunds</td></tr>
<tr><td colspan="2">

Distributor: PRC
Director: Arthur Ripley
Released: June 30, 1942

</td><td>Foquet</td><td>Marcel Dalio</td></tr>
<tr><td></td><td></td><td>Madame Bonne</td><td>Marcelle Corday</td></tr>
<tr><td></td><td></td><td>Charendon</td><td>Edward Ashley</td></tr>
</table>

Roddy McDowall, Anne Baxter, Monte Woolley and Otto Preminger in **The Pied Piper** (20th Century-Fox).

Roger Dickinson	Morton Lowry	Anna	Julika
Madame Rougeron	Odette Myrtil	Waiter	Wilson Benge
Railroad Official	Jean Del Val	Major Domo	Brandon Hurst
Barman	George Davis	Medford	Thomas Louden
Lieutenant	Robert O. Davis		
Military Policeman	Henry Rowland		

Roger Dickinson .... Morton Lowry
Madame Rougeron .... Odette Myrtil
Railroad Official .... Jean Del Val
Barman .... George Davis
Lieutenant .... Robert O. Davis
Military Policeman .... Henry Rowland
Aide .... Helmut Dantine
German Soldier .... Otto Reichow
German Soldier .... Henry Guttman
Sergeant .... Hans von Morhart
Sergeant .... Hans von Twardowski
Officer At Road .... William Yetter
Servant .... Adrienne d'Ambricourt
Proprietress .... Mici Gory
Fisherman .... Jean De Briac
Soldier .... Ernst Hausman

Anna .... Julika
Waiter .... Wilson Benge
Major Domo .... Brandon Hurst
Medford .... Thomas Louden

Distributor: 20th Century-Fox
Director: Irving Pichel
Released: July 8, 1942

LITTLE TOKYO, U. S. A.

Michael Steele .... Preston Foster
Maris Hanover .... Brenda Joyce
Takimura .... Harold Huber
Hendricks .... Don Douglas

Teru	June Duprez
Kingoro	George E. Stone
Satsuma	Abner Biberman
Marsten	Charles Tannen
Jerry	Frank Orth
Suma	Edward Soohoo

Preston Foster with Brenda Joyce in **Little Tokyo, U.S.A.** (20th Century-Fox).

Shadow	Beal Wong
Mrs. Satsuma	Daisy Lee
Fujiama	Leonard Strong
Captain Wade	J. Farrell MacDonald
Oshima	Richard Loo
Okono	Sen Yung
Mrs. Okono	Melie Chang

Distributor: 20th Century-Fox
Director: Otto Brower
Released: July 8, 1942

ATLANTIC CONVOY

Capt. Morgan	Bruce Bennett
Lida Adams	Virginia Field
Carl Hansen	John Beal
Sandy Brown	Clifford Severn
Gregory	Larry Parks
Eddie	Stanley Brown
Bert	Lloyd Bridges
Otto	Victor Kilian
Commander von Smith	Hans Schumm

Gunther	Erik Rolf
Radio Operator	Eddie Laughton

Distributor: Columbia
Director: Lew Landers
Released: July 10, 1942

JOAN OF OZARK

Judy	Judy Canova
Cliff Little	Joe E. Brown
Eddie McCabe	Eddie Foy, Jr.
Philip Munson	Jerome Cowan
Guido	Alexander Granach
Marie	Anne Jeffreys
Otto	Otto Reichow
Kurt	Wolfgang Zilzer
Leonard Jones	Donald Curtis
Hans	Hans von Twardowski
Major Fadden	Harry Hayden

Distributor: Republic
Director: Joseph Santley
Released: July 15, 1942

PANAMA HATTIE

Red	Red Skelton
Hattie Maloney	Ann Sothern
Rags	Rags Ragland

Virginia Field, John Beal and Victor Kilian in **Atlantic Convoy** (Columbia).

Joe E. Brown, Jerome Cowan, Hans von Twardowski, Alexander Granach, Wolfgang Zilzer and William von Brincken in **Joan of Ozark** (Republic).

Rowdy	Ben Blue	Congo Jack	Stuart Erwin
Leila Tree	Marsha Hunt	Enid	Peggy Moran
Flo	Virginia O'Brien	Kirk	Don Terry
Jay Perkins	Alan Mowbray	Coutlass	Richard Lane
Dick Bulliett	Dan Dailey, Jr.	Kalu	Jules Bledsoe
Geraldine Bulliett	Jackie Horner	Juma	Turhan Bey
Lucas Kefler	Carl Esmond	Malimi	Dorothy Dandridge
Lena Horne	Herself	King Malaba	Ernest Whitman
The Berry Brothers	Themselves	Col. Robinson	Ed Stanley
		Chief Madjeduka	Jess Lee Brooks
		Taroka Leader	Napoleon Simpson

Distributor: M-G-M
Director: Norman Z. McLeod
Released: July 22, 1942

Distributor: Universal
Director: Christy Cabanne
Released: July 22, 1942

DRUMS OF THE CONGO

Dr. Ann Montgomery .... Ona Munson

PRIORITIES ON PARADE

Donna D'Arcy .... Ann Miller

Red Skelton, Ann Sothern, Rags Ragland and Ben
Blue in **Panama Hattie** (M-G-M).

Stuart Erwin, Ona Munson, Don Terry and Richard
Lane in **Drums of the Congo** (Universal).

Jerry Colonna and Vera Vague in **Priorities on Parade** (Paramount).

Marguerite Chapman, Louise Allbritton and Catherine Craig in **Parachute Nurse** (Columbia).

Johnny Draper	....	Johnnie Johnston
Jeep Jackson	....	Jerry Colonna
Lee Davis	....	Betty Rhodes
Mariposa Ginsbotham	....	Vera Vague
Harvey Erkimer	....	Harry Barris
Sticks O'Hara	....	Eddie Quillan
Push Gasper	....	Dave Willock
Cornetist	....	Nick Cochrane
Stage Manager	....	Rod Cameron
E. V. Hartley	....	Arthur Loft
Specialty Act	....	The Debonaires
Col. Reeves	....	William Forrest
1st Examiner	....	Warren Ashe
2nd Examiner	....	Charles Halton
Jones	....	Lee Shumway

Distributor: Paramount

Director: Albert S. Rogell
Released: July 23, 1942

PARACHUTE NURSE

Glenda White	....	Marguerite Chapman
Lieutenant Woods	....	William Wright
Dottie Morrison	....	Kay Harris
Jane Morgan		Lauretta M. Schimmoler
Helen Ames	....	Louise Albritton
Sergeant Peters	....	Frank Sully
Ruby Stark	....	Diedra Vale
Gretchen Ernst	....	Evelyn Wahl
Katherine Webb	....	Shirley Patterson
Mary Mack	....	Eileen O'Hearn
Nita Dominick	....	Roma Aldrich

Allen Jung, Douglas Fowley and Clark Gable in **Somewhere I'll Find You** (M-G-M).

Leo Carrillo, Andy Devine, Don Terry and Edgar Barrier in **Danger in the Pacific** (Universal).

Edward Arnold, Van Johnson, Fay Bainter, Jean Rogers and Richard Ney in **The War Against Mrs. Hadley** (M-G-M).

Wendie Holmes	Marjorie Reardon
Lieutenant Mullins	Catherine Craig
Major Devon	Douglas Wood
Lieutenant Tucker	Forrest Tucker

Distributor: Columbia
Director: Charles Barton
Released: August 6, 1942

DANGER IN THE PACIFIC

Leo Marzell	Leo Carrillo
Andy Parker	Andy Devine
David Lynd	Don Terry
Jane Claymore	Louise Albritton
Zambesi	Edgar Barrier
Tagani	Turhan Bey
Commissioner	Holmes Herbert
Storekeeper	David Hoffman

Joseph Cotton, Delores Del Rio and Eustace Wyatt in **Journey Into Fear** (RKO).

Manolo	Paul Dubov
Lobo	Neyle Marx

John Litel, Lee Shumway and Richard Scott in **Invisible Agent** (Universal).

Dan Dailey, Marjorie Lord and Edmund MacDonald in **Timber** (Universal).

Distributor: Universal
Director: Lewis D. Collins
Released: August 6, 1942

Jonathan Davis	Clark Gable
Paula Lane	Lana Turner
Kirk Davis	Robert Sterling
Willie Manning	Reginald Owen
Eve Manning	Lee Patrick
George L. Stafford	Charles Dingle
Mama Lugovska	Tamara Shayne
Dorloff	Leonid Kinskey
Penny	Diana Lewis
Nurse Winifred	Molly Lamont
Crystal Jones	Patricia Dane
Miss Coulter	Sara Haden
Prof. Anatole	Richard Kean
Pearcley	Francis Sayles
Bartender	Tom O'Grady
Waiter	Donald Kerr

Wanda McKay, John Beal, J. Farrell MacDonald and Warren Hymer in **One Thrilling Night** (Monogram).

Penny's Companion	Gayne Whitman
Boy	Grady Sutton
Girl	Dorothy Morris
Thomas Chang	Keye Luke
Fred Kirsten	Miles Mander
Ming	Eleanor Soohoo
Sam Porto	Allen Jung
Captain	Douglas Fowley
Felipe Morel	Benny Inocencio
Lieut. Hall	Van Johnson
Manuel Ortega	Angel Cruz
Sgt. Purdy	Keenan Wynn
Slim	Frank Faylen
Pete Brady	J. Lewis Smith
Chinese Doctor	Lee Tung Foo

James Ellison and Virginia Bruce in **Careful, Soft Shoulders** (20th Century-Fox).

Edward Norris with Kay Harris in **Sabotage Squad** (Columbia).

Sally	Frances Rafferty
Millie	Dorothy Morris
Bennett	Halliwell Hobbes
Cook	Connie Gilchrist
Peters	Horace McNally
Dr. Leonard Meecham	Miles Mander
Louie	Rags Ragland
Bob	Mark Daniels
Messenger Boy	Carl Switzer

Distributor: M-G-M
Director: Harold S. Bacquet
Released: August 7, 1942

Distributor: M-G-M
Director: Wesley Ruggles
Released: August 6, 1942

THE WAR AGAINST MRS. HADLEY

Elliott Fulton	Edward Arnold
Stella Hadley	Fay Bainter
Theodore Hadley	Richard Ney
Patricia Hadley	Jean Rogers
Mrs. Michael Fitzpatrick	Sara Allgood
Cecilia Talbot	Spring Byington
Michael Fitzpatrick	Van Johnson
Mrs. Laura Winters	Isobel Elsom

Jack Oakie and Sonja Henie in **Iceland** (20th Century-Fox).

Albert Dekker, Brian Donlevy, Walter Abel, Mac-
Donald Carey and Robert Preston in **Wake Island**
(Paramount).

JOURNEY INTO FEAR

Graham	Joseph Cotton
Josette	Dolores Del Rio
Stephanie	Ruth Warrick
Mme. Mathews	Agnes Moorehead
Gogo	Jack Durant
Kopeikin	Everett Sloane
Haller	Eustace Wyatt
Mathews	Frank Readick
Kuvetli	Edgar Barrier
Banat	Jack Moss
Purser	Stefan Schnabel
Oo Lang Sang	Hans Conried
Steward	Robert Meltzer
Ship's Captain	Richard Bennett
Col. Haki	Orson Welles

Distributor: RKO
Director: Norman Foster
Released: August 7, 1942

INVISIBLE AGENT

Maria Sorenson	Ilona Massey
Frank Raymond	Jon Hall
Baron Ikito	Peter Lorre
Conrad Stauffer	Sir Cedric Hardwicke
Karl Heiser	J. Edward Bromberg
Arnold Schmidt	Albert Basserman
John Gardiner	John Litel
Sir Alfred Spencer	Holmes Herbert
Surgeon	Keye Luke

Distributor: Universal
Director: Edwin L. Marin
Released: August 7, 1942

TIMBER

Quebec	Leo Carrillo
Arizona	Andy Devine
Kansas	Dan Dailey, Jr.
Yvette Lacour	Marjorie Lord
Pierre Lacour	Edmund MacDonald
Dan Crowley	Wade Boteler
Jules Fabian	Nestor Paiva
Pop Turner	Paul E. Burns
Joe Radway	James Seay
Ann Barrows	Jean Phillips
Bill Cormack	William Hall
Sandy	Walter Sande

Distributor: Universal
Director: Christy Cabanne
Released: August 7, 1942

ONE THRILLING NIGHT

Horace Jason	John Beal
Millie Jason	Wanda McKay
Frankie Saxton	Tom Neal
Dottie	Barbara Pepper
Pat Callahan	Warren Hymer
Sgt. Haggerty	J. Farrell MacDonald
Pete	Ernie Adams
Joe	Lynton Brent
Duke Keesler	Jerome Sheldon
Tubby	Jimmy O'Gatty

Distributor: Monogram
Director: William Beaudine
Released: August 8, 1942

SABOTAGE SQUAD

Lieutenant John Cronin	Bruce Bennett
Edith Cassell	Kay Harris
Eddie Miller	Eddie Norris
Carlyle Harrison	Sidney Blackmer
Chief Hanley	Don Beddoe
Robert Fuller	John Tyrell
Chuck Brown	George McKay

Conrad	Robert Emmett Keane
Felix	Eddie Laughton

Distributor: Columbia
Director: Lew Landers
Released: August 11, 1942

CAREFUL, SOFT SHOULDERS

Connie Mathers	Virginia Bruce
Thomas Aldrich	James Ellison
Mr. Fortune	Aubrey Mather
Agatha Mathers	Sheila Ryan
Elliott Salmon	Ralph Byrd
Milo	Sigurd Tor
Joe	Charles Tannen
Mr. Aldrich	William B. Davidson
Mrs. Ipswich	Dale Winter

Distributor: 20th Century-Fox
Director: Oliver H. P. Garrett
Released: August 12, 1942

ICELAND

Katina Jonsdottir	Sonja Henie
Corporal James Murfin	John Payne
Slip Riggs	Jack Oakie
Papa	Felix Bressart
Helga	Osa Massen
Adele Wynn	Joan Merrill
Tegnar	Fritz Feld
Sammy Kaye and his Orchestra	Themselves
Sverdrup Svensson	Sterling Holloway
Grandma	Adeline DeWalt Reynolds
Valtyr's Father	Ludwig Stossel
Valtyr	Duke Adlon
Aunt Sophie	Ilka Gruning
Skating Partner	Eugene Turner
Sergeant	James Flavin
Sentry	William Haade
Master Sergeant	James Bush
Canteen Girl	Carol Curtis Brown

Distributor: 20th Century-Fox
Director: Bruce Humberstone
Released: August 12, 1942

WAKE ISLAND

Major Caton	Brian Donlevy
Lieutenant Cameron	MacDonald Carey
Joe Doyle	Robert Preston
Smacksie Randall	William Bendix
Shad McCloskey	Albert Dekker
Commander Roberts	Walter Abel
Probenzki	Mikhail Rasumny

Robert Young with Jeanette MacDonald in **Cairo** (M-G-M).

Private Cunkel	Don Castle
Captain Lewis	Rod Cameron
Sergeant	Bill Goodwin
Sally Cameron	Barbara Britton
Captain Patrick	Damian O'Flynn
Johnny Rudd	Frank Albertson
Private Warren	Phillip Terry
Corp. Goebbels	Philip Van Zandt
Sparks Wilcox	Keith Richards
Colonel Cameron	Willard Robertson
Tommy	Marvin Jones
Squeaky Simpkins	Jack Chapin
Triunfo	Rudy Robles
Pete Hogan	John Sheehan
George Nielson	Charles Trowbridge
Cynthia Caton	Mary Thomas
Miss Pringle	Mary Field
Mr. Saburo Kurusu	Richard Loo
Tex Hannigan	Earle Tex Harris
Girl At Inn	Hillary Brooke
Girl At Inn	Patty McCarty
Major Johnson	William Forrest

Dr. Parkman	Jack Mulhall
Colonel	Ivan Miller
Captain	Hugh Beaumont
Commander	Edward Earle
Wounded Marine	James Brown
Rodrigo	Angel Cruz
Gordon	Anthony Nace
First Lieutenant	Hollis Bane
Wounded Marine	Frank Faylen
Marine	Dane Clark
Sight Setter	Alan Hale, Jr.

Distributor: Paramount
Director: John Farrow
Released: August 12, 1942

CAIRO

Marcia Warren	Jeanette MacDonald
Homer Smith	Robert Young
Cleona Jones	Ethel Waters
Philo Cobson	Reginald Owen
O. H. P. Boggs	Grant Mitchell
Teutonic Gentleman	Lionel Atwill
Ahmed Ben Hassan	Edward Ciannelli
Ludwig	Mitchell Lewis
Hector	Dooley Wilson
Bernie	Larry Nunn
Colonel Woodhue	Dennis Hoey
Mrs. Morrison	Mona Barrie
Strange Man	Rhys Williams
Mme. Laruga	Cecil Cunningham
Bartender	Harry Worth
Alfred	Frank Richards

Distributor: M-G-M
Director: W. S. Van Dyke II
Released: August 17, 1942

BERLIN CORRESPONDENT

Karen Hauen	Virginia Gilmore
Bill Roberts	Dana Andrews
Carla	Mona Maris
Captain Carl von Rau	Martin Kosleck
Dr. Dietrich	Sig Rumann
Weiner	Kurt Katch
Mr. Hauen	Erwin Kalser
Manager	Torben Meyer

Dana Andrews with Virginia Gilmore in **Berlin Correspondent** (20th Century-Fox).

Gruber	William Edmunds
Gunther	Hans Schumm
English Prisoner	Leonard Mudie
Actor	Hans von Morhart
Doctor	Curt Furberg
Pilot	Henry Rowland
Prisoner	Christian Rub

Distributor: 20th Century-Fox
Director: Eugene Forde
Released: August 17, 1942

HILLBILLY BLITZKRIEG

Snuffy Smith	Bud Duncan

Barney Google	Cliff Nazarro
Sergeant Gatling	Edgar Kennedy
Julie James	Doris Linden
Professor James	Lucien Littlefield
Corporal Bruce	Alan Baldwin
Marlene Zara	Nicolle Andre
Missouri	Jimmie Dodd
Dinky	Teddy Mangean
Boller	Jerry Jerome
Hertle	Jack Carr
Luke	Frank Austin

Distributor: Monogram
Director: Roy Mack
Released: August 17, 1942

Alan Baldwin, Jimmie Dodd, Edgar Kennedy and Bud Duncan in **Hillbilly Blitz Kreig** (Monogram).

SWEETHEART OF THE FLEET

Phoebe Weyms	Joan Davis
Jerry Gilbert	Jinx Falkenburg
Kitty Leslie	Joan Woodbury
Brenda	Blanche Stewart
Cobina	Elvia Allman
Lt. Philip Blaine	William Wright
Ensign George Landers	Robert Stevens
Gordon Crouse	Tim Ryan
Hambone	George McKay
Daffy Dill	Walter Sande
Chumley	Dick Elliott
Commander Hawes	Charles Trowbridge
Bugsy	Tom Seidel

Distributor: Columbia
Director: Charles Barton
Released: August 17, 1942

William Wright, Joan Davis, Joan Woodbury, Tim Ryan, Robert Stevens, Jinx Falkenburg, Dick Elliott and Charles Trowbridge in **Sweetheart of the Fleet** (Columbia).

Humphrey Bogart with Mary Astor in **Across the Pacific** (Warner Bros.).

ACROSS THE PACIFIC

Rick Leland	Humphrey Bogart
Alberta Marlow	Mary Astor
Dr. Lorenz	Sydney Greenstreet
A. V. Smith	Charles Halton
Joe Totsuiko	Victor Sen Yung
Sugi	Roland Got
Sam Wing On	Lee Tung Foo
Captain Morrison	Frank Wilcox
Colonel Hart	Paul Stanton
Canadian Major	Lester Matthews
Court-Martial President	John Hamilton
Tall Thin Man	Tom Stevenson
Captain Harkness	Roland Drew
Dan Morton	Monte Blue
Captain Higoto	Chester Gan
First Officer Miyuma	Richard Loo
Steamship Office Clerk	Keye Luke
T. Oki	Kam Tong
Chief Engineer Mitsudo	Spencer Chan
Filipino Assassin	Rudy Robles

Distributor: Warner Bros—First National
Director: John Huston
Released: August 18, 1942

DESPERATE JOURNEY

Flight Lieutenant Terence Forbes	Errol Flynn
Flying Officer Johnny Hammond	Ronald Reagan
Kaethe Brahms	Nancy Coleman
Major Otto Baumeister	Raymond Massey

Ronald Reagan, Nancy Coleman, Errol Flynn and Arthur Kennedy in **Desperate Journey** (Warner Bros.).

Flight Sergeant Kirk Edwards	Alan Hale
Flying Officer Jed Forrest	Arthur Kennedy
Flight Sergeant Lloyd Hollis	Ronald Sinclair
Dr. Mather	Albert Basserman
Preuss	Sig Rumann
Squadron Leader Lane Ferris	Patrick O'Moore
Dr. Herman Brahms	Felix Basch
Frau Brahms	Ilka Gruning
Frau Raeder	Elsa Basserman
Captain Coswick	Charles Irwin
Squadron Leader Clark	Richard Fraser
Kruse	Robert O. Davis
Heinrich Schwartzmuller	Henry Victor
Assistant Plotting Officer	Bruce Lester
Wing Commander	Lester Matthews
Hesse	Kurt Katch
Gestapo	Hans Schumm
German Co-Pilot	Helmut Dantine
Squadron Commander	Barry Bernard

Distributor: Warner Bros.—First National
Director: Raoul Walsh
Released: August 18, 1942

George Meeker, Cary Grant and Faye Emerson in **Secret Enemies** (Warner Bros.).

110

SECRET ENEMIES

Carl Becker .... Craig Stevens
Paula Fengler .... Faye Emerson
John Trent .... John Ridgely
Jim Jackson .... Charles Lang
Dr. Woodford .... Robert Warwick
Henry Bremmer .... Frank Reicher
Hans .... Rex Williams
Counter-Espionage Man .... Frank Wilcox
Rudolph .... George Meeker
Fred .... Roland Drew
Travers .... Addison Richards
Capt. Jarrett .... Cliff Clark
Hugo .... Monte Blue

Distributor: Warner Bros.

Director: Ben Stoloff
Released: August 18, 1942

BUSSES ROAR

Sergeant Ryan .... Richard Travis
Reba Richards .... Julie Bishop
Eddie Sloan .... Charles Drake
Norma .... Eleanor Parker
Betty .... Elisabeth Fraser
Dick Remick .... Richard Fraser
Hoff .... Peter Whitney
Detective Quinn .... Frank Wilcox
Sunshine .... Willie Best
Jerry Silva .... Rex Williams
Danny .... Harry Lewis

Richard Travis and Julie Bishop in **Busses Roar** (Warner Bros.).

James Seay, William Gargan and Felix Basch in **Enemy Agents Meet Ellery Queen** (Columbia).

ENEMY AGENTS MEET ELLERY QUEEN

Ellery Queen	William Gargan
Nikki Porter	Margaret Lindsay
Inspector	Charley Grapwin
Mrs. Van Dorn	Gale Sondergaard
Paul Gillette	Gilbert Roland
Heinrich	Sig Rumann
Sergeant Velie	James Burke
Morse	Ernest Dorian
Helm	Felix Basch
Commodore Lang	Minor Watson
Commissioner Bracken	John Hamilton
Sergeant Stevens	James Seay
Reece	Louis Donath

The Moocher	Bill Kennedy
Nick Stoddard	George Meeker
Mrs. Dipper	Vera Lewis
Henry Dipper	Harry C. Bradley
First Old Maid	Lottie Williams
Second Old Maid	Leah Baird
Yamanito	Chester Gan

Distributor: Warner Bros.
Director: D. Ross Lederman
Released: August 18, 1942

Oscar O'Shea and J. Edward Bromberg in **Halfway to Shanghai** (Universal).

Distributor: Columbia
Director: James Hogan
Released: August 26, 1942

THEY RAID BY NIGHT

Capt. Robert Owen	Lyle Talbot
Inga	June Duprez
Oberst von Ritter	Victor Varconi
Lieutenant Falken	George Neise
Harry	Charles Rogers
General Heden	Paul Baratoff
Captain Deane	Leslie Dennison
Doctor	Crane Whitley
Dalberg	Sven Hugo Borg

Victor Varconi, Sigfrid Tor, Lyle Talbot, Richard Scott and George Neise in **They Raid by Night** (PRC).

Donna Reed, Ann Harding, Reginald Denny and
Stanley Ridges in **Eyes in the Night** (M-G-M).

General Lloyd	Eric Wilton	Colonel Blympton	Henry Stephenson
Braun	Pierce Lyden	Yinpore	J. Edward Bromberg
Beggar	John Beck	Karl Zerta	George Zucco
Sentry	William Kellogg	Jonathan Peale	Charles Wagenheim
Von Memel	Robert C. Fisher	Nikolas	Alexander Granach
German Lieutenant	Sigfrid Tor	Otto Van Shact	Lionel Royce
Lammet	Brian O'Hara	Mr. Wu	Willie Fung
		Mr. McIntyre	Oscar O'Shea
		Caroline Wrallins	Charlotte Wynters
		Mrs. McIntyre	Mary Gordon
		Marion Mills	Fay Helm
		Conductor	Frank Lackteen

Distributor: PRC
Director: Spencer Gordon Bennett
Released: September 3, 1942

HALF WAY TO SHANGHAI

Alexander Barton	Kent Taylor
Vicky Neilson	Irene Hervey

Distributor: Universal
Director: John Rawlins
Released: September 4, 1942

Nigel Bruce, Evelyn Ankers and Basil Rathbone in **Sherlock Holmes and the Voice of Terror** (Universal).

EYES IN THE NIGHT

Duncan Maclain	Edward Arnold
Norma Lawry	Ann Harding
Barbara Lawry	Donna Reed
Cheli Scott	Katherine Emery
Gabriel Hoffman	Horace McNally
Marty	Allen Jenkins
Hansen	Stanley C. Ridges
Stephen Lawry	Reginald Denny
Paul Gerente	John Emery
Vera Hoffman	Rosemary De Camp
Boyd	Eric Rolf
Busch	Barry Nelson
Victor	Reginald Sheffield
Anderson	Steve Geray
Allistair	Mantan Moreland
'Friday'	Himself

Distributor: M-G-M
Director: Fred Zinnemann
Released: September 9, 1942

SHERLOCK HOLMES AND THE VOICE OF TERROR

Sherlock Holmes	Basil Rathbone
Doctor Watson	Nigel Bruce
Kitty	Evelyn Ankers
Sir Evan Barham	Reginald Denny
Meade	Thomas Gomez

Gen. Jerome Lawford	Montagu Love
Anthony Lloyd	Henry Daniell
Fabian Prentiss	Olaf Hytten
Capt. Roland Shore	Leyland Hodgson

Distributor: Universal
Director: John Rawlins
Released: September 16, 1942

MANILA CALLING

Lucky Matthews	Lloyd Nolan
Edna Fraser	Carole Landis
Jeff Bailey	Cornel Wilde
Tom O'Rourke	James Gleason
Heller	Martin Kosleck
Corbett	Ralph Byrd
Fillmore	Charles Tannen
Jamison	Ted North
Gillman	Elisha Cook, Jr.
Santora	Harold Huber
Wayne Ralston	Lester Matthews
Watson	Louis Jean Heydt
Armando	Sen Yung

Distributor: 20th Century-Fox
Director: Herbert I. Leeds
Released: September 18, 1942

Lloyd Nolan and Carole Landis in **Manila Calling** (20th Century-Fox).

Lyle Latell, Patsy Moran, John Shelton and Gale Storm in **Foreign Agent** (Monogram).

FOREIGN AGENT

Jimmy	John Shelton
Mitzi	Gale Storm
Okura	Ivan Lebedeff
Werner	Hans Schumm
Davis	William Halligan
Nick	George Travell
Joan	Patsy Moran
Eddie	Lyle Latell
Stevens	Herb Rawlinson
McCall	Kenneth Harlan
Editor	Jack Mulhall
Carl Beck	David Clarke

Distributor: Monogram

Director: William Beaudine
Released: September 21, 1942

FLYING TIGERS

Jim Gordon	John Wayne
Woody Jason	John Carroll
Brooke Elliott	Anna Lee
Hap	Paul Kelly
Alabama	Gordon Jones
Verna Bales	Mae Clarke
Colonel Lindsay	Addison Richards
Blackie Bales	Edmund MacDonald
Dale	Bill Shirley
Reardon	Tom Neal

McCurdy	Malcolm MacTaggart
Barton	David Bruce
Mike	Chester Gan
McIntosh	James Dodd
Tex	Gregg Barton
Selby	John James

Distributor: Republic
Director: David Miller
Released: September 23, 1942

Anna Lee and John Wayne in **Flying Tigers** (Republic).

COUNTER-ESPIONAGE

Michael Lanyard	Warren William
Jameson	Eric Blore
Pamela	Hillary Brooke
Inspector Crane	Thurston Hall
Dickens	Fred Kelsey
Anton Schugg	Forrest Tucker
Inspector Stephens	Matthew Boulton
Gustave Sossel	Kurt Katch
Kent Wells	Morton Lowry
Harvey Leeds	Leslie Denison
George Barrow	Billy Bevan
Sir Stafford Hart	Stanley Logan
Police Constable Hopkins	Tom Stevenson

Distributor: Columbia
Director: Edward Dmytryk
Released: September 26, 1942

TOP SERGEANT

Frenchy Devereaux	Leo Carrillo
Andy Jarrett	Andy Devine
Dick Manson	Don Terry
Helen Gray	Elyse Knox
Al Bennett	Don Porter
Colonel Gray	Addison Richards
Tony Gribaldi	Bradley Page
Jack Manson	Gene Garrick
Cruston	Alan Hale, Jr.
Roy	Roy Harris
Phil	Richard Davies
Prosecuting Officer	Emmett Vogan

Distributor: Universal
Director: Christy Cabanne
Released: October 1, 1942

THE YANKS ARE COMING

Gil Whitney	Henry King
Rita Edwards	Mary Healy
Sammy Winkle	Little Jackie Heller
Butch	Maxie Rosenbloom
Bob Reynolds	William Roberts
Parky	Parkyarkarkus
Peggy	Dorothy Dare
Vicki	Lynn Starr
Flora	Jane Novak
Corporal Jenks	Charles Purcell

Warren William and Hillary Brooke in **Counter-Espionage** (Columbia).

Captain Brown	Forrest Taylor	Bates	Edward Gargan
Sergeant Callahan	David O'Brien	Grimes	Eddie Dunn
Lew Pollack	As Himself	Arlette	Charlotte Wynters

Distributor: PRC
Director: Alexis Thur-Taxis
Released: October 5, 1942

FALCON'S BROTHER

Gay Lawrence	George Sanders
Tom Lawrence	Tom Conway
Marcia Brooks	Jane Randolph
Lefty	Don Barclay
Donovan	Cliff Clark

Paul Harrington	James Newill
Jerry	Keye Luke
Carmela	Amanda Varela
Valdez	George Lewis
Diane Medford	Gwili Andre
Savitski	Andre Charlot
Miss Ross	Mary Halsey
Pat Moffett	Charles Arnt

Distributor: RKO
Director: Stanley Logan
Released: October 5, 1942

Don Terry and Don Porter in **Top Sergeant** (Universal).

Forrest Taylor, William Roberts and Mary Healy in
The Yanks Are Coming (PRC).

BLONDIE FOR VICTORY

Blondie	Penny Singleton
Dagwood	Arthur Lake
Baby Dumpling	Larry Simms
Daisy	Daisy
Cookie	Majelle White
Hershel Smith	Stuart Erwin
J. C. Dithers	Jonathan Hale
Alvin Fuddle	Danny Mummert
Sergeant	Edward Gargan
Miss Clabber	Renie Riano
Mr. Crumb	Irving Bacon
Mr. Green	Harrison Greene
Hoarder	Charles Wagenheim

Distributor: Columbia

Director: Frank R. Strayer
Released: October 9, 1942

TEXAS TO BATAAN

Dusty	John King
Davy	Dave Sharpe
Alibi	Max Terhune
Dallas	Marjorie Manning
Tad	Budd Buster
Capt. Anders	Ken Duncan
Cookie	Escolastico Baucin
Richards	Frank Ellis
Engel	Carl Mathews
Miller	Guy Kingsford

Distributor: Monogram
Director: Robert Tansey
Released: October 13, 1942

SEVEN DAYS LEAVE

Johnny Grey	Victor Mature
Terry	Lucille Ball
Gildersleeve	Harold Peary
Mapy	Mapy Cortes
Ginny	Ginny Simms
Mickey	Marcy McGuire
Jackson	Peter Lind Hayes
Ralph Bell	Walter Reed
Sergeant Mead	Wallace Ford

Penny Singleton and Arthur Lake in **Blondie for Victory** (Columbia).

Jane Randolph and Tom Conway in **The Falcon's Brother** (RKO).

Bitsy	Arnold Stang
Clarky	Buddy Clark
Charles	Charles Victor
Gifford	King Kennedy
Andre	Charles Andre
Justice Of Peace	Harry Holman
Capt. Collins	Addison Richards

Distributor: RKO
Director: Tim Whelan
Released: October 15, 1942

THE NAVY COMES THROUGH

Mallory	Pat O'Brien

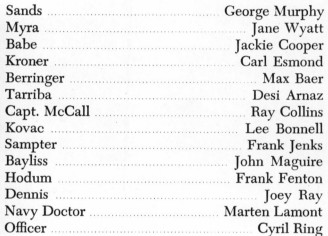

Sands	George Murphy
Myra	Jane Wyatt
Babe	Jackie Cooper
Kroner	Carl Esmond
Berringer	Max Baer
Tarriba	Desi Arnaz
Capt. McCall	Ray Collins
Kovac	Lee Bonnell
Sampter	Frank Jenks
Bayliss	John Maguire
Hodum	Frank Fenton
Dennis	Joey Ray
Navy Doctor	Marten Lamont
Officer	Cyril Ring

Distributor: RKO
Director: A. Edward Sutherland
Released: October 15, 1942

Dave Sharpe with Escolastico Baucin in **Texas to Bataan** (Monogram).

Arnold Stang, Victor Mature, Harold Peary and Peter Lind Hayes in **Seven Days Leave** (RKO).

Pat O'Brien with Jane Wyatt in **The Navy Comes Through** (RKO).

Noel Coward in **In Which We Serve** (United Artists).

...ne, Bobby Watson and Joe Devlin in The Devil With Hitler (United Art-

Colonel MacDonald	Jack Holt		
Lady Stackhouse	Dame May Whitty		
Gramps	George Barbier		
George Lockwood	Richard Haydn		
Barratt	Reginald Denny		
Cadet Hackzell	Ted North		
Blonde	Janis Carter		
Chinese Cadet	Archie Got		
Chinese Cadet	Lawrence Ung		
Doctor	Montague Shaw		
Mrs. Blake	Nana Bryant		
Saleswoman	Iris Adrian		
Nurse	Viola Moore		
Ellen	Connie Leon		
Messenger	Walter Tetley		
English Cadet	Billy McGuire		
English Cadet	Richard Woodruff		

Distributor: 20th Century-Fox
Director: William A. Wellman
Released: October 19, 1942

THE DEVIL WITH HITLER

The Devil	Alan Mowbray
Hitler	Bobby Watson
Suki Yaki	George E. Stone
Mussolini	Joe Devlin
Linda	Marjorie Woodworth
Walter	Douglas Fowley
Louis	Herman Bing
Julius	Sig Arno

Distributor: United Artists

James Ellison, Jane Wyatt and George Cleveland in
Army Surgeon (RKO).

Laraine Day, Margaret O'Brien, Robert Young and
William Severn in **Journey for Margaret** (M-G-M).

Director: Gordon Douglas
Released: October 22, 1942

Distributor: RKO-Radio
Director: A. Edward Sutherland
Released: October 26, 1942

ARMY SURGEON

Capt. James Mason	James Ellison
Beth Ainsley	Jane Wyatt
Lt. Philip Harvey	Kent Taylor
Bill Drake	Walter Reed
Brooklyn	James Burke
Major Wishart	Jack Briggs
Major Peterson	Cyril Ring
Ship Orderly	Eddie Dew
Flowerwoman	Ann Codee
Soldier	Russell Wade
Soldier	Richard Martin

JOURNEY FOR MARGARET

John Davis	Robert Young
Nora Davis	Laraine Day
Trudy Strauss	Fay Bainter
Anya	Signe Hasso
Margaret	Margaret O'Brien
Herbert V. Allison	Nigel Bruce
Peter Humphreys	William Severn
Rugged	G. P. Huntley, Jr.
Mrs. Barrie	Doris Lloyd
Mr. Barrie	Halliwell Hobbes

Susan Fleming	Jill Esmond
Fairoaks	Charles Irwin
Mrs. Bailey	Elisabeth Risdon
Frau Weber	Lisa Golm
Man	Herbert Evans

Cary Grant, Albert Dekker and Ginger Rogers in **Once Upon a Honeymoon** (RKO).

Child	Clare Sandars
Censor	Leyland Hodgson
Woman	Anita Bolster
Warden	Matthew Boulton
Nurse	Lilyan Irene
Manager	Olaf Hytten
Nurse	Ottola Nesmith
Surgeon	John Burton
Steward	Colin Kenny
Porter	Jimmy Aubrey
Mrs. Harris	Heather Thatcher
Isabel	Joan Kemp
Hans	Norbert Muller
Policeman	Al Ferguson
Nora's Mother	Bea Nigro
Stage Manager	Cyril Delavanti
Mme. Bornholm	Jody Gilbert
Everton	Crauford Kent
Japanese Statesman	Keye Luke
Air Raid Warden	David Thursby
Police Captain	Henry Guttman

Distributor: M-G-M
Director: W. S. Van Dyke
Released: October 28, 1942

ONCE UPON A HONEYMOON

Katie	Ginger Rogers
Pat	Cary Grant
Baron von Luber	Walter Slezak
Leblanc	Albert Dekker
Borelski	Albert Basserman
Elsa	Ferike Boros
Cumberland	Harry Shannon
Kleinoch	John Banner

Distributor: RKO
Director: Leo McCarey
Released: November 4, 1942

LADY FROM CHUNGKING

Kwan Mei	Anna May Wong
General Kaimura	Harold Huber
Lavara	Mae Clarke
Rodney Carr	Rick Vallin
Pat O'Rourke	Paul Bryar
Lieutenant Shimoto	Ted Hecht
Hans Gruber	Louis Donath
Chen	James Leong

Ludwig Donath, Rick Vallin and Mae Clarke in **Lady from Chungking** (PRC).

Mochow	Archie Got
Lu-Chi	Walter Soo Hoo

Distributor: PRC
Director: William Nigh
Released: November 9, 1942

Brian Donlevy, Diana Barrymore and Arthur Gould-Porter in **Nightmare** (Universal).

NIGHTMARE

Leslie Stafford	Diana Barrymore
Dan Shane	Brian Donlevy
Captain Stafford	Henry Daniell
Angus	Eustace Wyatt
Sergeant	Arthur Shields
Lord Abbington	Gavin Muir
Inspector Robbins	Stanley Logan
Abbington's Butler	Ian Wolfe
Hans	Hans Conried
Carl	John Abbott
Jock	David Clyde
Angus' Wife	Elspeth Dudgeon
London Cabby	Harold de Becker
Money Changer	Ivan Simpson
London Bobby	Keith Hitchcock
Freddie	Arthur Gould-Porter
Mrs. McDonald	Anita Bolster
Mrs. Bates	Lydia Bilbrook
Gladys	Pax Walker
Old Gaffer	Bobbie Hale

Distributor: Universal
Director: Tim Whelan
Released: November 10, 1942

SEVEN MILES FROM ALCATRAZ

Champ Larkin	James Craig
Anne Porter	Bonita Granville
Jimbo	Frank Jenks
Stormy	Cliff Edwards

Erford Gage, George Cleveland, Cliff Edwards, Frank
Jenks, Bonita Granville and James Craig in **Seven
Miles from Alcatraz** (RKO).

Capt. Porter	George Cleveland	Pearl	Marie McDonald
Paul Brenner	Erford Gage	Ernest Higgins	Lloyd Corrigan
Baroness	Tala Birell	Eddie	Russell Hoyt
Fritz Weinermann	John Banner	Angelo Palacio	Dave Willock
Max	Otto Reichow	Kesselman	John Wengraf
		Kilpatrick	Miles Mander
Distributor: RKO		Sergeant	Charles Cane
Director: Edward Dmytryk		Little Man	Virginia Brissac
Released: November 10, 1942		First Killer	Al Hill
		Second Killer	Fred Kohler, Jr.
		Johnny	Jack Roberts
LUCKY JORDAN		Gas Station Attendant	Clem Bevans
		Charles	Olaf Hytten
Lucky Jordan	Alan Ladd	Miller	William Halligan
Jill Evans	Helen Walker	Mrs. Magotti	Kitty Kelly
Slip Moran	Sheldon Leonard	Joe Maggotti	George Humbert
Annie	Mabel Paige	Maid At Hollyhock School	Dorothy Dandridge

Helen Walker, Alan Ladd and Marie McDonald in **Lucky Jordan** (Paramount).

Harrison	Joseph Downing
Girl In Back Room	Carol Hughes
Army Guard	Ralph Dunn
Man	Edward Earle
Army Guard	Lyle Latell
Private Secretary	Edythe Elliott
Big-Ears	John Harmon
Colonel	John Hamilton
Colonel	Roy Gordon
Pearl's Boy Friend	Kirk Alyn
Hearndon	Arthur Loft
Florist	Ronnie Rondell
Sentry	Terry Ray
Helen	Sara Berner
Commanding Officer	William Forrest
Woman	Ethel Clayton
Gunman	Anthony Caruso
Saleslady In Toy Shop	Georgia Backus
Girl	Yvonne DeCarlo

Distributor: Paramount
Director: Frank Tuttle
Released: November 16, 1942

FALL IN

William Tracy, Joe Sawyer, Robert Barrat, Jean Porter

Distributor: United Artists
Director: William McGann
Released: November 20, 1942

CASABLANCA

Rick Blaine	Humphrey Bogart
Ilsa Lund Laszlo	Ingrid Bergman
Victor Laszlo	Paul Henreid
Captain Louis Renault	Claude Rains
Maj. Heinrich Strasser	Conrad Veidt
Senor Ferrari	Sydney Greenstreet
Ugarte	Peter Lorre
Carl	S. Z. Sakall
Yvonne	Madeleine LeBeau
Sam	Dooley Wilson
Annina Brandel	Joy Page
Berger	John Qualen
Sascha	Leonid Kinsky
Jan Brandel	Helmut Dantine
Dark European	Curt Bois
Croupier	Marcel Dalio
Singer	Corinna Mura
Mr. Leuchtag	Ludwig Stossel
Mrs. Leuchtag	Ilka Gruning
Senor Martinez	Charles La Torre
Arab Vendor	Frank Puglia
Abdul	Dan Seymour
Blue Parrot Waiter	Oliver Prickett
German Banker	Gregory Gay
Friend	George Meeker
Contact	William Edmunds
Banker	Torben Meyer
Waiter	Gino Corrado
Casselle	George Dee
Englishwoman	Norma Varden

William Tracy and Joe Sawyer in **Fall In** (United Artists).

Paul Henreid, Ingrid Bergman and Humphrey Bogart
in **Casablanca** (Warner Bros.).

Fydor		Leo Mostovoy
Heinz		Richard Ryen
Headwaiter		Martin Garralaga
Prosperous Man		Olaf Hytten
American		Monte Blue
Vendor		Michael Mark
Dealer		Leon Belasco
Native		Paul Porcasi
German Officer		Hans von Twardowski
French Officer		Albert Morin
Customer		Creighton Hale
German Officer		Henry Rowland

Distributor: Warner Bros.
Director: Michael Curtiz
Released: November 27, 1942

REUNION

Michele De La Becque	Joan Crawford
Pat Talbot	John Wayne
Robert Cartot	Philip Dorn
Schultz	Reginald Owen
General Hugo Schroeder	Albert Bassermann
Ulrich Windler	John Carradine
Juliette	Ann Ayars
Durand	J. Edward Bromberg
Paul Grebeau	Moroni Olsen
Emile Fleuron	Henry Daniell
Anton Stregel	Howard da Silva
Honore	Charles Arnt
Martin	Morris Ankrum
Genevieve	Edith Evanson

Captain	Ernest Dorian
Clothilde	Margaret Laurence
Mme. Montanot	Odette Myrtil
Soldier	Peter Whitney

Distributor: M-G-M
Director: Jules Dassin
Released: December 2, 1942

Joan Crawford and John Wayne in **Reunion** (M-G-M).

MADAME SPY

Joan Bannister	Constance Bennett
David Bannister	Don Porter
Peter	John Litel
Mike Reese	Edward Brophy
Carl Gordon	John Eldredge
Bill Drake	Edmund MacDonald
Alicia Rolf	Nana Bryant
Winston	Jimmy Conlin
Harrison Woods	Selmer Jackson
Miro	Nino Pepitone
Inspector Varden	Cliff Clark
Martin	John Dilson

Distributor: Universal
Director: Roy William Neill
Released: December 2, 1942

CHINA GIRL

Miss Young	Gene Tierney

Johnny Williams	George Montgomery
Captain Fifi	Lynn Bari
Major Bull Weed	Victor McLaglen
Jones	Alan Baxter
Jarubi	Sig Ruman
Shorty	Myron McCormick
Chinese Boy	Bobby Blake
Entertainer	Ann Pennington
Dr. Young	Philip Ahn
Haines	Tom Neal
Japanese Colonel	Paul Fung
Desk Clerk	Lal Chand Mehra
Doctor	Kam Tong

Distributor: 20th Century-Fox
Director: Henry Hathaway
Released: December 9, 1942

Mary Kelley and Constance Bennett in **Madame Spy** (Universal).

STAND BY FOR ACTION

Lieut. Gregg Masterman	Robert Taylor
Lt. Cmdr. M. J. Roberts	Brian Donlevy
Rear Admiral Stephen Thomas	Charles Laughton
Chief Yeoman H. Johnson	Walter Brennan
Audrey Carr	Marilyn Maxwell
Commander Stone	Henry O'Neill
Mary Collins	Marta Linden
Chief Boatswain's Mate Jenks	Chill Wills
Captain Ludlow	Douglas Dumbrille
Ensign Lindsay	Richard Quine
Flag Lieutenant Dudley	William Tannen
Ensign Martin	Douglas Fowley
Lieutenant Tim Ryan	Tim Ryan

Lieutenant Royce	Dick Simmons	Walter Sibley	Richard Fraser
Pharmacist's Mate 'Doc' Miller	Byron Foulger	Dr. Wolf	Paul Cavanagh
Carp.'s Mate 'Chips'	Hobart Cavanaugh	General Devon	Lumsden Hare
Susan Garrison	Inez Cooper	Dr. Ferris	John Abbott
Chief Quartermaster Rankin	Ben Welden	Nurse Kruger	Mary Field
Chief Signalman	Harry Fleischman	Eric	Rex Williams
		Mr. Tanner	Joan Winfield
		Inspector Cady	Charles Irwin
		Oliver	Peggy Carson
		Sammy	Walter Tetley
		Constable	Art Foster
		Ryan	Creighton Hale
		Fletcher	Frank Mayo

Distributor: M-G-M
Director: Robert Z. Leonard
Released: December 10, 1942

GORILLA MAN

Capt. Craig Killian	John Loder
Patricia Devon	Marian Hall
Janet Devon	Ruth Ford

Distributor: Warner Bros.
Director: D. Ross Lederman
Released: December 11, 1942

Gene Tierney and George Montgomery in **China Girl**
(20th Century-Fox).

Walter Brennan, Robert Taylor, Brian Donlevy and
Charles Laughton in **Stand By For Action** (M-G-M).

COMMANDOS STRIKE AT DAWN

Erik Toresen	Paul Muni
Judith Bowen	Anna Lee
Mrs. Bergesen	Lillian Gish
Admiral Bowen	Sir Cedric Hardwicke
Robert Bowen	Robert Coote
Bergesen	Ray Collins
Hilma Arnesen	Rosemary DeCamp
Gunner Korstad	Richard Derr
German Captain	Alexander Knox
Pastor	Rod Cameron
Lars Arnesen	Louis Jean Heydt
Anna Korstad	Elizabeth Fraser
Johan Garmo	Erville Alderson
Schoolteacher	George Macready
Mrs. Olav	Barbara Everest
German Colonel	Arthur Margetson
Solveig Toresen	Ann Carter
Mrs. Korstad	Elsa Janssen
Mr. Korstad	Ferdinand Munier
Alfred Korstad	John Arthur Stockton
Young Soldier	Lloyd Bridges
Otto	Walter Sande
Thirsty Soldier	Philip Van Zandt

Distributor: Columbia
Director: John Farrow
Released: December 18, 1942

LONDON BLACKOUT MURDERS

Jack Rawlings	John Abbott

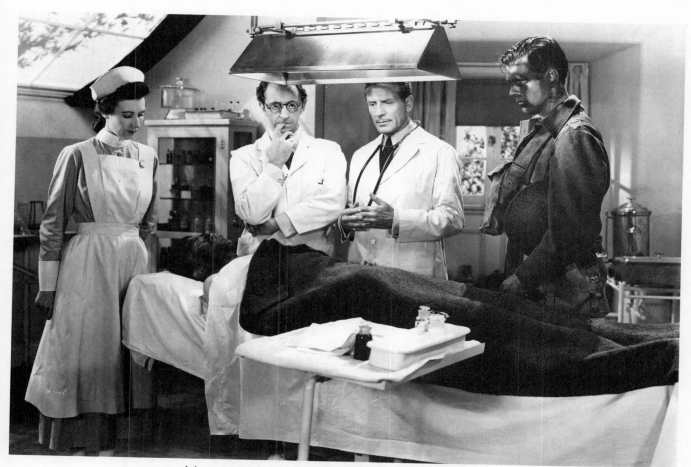

Mary Field, John Loder (on the table), John Abbott, Paul Cavanagh and Richard Fraser in **The Gorilla Man** (Warner Bros.).

Paul Muni, Anna Lee, Elizabeth Fraser and Robert Coote in **Commandos Strike at Dawn** (Columbia).

Billy Bevan with John Abbott in **London Blackout Murders** (Republic).

133

Ralph Bellamy in **The Great Impersonation** (Universal).

Mary Tillet	Mary McLeod
Inspector Harris	Lloyd Corrigan
Madison	Lester Matthews
Mrs. Pringle	Anita Bolster
Peter Dongen	Louis Borell
Air Raid Warden	Billy Bevan
Supt. Neil	Lumsden Hare
Caldwell	Frederic Worlock
George	Carl Harbord
Constable	Keith Hitchcock
Doctor	Tom Stevenson

Distributor: Republic
Director: George Sherman
Released: December 21, 1942

THE GREAT IMPERSONATION

Sir Edward Dominey	
	Ralph Bellamy
Baron von Ragenstein	
Muriel	Evelyn Ankers
Sir Ronald	Aubrey Mather
Bardinet	Edward Norris
Baroness Stephanie	Kaaren Verne
Seaman	Henry Daniell
Dr. Schmidt	Ludwig Stossel
Lady Leslie	Mary Forbes
Sir Tristram	Rex Evans
Mangan	Charles Coleman
Hofmann	Robert O. Davis
Yardly	Charles Irwin

Stengel .... Fred Vogeding
Nazi Soldier .... Victor Zimmerman

Distributor: Universal
Director: John Rawlins
Released: December 21, 1942

JOHNNY DOUGHBOY

Ann Winters
.... Jane Withers
Penelope Ryan
Oliver Lawrence .... Henry Wilcoxon
Johnny Kelly .... Patrick Brook
Harry Fabian .... William Demarest
'Biggy' Bigsworth .... Ruth Donnelly
Mammy .... Etta McDaniel
Jennifer .... Joline Westbrook
Also: Bobby Breen, 'Alfalfa' Switzer, Baby Sandy,
'Spanky' McFarland, Butch and Buddy,
Cora Sue Collins, Robert Coogan, Grace
Costello, The Falkner Orchestra, Karl Kiffe.

Distributor: Republic
Director: John H. Auer
Released: December 24, 1942

QUIET PLEASE, MURDER

Fleg .... George Sanders
Myra Blandy .... Gail Patrick
McByrne .... Richard Denning
Kay .... Lynne Roberts
Martin Cleaver .... Sidney Blackmer
Pahsen .... Kurt Katch
Miss Oval .... Margaret Brayton
Hollis .... Charles Tannen
Mr. Walpole .... Byron Foulger
Vance .... Arthur Space
Benson .... George Wolcott
Webley .... Chick Collins
Stock Boy .... Bud McCallister
Gannett .... Bud Geary
Stover .... Harold R. Goodwin
Detective .... James Farley
Policeman .... Jack Cheatham
Housewife .... Minerva Urecal
Husband .... Bert Roach
Rebescu .... Paul Porcasi

Lucas .... Theodore von Eltz

Distributor: 20th Century-Fox
Director: John Larkin
Released: December 24, 1942

WHEN JOHNNY COMES MARCHING HOME

Johnny Kovacs .... Allan Jones

Jane Withers with Patrick Brook in **Johnny Dough-boy** (Republic).

Marilyn .... Gloria Jean
Frankie .... Donald O'Connor
Joyce .... Jane Frazee
Dusty .... Peggy Ryan
Tommy Bridges .... Richard Davies
Hamilton Wellman .... Clyde Fillmore
Diana Wellman .... Marla Shelton
Trullers .... Olin Howlin
Ma Flanagan .... Emma Dunn
Also: The Four Step Brothers and Phil Spitalny
and his Hour of Charm All-Girl Orchestra
with Evelyn and Her Magic Violin.

George Sanders, Byron Foulger, Richard Denning, Gail Patrick and Lynne Roberts in **Quiet Please, Murder** (20th Century-Fox).

Distributor: Universal
Director: Charles Lamont
Released: December 24, 1942

SHERLOCK HOLMES AND THE SECRET WEAPON

Sherlock Holmes .... Basil Rathbone
Doctor Watson .... Nigel Bruce
Moriarity .... Lionel Atwill
Charlotte Eberti .... Kaaren Verne
Dr. Franz Tobel .... William Post, Jr.
Lestrade .... Dennis Hoey
Sir Reginald .... Holmes Herbert
Mrs. Hudson .... Mary Gordon

Distributor: Universal

Director: Roy William Neill
Released: December 28, 1942

STAR SPANGLED RHYTHM

Pop Webster .... Victor Moore
Polly Judson .... Betty Hutton
Jimmy Webster .... Eddie Bracken
Frisbee .... Walter Abel
Hi-Pockets .... Gil Lamb
Mimi .... Cass Daley
Sarah .... Anne Revere
Mr. Freemont .... Edward Fielding
Mac .... Edgar Dearing
Duffy .... William Haade
Sailor .... Maynard Holmes
Sailor .... James Millican

Peggy Ryan, Allan Jones, Donald O'Connor and Gloria Jean in **When Johnny Comes Marching Home** (Universal).

Tommy	Eddie Johnson
Casey	Arthur Loft
Captain Kingsley	Boyd Davis
Officer	Eddie Dew
Officer	Rod Cameron

Susanna Foster, Robert Preston, Louise LaPlanche, Donivee Lee, Christopher King, Alice Kirby, Marcella Phillips, Frank Faylen, Woodrow W. Strode, Marion Martin, Chester Clute.

Also: Bing Crosby, Bob Hope Fred MacMurray, Franchot Tone, Ray Milland, Dorothy Lamour, Paulette Goddard, Vera Zorina, Mary Martin, Dick Powell, Veronica Lake, Alan Ladd, William Bendix, Jerry Colonna, MacDonald Carey, Susan Hayward, Rochester, Marjorie Reynolds, Betty Rhodes, Dona Drake, Don Castle, Lynne Overman, Gary Crosby, Johnnie Johnston, Ernest Truex, Katherine Dunham, Slim and Slam, Arthur Treacher, Walter Catlett, Sterling Holloway, Tom Dugan, Paul Porcasi, Richard Loo, Golden Gate Quartet, Walter Dare Wahl and Company, Cecil B. DeMille, Preston Sturges, Ralph Murphy, Barney Dean, Jack Hope, Albert Dekker, Cecil Kellaway, Ellen Drew, Jimmy Lydon, Charles Smith, Frances Gifford,

Basil Rathbone, Kaaren Verne and Nigel Bruce in **Sherlock Holmes and the Secret Weapon** (Universal).

Marjorie Reynolds, center, and chorus in **Star Spangled Rhythm** (Paramount).

Eduardo Ciannelli and Bob Hope in **They Got Me Covered** (RKO).

Victor Sen Yung, Ellen Drew, Stephen Geray, Robert Preston and Otto Kruger in **Night Plane from Chungking** (Paramount).

Tim Holt and Bonita Granville in **Hitler's Children** (RKO).

Distributor: Paramount	
Director: George Marshall	
Released: December 31, 1942	

THEY GOT ME COVERED

Robert Kittredge	Bob Hope
Christina Hill	Dorothy Lamour
Mrs. Vanescu	Lenore Aubert
Fauscheim	Otto Preminger
Baldanacco	Edward Ciannelli
Gloria	Marion Martin
Little Old Man	Donald Meek
Sally	Phyllis Ruth
Nichimuro	Philip Ahn
Mason	Donald MacBride
Helen	Mary Treen
Mildred	Bettye Avery
Lucille	Margaret Hayes
Laura	Mary Byrne
Holtz	William Yetter
Faber	Henry Guttman
Gypsy Woman	Florence Bates
Hotel Manager	Walter Catlett
Vanescu	John Abbott
Red	Frank Sully

Distributor: RKO
Director: David Butler
Released: January 4, 1943

NIGHT PLANE FROM CHUNGKING

Captain Nick Stanton	Robert Preston

Hans Schumm, Elmer Jack Semple, Carl Esmond,
Ted North, Joan Bennett and J. Norton Dunn in
Margin for Error (20th Century-Fox).

Ann Richards	Ellen Drew	Anna Muller	Bonita Granville
Rev. Dr. van der Lieden	Stephen Geray	Professor Nichols	Kent Smith
Captain Po	Sen Yung	Colonel Henkel	Otto Kruger
Madame Wu	Soo Yong	The Bishop	H. B. Warner
Albert Pasavy	Otto Kruger	Franz Erhart	Lloyd Corrigan
Major Brissac	Ernest Dorian	Doctor Schmidt	Erford Gage
Countess Olga Karagin	Tamara Geva	Doctor Graf	Hans Conreid
Lieut. Tang	Allen Jung	Brenda	Nancy Gates
		Nazi Major	Gavin Muir
		Murph	Bill Burrud
		Irwin	Jimmy Zaner
		Gestapo Man	Richard Martin
		Arresting Sergeant	Goetz Van Eyck
		Gestapo Officer	John Merton
		Plane Dispatcher	Max Lucke
		N. S. V. Worker	Anna Loos
		Mother	Bessie Wade

Distributor: Paramount
Director: Ralph Murphy
Released: January 4, 1943

HITLER'S CHILDREN

Karl Bruner .... Tim Holt

Boys	Orley Lindgren
	Billy Brow
	Chris Wren
Mr. Muller	Egon Brecher
Mrs. Muller	Elsa Janssen
American Vice Consul	William Forrest
Young Matrons	Ariel Heath
	Rita Corday
Bit	Mary Stuart
Lieutenant S. A.	Roland Varno
Whipping Sergeant	Crane Whitley
Chief Trial Judge	Edward Van Sloan
Radio Announcer	Douglas Evans
Magda	Carla Boehm
Storm Trooper	Bruce Cameron

Morton Lowry, Melville Cooper, Henry Fonda, Allyn Joslyn, Thomas Mitchell and Bramwell Fletcher in **Immortal Sergeant** (20th Century-Fox).

Merrill Rodin, Anna Sten and Patricia Priest in **Chetniks** (20th Century-Fox).

Otto Horst	Howard Freeman
Frieda	Poldy Dur
Dr. Jennings	Clyde Fillmore
Mrs. Finkelstein	Ferike Boros
Solomon	Joe Kirk
Fritz	Hans von Twardowski
Saboteur	Ted North
Saboteur	Elmer Jack Semple
Saboteur	J. Norton Dunn
Kurk Moeller	Hans Schumm
Captain Mulrooney	Ed McNamara
Coroner	Selmer Jackson

Distributor: 20th Century-Fox
Director: Otto Preminger
Released: January 8, 1943

First Matron	Betty Roadman
Chief Matron	Kathleen Wilson
Boy	Harry McKim
Gestapo Officer	John Stockton

Distributor: RKO
Director: Edward Dmytryk
Released: January 6, 1943

MARGIN FOR ERROR

Sophie Baumer	Joan Bennett
Moe Finkelstein	Milton Berle
Karl Baumer	Otto Preminger
Baron von Alvenstor	Carl Esmond

Carol Hughes, Joseph Allen Jr., Roscoe Karns and Joan Blair in **My Son, the Hero** (PRC).

Johnny Sheffield, Stanley Ridges, Sig Rumann and
Johnny Weissmuller in **Tarzan Triumphs** (RKO).

CHETNIKS

Gen. Draja Mihailovitch	Philip Dorn
Lubitca Mihailovitch	Anna Sten
Alexis	John Sheppard
Natalia	Virginia Gilmore
Colonel Brockner	Martin Kosleck
General von Bauer	Felix Basch
Major Danilov	Frank Lackteen
Nada	Patricia Prest
Mirko	Merrill Rodin
Captain Savo	Leroy Mason

Distributor: 20th Century-Fox
Director: Louis King
Released: January 11, 1943

IMMORTAL SERGEANT

Corporal Colin Spence	Henry Fonda
Valentine	Maureen O'Hara
Sergeant Kelly	Thomas Mitchell
Cassidy	Allyn Joslyn
Benedict	Reginald Gardiner
Pilcher	Melville Cooper
Symes	Bramwell Fletcher
Cottrell	Morton Lowry
Specialty Dancer	Bob Mascagno
Specialty Dancer	Italia Denubila
Nurse	Jean Prescott

Distributor: 20th Century-Fox
Director: John Stahl

MY SON, THE HERO

Gerty .... Patsy Kelly
Big Time .... Roscoe Karns
Cynthia .... Joan Blair
Linda .... Carol Hughes
Kid Slug .... Maxie Rosenbloom
Tony .... Luis Alberni
Michael .... Joseph Allen, Jr.
Nancy .... Lois Collier
Lambie .... Jennie Le Gon
Nicodemus .... Nick Stewart
Manager .... Hal Price
Night Clerk .... Al St. John
Rositta .... Elvira Curci
Mrs. Olmstead .... Isobel La Mel
Girl Reporter .... Maxine Leslie

Distributor: PRC
Director: Edgar C. Ulmer
Released: January 20, 1943

TARZAN TRIUMPHS

Tarzan .... Johnny Weissmuller
Boy .... Johnny Sheffield
Zandra .... Frances Gifford
Col. von Reichart .... Stanley Ridges
Sergeant .... Sig Ruman
Patriarch .... Pedro de Cordoba
Bausch .... Philip Van Zandt
Archmet .... Stanley Brown
Schmidt .... Rex Williams
Cheta .... Herself

Distributor: RKO
Director: William Thiele
Released: January 20, 1943

MISS V FROM MOSCOW

Vera Marova .... Lola Lane
Capt. Anton Kleis .... Noel Madison
Steve Worth .... Howard Banks
Henri Davallier .... Paul Weigel
Col. Wolfgang Heinrich .... John Vosper

Mme. Finchon .... Anna Demetrio
Capt. Richter .... William Vaughn
Pierre .... Juan De La Cruz
Minna .... Kathryn Sheldon

Albert Sharpe and Lola Lane in **Miss V from Moscow** (PRC).

Gerald Naughton .... Victor Kendell
Dr. Suchevsky .... Richard Kipling

Distributor: PRC
Director: Albert Herman
Released: January 21, 1943

FLIGHT FOR FREEDOM

Tonie Carter .... Rosalind Russell
Randy Britton .... Fred MacMurray
Paul Turner .... Herbert Marshall
Johnny Salvini .... Eduardo Ciannelli
Admiral Graves .... Walter Kingsford
Pete .... Damian O'Flynn
Bill .... Jack Carr
Mac .... Matt McHugh
Mr. Yokohata .... Richard Loo
Flyer .... Charles Lung

Distributor: RKO
Director: Lothar Mendes
Released: February 4, 1943

Rosalind Russell in **Flight for Freedom** (RKO).

AMAZING MRS. HOLLIDAY

Ruth	Deanna Durbin
Tom	Edmond O'Brien
Timothy	Barry Fitzgerald
Henderson	Arthur Treacher
Commodore	Harry Davenport
Edgar	Grant Mitchell
Karen	Frieda Inescourt
Louise	Elisabeth Risdon
Ferguson	Jonathan Hale
Lucy	Esther Dale
Jeff	Gus Schilling
Dr. Kirke	J. Frank Hamilton

The Children: Christopher Severn, Yvonne Severn, Vido Rich, Mila Rich, Teddy Infuhr, Linda Bieber, Diane Dubois, Bill Ward and the Chinese Baby.

Frank O'Connor, Harry Davenport, Arthur Treacher and Barry Fitzgerald in **The Amazing Mrs. Holliday** (Universal).

John Hubbard, Robin Raymond and Olin Howlin in
Secrets of the Underground (Republic).

Distributor: Universal
Director: Bruce Manning
Released: February 10, 1943

Director: William Morgan
Released: February 18, 1943

SECRETS OF THE UNDERGROUND

P. Cadwallder Jones	John Hubbard
Terry	Virginia Grey
Maurice	Lloyd Corrigan
Paul Panois	Miles Mander
Oscar	Olin Howlin
Joe	Ben Welden
Mrs. Perkins	Marla Shelton
Kermit	Neil Hamilton
Cleary	Ken Christy
Maxie	Dick Rich

Distributor: Republic

THE MYSTERIOUS DOCTOR

Sir Henry Leland	John Loder
Letty Carstairs	Eleanor Parker
Lt. Christopher Hilton	Bruce Lester
Dr. Frederick Holmes	Lester Matthews
Hugh Penhryn	Forrester Harvey
Bart Raymond	Matt Willis
Saul Bevans	Art Foster
Herbert	Clyde Cook
Luke	Creighton Hale
Ruby	Phyllis Barry
Tom Andrews	David Clyde
The Peddler	Harold de Becker
Simon Tewksbury	Frank Mayo

Lester Matthews, Forrester Harvey and John Loder
in **The Mysterious Doctor** (Warner Bros.).

Roger .... Hank Mann
Orderly .... DeWolf Hopper
Watson .... Jack Mower
The Commandant .... Crauford Kent

Distributor: Warner Bros.
Director: Ben Stoloff
Released: March 3, 1943

THE MOON IS DOWN

Col. Lanser .... Sir Cedric Hardwicke
Mayor Orden .... Henry Travers
Dr. Winter .... Lee J. Cobb
Molly Morden .... Doris Bowden
Madame Orden .... Margaret Wycherly
Lieut. Tonder .... Peter Van Eyck

Alex Morden .... William Post, Jr.
Capt. Loft .... Henry Rowland
George Corell .... E. J. Ballentine
Inn Keeper .... Irving Pichel
Peder's Wife .... Violette Wilson
Capt. Bentick .... Hans Schumm
Major Hunter .... Ernest Dorian
Lieut. Prackle .... John Banner
Annie .... Helene Thimig
Joseph .... Ian Wolfe
Orderly .... Kurt Krueger
Albert .... Jeff Corey
Schumann .... Louis Arco
Moeller .... Ernst Hausman
Ole .... Charles McGraw
Foreman .... Trevor Bardette
Staff Officer .... John Mylong

Sergeant	Otto Reichow
Sergeant	Sven Hugo Borg
Mother	Dorothy Peterson

Distributor: 20th Century-Fox
Director: Irving Pichel
Released: March 10, 1943

HE'S MY GUY

Van Moore	Dick Foran
Terry Allen	Irene Hervey
Madge Donovan	Joan Davis
Sparks	Fuzzy Knight
Kirk	Lon Douglas

| Johnson | Samuel S. Hinds |
| Elwood | William Halligan |

Also: Gertrude Niesen, Diamond Brothers, Mills Brothers, Louis Da Pron, Lorraine Krueger, Dorene Sisters.

Distributor: Universal
Director: Edward F. Cline
Released: March 11, 1943

ASSIGNMENT IN BRITTANY

Capt. Metard	
Bertrand Conlay	Pierre Aumont
Anne Pinot	Susan Peters

Doris Bowden, Otto Reichow and Sven Hugo Borg in
The Moon is Down (20th Century-Fox).

Joan Davis, Fuzzy Knight and Irene Hervey in **He's My Guy** (Universal).

Susan Peters and Jean Pierre Aumont in **Assignment in Brittany** (M-G-M).

Charles Laughton with Una O'Connor in **This Land is Mine** (RKO).

Alan Ladd, Iris Wong and Loretta Young in **China**
(Paramount).

Kerenor .... Richard Whorf
Mme. Corlay .... Margaret Wycherly
Elise .... Signe Hasso
Col. Trane .... Reginald Owen
Capt. Deichgraper .... John Emery
Capt. Holz .... George Couloris
Albertine .... Sarah Padden
Col. Fournier .... Miles Mander
Henri .... George Brest
Etienne .... Darryl Hickman

Distributor: M-G-M
Director: Jack Conway
Released: March 11, 1943

THIS LAND IS MINE

Albert Lory .... Charles Laughton
Louise Martin .... Maureen O'Hara
George Lambert .... George Sanders
Major von Keller .... Walter Slezak
Paul Martin .... Kent Smith
Mrs. Emma Lory .... Una O'Connor
Prof. Sorel .... Philip Merivale
Mayor .... Thurston Hall
Prosecutor .... George Coulouris
Julie Grant .... Nancy Gates
Judge .... Ivan Simpson
Edmund Lorraine .... John Donat

Lt. Schwartz	Frank Alten	Corp. Peterson	Ward Wood
Little Man	Leo Bulgakov	Pvt. Chester	Ray Montgomery
Mr. Lorraine	Wheaton Chambers	Sgt. Joe Winocki	John Garfield
Mrs. Lorraine	Cecil Weston	Lt. Tex Rader	James Brown

Distributor: RKO
Director: Jean Renoir
Released: March 17, 1943

CHINA

Carolyn Grant	Loretta Young
Mr. Jones	Alan Ladd
Johnny Sparrow	William Bendix
First Brother-Lin Cho	Philip Ahn
Kwan Su	Iris Wong
Third Brother-Lin Wei	Sen Yung
Tan Ying	Marianne Quon
Student	Jessie Tai Sing

Distributor: Paramount
Director: John Farrow
Released: March 19, 1943

A bombing scene from **Air Force** (Paramount).

AIR FORCE

Capt. Mike Quincannon	John Ridgely
Lt. Bill Williams	Gig Young
Lt. Tommy McMartin	Arthur Kennedy
Lt. Munchauser	Charles Drake
Sgt. Robby White	Harry Carey
Corp. Weinberg	George Tobias

Corp. Peterson	Ward Wood
Pvt. Chester	Ray Montgomery
Sgt. Joe Winocki	John Garfield
Lt. Tex Rader	James Brown
Major Mallory	Stanley Ridges
Colonel	Willard Robertson
Colonel Blake	Moroni Olsen
Sgt. J. J. Callahan	Edward Brophy
Major W. G. Roberts	Richard Lane
Lt. P. T. Moran	Bill Crago
Susan McMartin	Faye Emerson
Major Daniels	Addison Richards
Major A. M. Bagley	James Flavin
Mary Quincannon	Ann Doran
Mrs. Chester	Dorothy Peterson
Marine With Dog	James Millican
Jack Harper	William Forrest
Corporal, Demolition Sqd.	Murray Alper
Officer At Hickam Field	George Neise
Marine	Tom Neal
Quincannon's Son	Henry Blair
Control Officer	Warren Douglas
Nurse	Ruth Ford
Second Nurse	Leah Baird
Sergeant	William Hopper
Sergeant	Sol Gorss
Control Officer	James Bush
Ground Control Man	George Offerman, Jr.
Joe	Walter Sande
First Lieutenant	Theodore von Eltz
Second Lieutenant	Ross Ford
Co-Pilot	Rand Brooks
Nurse	Lynne Baggett

Distributor: Warner Bros.
Director: Howard Hawks
Released: March 20, 1943

IT AIN'T HAY

Grover	Bud Abbott
Wilbur Hoolihan	Lou Costello
Kitty McCloin	Grace McDonald
King O'Hara	Cecil Kellaway
Gregory Warner	Eugene Pallette
Peggy Princess O'Hara	Patsy O'Connor
Private Joe Collins	Leighton Noble
Umbrella Sam	Shemp Howard
Colonel Brainard	Samuel S. Hinds
Harry The Horse	Eddie Quillan

Leighton Noble with Grace McDonald in **It Ain't Hay** (Universal).

Slicker	Richard Lane	Sergt. Jones	Keith Richards
Chauncey The Eye	David Hacker	Private Laswell	Billy Benedict
Big Hearted Charlie	Andrew Tombes	Barclay	Ralph Sanford
Major Harper	Pierre Watkin		
Banker	William Forrest		
Reilly	Wade Boteler		
Grant	Selmer Jackson		

Distributor: Paramount
Director: William H. Pine
Released: March 22, 1943

Distributor: Universal
Director: Erle C. Kenton
Released: March 22, 1943

HANGMEN ALSO DIE

Dr. Svoboda	Brian Donlevy
Prof. Novotny	Walter Brennan
Mascha Novotny	Anna Lee
Czaka	Gene Lockhart
Jan Horek	Dennis O'Keefe
Alois Gruber	Alexander Granach
Aunt Ludmilla	Margaret Wycherly
Mrs. Novotny	Nana Bryant
Beda Novotny	Billy Roy

AERIAL GUNNER

Foxy Pattis	Chester Morris
Ben Davis	Richard Arlen
Peggy Lunt	Lita Ward
Sandy Lunt	Jimmy Lydon
Gadget Blaine	Dick Purcell

Dick Purcell, Billy Benedict, Jimmy Lydon, Richard Arlen and Chester Morris in **Aerial Gunner** (Paramount).

Anna Lee and Brian Donlevy in **Hangmen Also Die** (United Artists).

Jean Parker, Chester Morris and Barry Sullivan in **High Explosive** (Paramount).

Roman Bohnen, Errol Flynn and Ann Sheridan in
Edge of Darkness (Warner Bros.).

Heydrich	Hans von Twardowski
Haas	Tonio Selwart
Dedic	Jonathan Hale
Gabby	Lionel Stander
Bartos	Byron Foulger
Landlady	Virginia Farmer
Schirmer	Louis Donath
Mrs. Dvorak	Sarah Padden
Dr. Pilar	Edmund MacDonald
Necval	George Irving
Worker	James Bush
Camp Officer	Arno Frey
Hostage	Lester Sharpe
Votruba	Arthur Loft
Viktorin	William Farnum
Ritter	Reinhold Scheunzel

Distributor: United Artists
Director: Fritz Lang
Released: March 23, 1943

HIGH EXPLOSIVE

Buzz Mitchell	Chester Morris
Connie Baker	Jean Parker
Mike Douglas	Barry Sullivan
Jimmy Baker	Rand Brooks
Doris Lynch	Barbara Lynn
Squichy Andrews	Ralph Sanford
Dave	Dick Purcell
Man	Vince Barnett
Joe	Addison Randall

Distributor: Paramount
Director: Frank McDonald
Released: March 23, 1943

EDGE OF DARKNESS

Gunnar Brogge	Errol Flynn

Karen Stensgard	Ann Sheridan
Dr. Martin Stensgard	Walter Huston
Katja	Nancy Coleman
Captain Koenig	Helmut Dantine
Gerd Bjarnesen	Judith Anderson
Anna Stensgard	Ruth Gordon
Johann Stensgard	John Beal

Tom Conway, Wynne Gibson and Harriett Hilliard in **The Falcon Strikes Back** (RKO).

Sixtus Andresen	Morris Carnovsky
Kaspar Torgersen	Charles Dingle
Lars Malken	Roman Bohnen
Pastor Aalesen	Richard Fraser
Knut Osterholm	Art Smith
Hammer	Tom Fadden
Major Ruck	Henry Brandon
Paul	Tonio Selwart
Frida	Helene Thimig
Jensen	Frank Wilcox
Mortensen	Francis Pierlot
Mrs. Mortensen	Lottie Williams
Petersen	Monte Blue
Solveig Brategaard	Dorothy Tree
Hulda	Virginia Christine
Helmut	Henry Rowland
German Captain	Kurt Katch
German Aviator	Kurt Krueger
German Soldier	Peter Van Eyck

Distributor: Warner Bros.—First National
Director: Lewis Milestone
Released: March 23, 1943

THE FALCON STRIKES BACK

Falcon	Tom Conway
Gwynne Gregory	Harriet Hilliard
Marcia Brooks	Jane Randolph
Smiley Dugan	Edgar Kennedy
Goldy	Cliff Edwards
Mia Bruger	Rita Corday
Rickey Davis	Erford Gage
Mrs. Lipton	Wynne Gibson
Jerry	Richard Loo
Bruno Steffen	Andre Charlot
Inspector Donovan	Cliff Clark
Bates	Ed Gargan

Distributor: RKO
Director: Edward Dmytryk
Released: March 24, 1943

THE PURPLE V

Joe Thorne	John Archer
Katti Forster	Mary McLeod
Thomas Forster	Fritz Kortner
Paul Forster	Rex Williams
Johann Keller	Kurt Katch
Otto Horner	Walter Sande
Oberst von Ritter	William Vaughn
Roger	Peter Lawford
Walter Heyse	Kurt Krueger
Marta	Eva Hyde
Mrs. Vogel	Irene Seidner

Peter Lawford, Mary McLeod and John Archer in **The Purple V** (Republic).

Distributor: Republic
Director: George Sherman
Released: March 25, 1943

CORREGIDOR

Jan Stockman	Otto Kruger
Dr. Royce Lee	Elissa Landi
Michael	Donald Woods
Sergeant Mahoney	Frank Jenks
Pinky	Rick Vallin
Hey Dutch	Wanda McKay
Captain	Ian Keith
Hyacinth	Ruby Dandridge

Brooklyn	Eddie Hall
Bronx	Charles Jordan
Filipino Lieutenant	Ted Hecht
Lieutenant No. 2	Frank Hagney
Priest	Frank Jaquet
General	Jack Rutherford
Soldier No. 1	John Grant
Soldier No. 2	Stan Jolley
No. 1 Boy	Jimmy Vilan
Marine	Gordon Hayes

Distributor: PRC
Director: William Nigh
Released: March 25, 1943

Donald Woods and Elissa Landi in **Corregidor** (PRC).

Annabella with Howard da Silva in **Tonight We Raid Calais** (20th Century-Fox).

TONIGHT WE RAID CALAIS

Odette	Annabella
Geoffrey Carter	John Sutton
M. Bonnard	Lee J. Cobb
Mme. Bonnard	Beulah Bondi
Widow Grelieu	Blanche Yurka
Sergeant Block	Howard da Silva
Jacques Grandet	Marcel Dalio
Mme. Grandet	Ann Codee
Danton	Nigel de Brulier
Maurice Bonnard	Robert Lewis
Captain	Richard Derr
Captain Baird	Leslie Denison
Bell Ringer	Billy Edmunds
Major West	Lester Matthews
Commander	Reginald Sheffield
Kurz	John Banner
English Pilot	Leslie Vincent
Lieutenant	Robert O. Davis
Lieutenant	George Lynn

Distributor: 20th Century-Fox
Director: John Brahm
Released: March 29, 1943

SHERLOCK HOLMES IN WASHINGTON

Sherlock Holmes	Basil Rathbone
Dr. Watson	Nigel Bruce
Nancy Partridge	Marjorie Lord
William Easter	Henry Daniell
Stanley	George Zucco
Lt. Pete Merriam	John Archer
Bart Lang	Gavin Muir
Detective Lt. Grogan	Edmund MacDonald
Howe	Don Terry
Cady	Bradley Page
Mr. Ahrens	Holmes Herbert
Santor Babcock	Thurston Hall

Distributor: Universal
Director: Roy William Neill
Released: March 31, 1943

THE MORE THE MERRIER

Connie Milligan	Jean Arthur
Joe Carter	Joel McCrea
Benjamin Dingle	Charles Coburn

Don Terry, Marjorie Lord and Bradley Page in **Sherlock Holmes in Washington** (Universal).

Charles J. Pendergast	Richard Gaines
Evans	Bruce Bennett
Pike	Frank Sully
Senator Noonan	Clyde Fillmore
Morton Rodakiewicz	Stanley Clements
Harding	Don Douglas
Miss Dalton	Ann Savage
Waiter	Grady Sutton
Dancer	Sugar Geise
Drunk	Don Barclay
Drunk	Frank Sully

Charles Coburn and Jean Arthur in **The More the Merrier** (Columbia).

Girl	Shirley Patterson	Taxi Driver	Jack Carr
Miss Bilby	Ann Doran	Hotel Clerk	Chester Clute
Waitress	Mary Treen	Head Waiter	Robert F. Hill
Barmaid	Gladys Blake	Police Captain	Eddy Chandler
Miss Allen	Kay Linaker	Dancer	Peggy Carroll
Miss Chasen	Nancy Gray	Caretaker	George Reed
Air Corps Captain	Byron Shores	Taxi Driver	Kitty McHugh
Miss Finch	Betzi Beaton		
Texan	Harrison Greene		
Southerner	Robert McKenzie		
Cattleman	Vic Potel		
Character	Lon Poff		
Senator	Frank LaRue		
Minister	Harry Bradley		
Miss Geeskin	Betty McMahan		
Dumpy Woman	Helen Holmes		
Fat Statistician	Marshall Ruth		
Second Statistician	Hal Gerard		
Reporter	Henry Roquemore		

Distributor: Columbia
Director: George Stevens
Released: April 7, 1943

PILOT NO. 5

George Braynor Collins	Franchot Tone
Freddie	Marsha Hunt
Vito S. Alesandro	Gene Kelly
Everett Arnold	Van Johnson

157

Franchot Tone, Marsha Hunt and Gene Kelly in
Pilot No. 5 (M-G-M).

Dean Jagger, Billy Marshall, Charles Wagenheim and
John Carradine in **I Escaped from the Gestapo**
(Monogram).

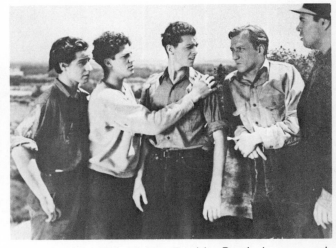

Bobby Jordan, Billy Halop, Freddie Bartholomew and
Huntz Hall in **Junior Army** (Columbia).

Winston Davis	Alan Baxter
Henry Willoughby Claven	Dick Simmons
Major Eichel	Steve Geray
Hank Durban	Howard Freeman
Nikola	Frank Puglia
American Soldier	William Tannen

Distributor: M-G-M
Director: George Sidney
Released: April 8, 1943

I ESCAPED FROM THE GESTAPO

Helen	Mary Brian
Lane	Dean Jagger
Martin	John Carradine
Gordan	Bill Henry
Bergen	Sidney Blackmer

Lokin	Anthony Warde
One-Arm Sailor	William Vine
Haft	Charles Wagenheim
Lunt	Billy Marshall
Rodt	Norman Willis
Gerard	Ian Keith
Olin	Peter Dunne
Billy	Spanky MacFarland
Domack	Edward Keane

Distributor: Monogram
Director: Harold Young
Released: April 15, 1943

JUNIOR ARMY

| Freddie Hewlett | Freddie Bartholomew |
| Jimmie Fletcher | Billy Halop |

Anne Baxter and Tyrone Power in **Crash Dive** (20th Century-Fox).

Fred MacMurray, Conrad Veidt and Joan Crawford
in **Above Suspicion** (M-G-M).

Cowboy	Bobby Jordan
Bushy Thomas	Huntz Hall
Major Carter	Boyd Davis
Cadet Capt. Rogers	William Blees

Cadet Sergeant Sable	Richard Noyes
Mr. Ferguson	Joseph Crehan
Saginaw Jake	Don Beddoe
Cadet Pell	Charles Lind
Cadet Baker	Billy Lechner
Cadet Wilbur	Peter Lawford
Horner	Robert O. Davis

Distributor: Columbia
Director: Lew Landers
Released: April 22, 1943

CRASH DIVE

Lieutenant Ward Stewart	Tyrone Power
Jean Hewlett	Anne Baxter
Lieutenant Commander Dewey Connors	
	Dana Andrews
McDonnell	James Gleason

Erich von Stroheim, Anne Baxter and Franchot Tone
in **Five Graves to Cairo** (Paramount).

Sig Rumann, Elsa Janssen, George Sanders and Ludwig Stossel in **They Came to Blow Up America** (20th Century-Fox).

Grandmother	Dame May Whitty
Brownie	Henry Morgan
Oliver Cromwell Jones	Ben Carter
Hammond	Charles Tannen
Captain Bryson	Frank Conroy
Doris	Florence Lake
Curly	John Archer
Crew Member	George Holmes
Butler	Minor Watson
Miss Bromley	Kathleen Howard
Lieutenant	David Bacon
Captain	Stanley Andrews
Clerk	Paul Burns
Sailor	Gene Rizzi

Distributor: 20th Century-Fox
Director: Archie Mayo
Released: April 22, 1943

ABOVE SUSPICION

Frances Myles	Joan Crawford
Richard Myles	Fred MacMurray
Hassert Seidel	Conrad Veidt
Sig von Aschenhausen	Basil Rathbone
Dr. Mespelbrunn	Reginald Owen
Peteer Galt	Richard Ainley
Countess	Cecil Cunningham
Aunt Ellen	Ann Shoemaker
Aunt Hattie	Sara Haden
Mr. A. Werner	Felix Bressart
Thornley	Bruce Lester
Frau Kleist	Johanna Hofer
Ottilie	Lotta Palfi

Distributor: M-G-M
Director: Richard Thorpe

Released: April 28, 1943

FIVE GRAVES TO CAIRO

John J. Bramble	Franchot Tone
Mouche	Anne Baxter
Farid	Akim Tamiroff

William Terry and Cheryl Walker in **Stage Door Canteen** (United Artists).

Field Marshal Rommel	Erich von Stroheim
Lieutenant Schwegler	Peter Van Eyck
General Sebastiano	Fortunio Bonanova
Major von Buelow	Konstantin Shayne
Major Lamprecht	Fred Nurney
British Colonel	Miles Mander
British Captain	Leslie Denison
British Captain	Ian Keith
English Tank Commander	Bud Geary
German Sergeant	Frederick Giermann
Schwegler (Body Guard)	Bill Mussetter
German Technician	John Royce
German Engineer	Otto Reichow
Rommel's Orderly	Clyde Jackman
Rommel's Orderly	Sam Waagenaar
German Soldier	Peter F. U. Pohlney
First Soldier	John Erickson
Second Soldier	Philip Ahlm
Third Soldier	Hans Maebus
Fourth Soldier	Roger Creed

Distributor: Paramount
Director: Billy Wilder
Released: May 4, 1943

THEY CAME TO BLOW UP AMERICA

Carl Steelman	George Sanders
Frau Reiker	Anna Sten
Craig	Ward Bond
Colonel Taeger	Dennis Hoey
Dr. Herman Baumer	Sig Ruman
Julius Steelman	Ludwig Stossel
Captain Kranz	Robert Barrat
Helga Lorenz	Poldy Dur
Heinrich Burkhardt	Ralph Byrd
Mrs. Henrietta Steelman	Elsa Janssen
Eichner	Rex Williams
Zellerbach	Charles McGraw
Commander Houser	Sven Hugo Borg
Schonzeit	Kurt Katch
Fritz	Otto Reichow
Zugholtz	Andre Charlot
Kranz' Aide	Arno Frey
Jones	Sam Wren
Theresa	Etta McDaniel
Gertzer	Peter Michael
Coast Guardsman	Dick Hogan
Saleslady	Lisa Golm
Schlegel	Wolfgang Zilzer

Distributor: 20th Century-Fox
Director: Edward Ludwig
Released: May 7, 1943

STAGE DOOR CANTEEN

Eileen	Cheryl Walker
Dakota	William Terry
Jean	Marjorie Riordan
California	Lon McCallister
Ella Sue	Margaret Early
Texas	Michael Harrison
Mamie	Dorothea Kent
Jersey	Fred Brady
Lillian	Marion Shockley
The Australian	Patrick O'Moore
Girl	Ruth Roman

Stars of the Stage Door Canteen:
Judith Anderson, Tallulah Bankhead, Ray Bolger, Katharine Cornell, Jane Darwell, Dorothy Fields, Arlene Francis, Lucile Gleason, Helen Hayes, Jean Hersholt, George Jessel, Tom Kennedy, Betty

Lawford, Alfred Lunt, Harpo Marx, Yehudi Menuhin, Ralph Morgan, Elliott Nugent, Dame May Whitty, Henry Armetta, Ralph Bellamy, Helen Broderick, Lloyd Corrigan, William Demarest, Gracie Fields, Vinton Freedley, Vera Gordon, Katharine Hepburn, Sam Jaffe, Roscoe Karns, Otto Kruger, Gertrude Lawrence, Bert Lytell, Elsa Maxwell, Ethel Merman, Alan Mowbray, Merle Oberon, Brock Pemberton, Selena Royle, Ned Sparks, Johnny Weissmuller, Ed Wynn, Kenny Baker, Edgar Bergen, Ina Claire, Jane Cowl, Virginia Field, Lynn Fontaine, Billy Gilbert, Virginia Grey, Hugh Herbert, Allen Jenkins, Virginia Kaye, June Lang, Gypsy Rose Lee, Aline MacMahon, Helen Menken, Paul Muni, Franklin Pangborn, George Raft, Martha Scott, Bill Stern, Arleen Whelan, Count Basie and his Band, Xavier Cugat and his Orchestra, with Lina Romay, Benny Goodman and his Orchestra with Peggy Lee, Kay Kyser and his Band, Freddy Martin and his Orchestra, Guy Lombardo and his Orchestra

Distributor: United Artist
Director: Frank Borzage
Released: May 12, 1943

BOMBARDIER

Major Chick Davis	Pat O'Brien
Capt. Buck Oliver	Randolph Scott
Burt Hughes	Anne Shirley
Tom Hughes	Eddie Albert
Jim Carter	Walter Reed

Pat O'Brien, Randolph Scott and Barton MacLane in
Bombardier (RKO).

Joe Connors	Robert Ryan
Sergeant Dixon	Barton MacLane
Jap Officer	Leonard Strong
Chito Rafferty	Richard Martin
Paul Harris	Russell Wade
Captain Rand	James Newill
Chaplain Craig	John Miljan
Instructor	Charles Russell

Also: Joseph King, Charles D. Brown, Lloyd Ingraham, Lee Shumway, Edward Peil, Herbert Heyes, Robert Middlemass, Neil Hamilton, Abner Biberman

Distributor: RKO-Radio
Director: Richard Wallace
Released: May 13, 1943

Eleanor Parker, Ann Harding and Walter Huston in **Mission to Moscow** (Warner Bros.).

Humphrey Bogart and Raymond Massey in **Action in the North Atlantic** (Warner Bros.).

ACTION IN THE NORTH ATLANTIC

Joe Rossi	Humphrey Bogart
Captain Steve Jarvis	Raymond Massey
Boats O'Hara	Alan Hale
Pearl	Julie Bishop
Mrs. Jarvis	Ruth Gordon
Chips Abrams	Sam Levene
Johnny Pulaski	Dane Clark
Whitey Lara	Peter Whitney
Cadet Robert Parker	Dick Hogan
Rear Admiral Hartridge	Minor Watson
Caviar Jinks	J. M. Kerrigan
Ensign Wright	Kane Richmond
German Sub Captain	William von Brincken
Goldberg	Chick Chandler

Cecil	George Offerman, Jr.
Lieutenant Commander	Don Douglas
Pete Larson	Art Foster
Aherne	Ray Montgomery
Tex Mathews	Glenn Strange
Sparks	Creighton Hale
Hennessy	Elliott Sullivan
McGonigle	Alec Craig
Captain Ziemer	Ludwig Stossel
Cherub	Dick Wessel
Captain Carpolis	Frank Puglia
Jenny O'Hara	Iris Adrian
Bartender	Irving Bacon
Lieutenant Commander	James Flavin

Thelma White, Catherine Craig and Chick Chandler in **Spy Train** (Monogram).

Abe Kashey with Bobby Watson in **That Nazty Nuisance** (United Artists).

Distributor: Warner Bros.-First National
Director: Lloyd Bacon
Released: May 17, 1943

MISSION TO MOSCOW

Joseph E. Davies	Walter Huston
Mrs. Davies	Ann Harding
Litvinov	Oscar Homolka
Freddie	George Tobias
Molotov	Gene Lockhart
Madame Molotov	Frieda Inescort
Emlem Davies	Eleanor Parker
Robert Grosjean	Richard Travis
Major Kamenev	Helmut Dantine
Vyshinsky	Victor Francen
Von Ribbentrop	Henry Daniell
Mrs. Litvinov	Barbara Everest
Winston Churchill	Dudley Field Malone
Krestinsky	Roman Bohnen
Tanya Litvinov	Maria Palmer
Colonel Faymonville	Moroni Olsen
Loy Henderson	Winor Watson
Kalinin	Vladimir Sokoloff
Dr. Botkin	Maurice Schwartz
Spendler	Jerome Cowan
Bukharin	Konstantin Shayne
Stalin	Mannart Kippen
Lady Chilston	Kathleen Lockhart
Timoshenko	Kurt Katch
Dr. Hjalmar Schact	Felix Basch
Judge Ulrich	Frank Puglia
Grinko	John Abbott
Secretary Cordell Hull	Charles Trowbridge

Distributor: Warner Bros.

Director: Michael Curtiz, Joseph E. Davies
Released: May 22, 1943

SPY TRAIN

Bruce	Richard Travis
Jane	Catherine Craig
Stu	Chick Chandler
Millie	Thelma White
Frieda	Evelyn Brent
Italian	Gerald Brock
Porter	Snowflake
Detective	Bill Hunter
Chief Nazi	Steve Roberts
Herman	Warren Hymer

Distributor: Monogram
Director: Harold Young
Released: May 25, 1943

THAT NAZTY NUISANCE

Hitler	Bobby Watson
Mussolini	Joe Devlin
Suki Yaki	Johnny Arthur
Kela	Jean Porter
Chief	Ian Keith
Von Popoff	Henry Victor
Spense	Emory Parnell
Benson	Frank Faylen
Guard	Ed 'Strangler' Lewis
Second Guard	Abe 'King Kong' Kashey
Goering	Rex Evans
Goebbels	Charles Rogers
Himmler	Wedgewood Nowell

Distributor: United Artists
Director: Glenn Tryon
Released: May 28, 1943

Lloyd Nolan, Robert Taylor and Thomas Mitchell in
Bataan (M-G-M).

BATAAN

Sergeant Bill Dane	Robert Taylor
Lt. Steve Bentley	George Murphy
Corp. Jake Feingold	Thomas Mitchell
Corp. Barney Todd	Lloyd Nolan
Capt. Lassiter	Lee Bowman
Leonard Purckett	Robert Walker
Felix Ramirez	Desi Arnaz
F. X. Matowski	Barry Nelson
Gilbert Hardy	Phillip Terry
Corp. Jesus Katigbay	Roque Espiritu
Wesley Epps	Kenneth Spencer
Yankee Salazar	J. Alex Havier
Sam Malloy	Tom Dugan
Lieutenant	Donald Curtis
Nurse	Lynne Carver
Nurse	Mary McLeod
Nurse	Dorothy Morris
Infantry Officer	Bud Geary

Willard Robertson, Brenda Marshall and George Raft in **Background to Danger** (Warner Bros.).

Wounded Soldier	Ernie Alexander
Machine Gunner	Phil Schumacher

Distributor: M-G-M

Dona Drake and orchestra in **Salute for Three** (Paramount).

Director: Tay Garnett
Released: May 28, 1943

BACKGROUND TO DANGER

Joe Barton	George Raft
Tamara	Brenda Marshall
Colonel Robinson	Sydney Greenstreet
Zaleshoff	Peter Lorre
Ana Remzi	Osa Massen
Hassan	Turhan Bey
McNamara	Willard Robertson
Mailler	Kurt Katch
Rashenko	Daniel Ocko
Old Turk	Pedro de Corboda
Syrian Vendor	Frank Puglia
Raeder	Steve Geray

Distributor: Warner Bros.
Director: Raoul Walsh
Released: June 9, 1943

SALUTE FOR THREE

Judy Adams	Betty Rhodes
Buzz McAllister	MacDonald Carey
Jimmy Gates	Marty May
Foggy	Cliff Edwards
Myrt	Minna Gombell
Dona	Dona Drake
Lorraine and Rognan	Lorraine and Rognan

Distributor: Paramount
Director: Ralph Murphy
Released: June 10, 1943

HITLER'S MADMAN (HANGMAN)

Jarmila	Patricia Morison
Heydrich	John Carradine
Karel	Alan Curtis
Hanka	Ralph Morgan
Mayor Bauer	Ludwig Stossel
Himmler	Howard Freeman
Nepomuk	Edgar Kennedy
Priest	Al Sheehan
Maria Bartonek	Elizabeth Russell
Dvorak	Jimmy Conlin
Mrs. Hank	Blanche Yurka
Clara Janek	Jorja Rollins
Janek	Victor Kilian
Mrs. Bauer	Johanna Hofer
Colonel	Wolfgang Zilzer
Professor	Tully Marshall

Distributor: M-G-M
Director: Douglas Sirk
Released: June 10, 1943

Alan Curtis, Patricia Morison and John Carradine in **Hitler's Madman** (M-G-M).

TWO TICKETS TO LONDON

Jeanne	Michele Morgan
Dan Driscoll	Alan Curtis
Fairchild	C. Aubrey Smith
MacCardle	Barry Fitzgerald
Roddy	Tarquin Oliver
Mrs. Tinkle	Mary Gordon
Ormsby	Robert Warwick
Brighton	Matthew Boulton
Mr. Tinkle	Oscar O'Shea
Emmie	Doris Lloyd
Kilgallen	Holmes Herbert
Nettleton	Stanley Logan

Alan Curtis and Michele Morgan in **Two Tickets to London** (Universal).

Treathcote .... Lester Matthews
Benson .... Harold de Becker
Royce .... John Burton
Dame Dunne Hartley .... Mary Forbes
Accordionist .... Dooley Wilson

Distributor: Universal
Director: Edwin L. Marin
Released: June 14, 1943

GHOSTS ON THE LOOSE

Mugs .... Leo Gorcey
Glimpy .... Huntz Hall
Danny .... Bobby Jordan
Emil .... Bela Lugosi

Betty .... Ava Gardner
Jack .... Ric Vallin
Hilda .... Minerva Urecal
Tony .... Wheeler Oakman
Stash .... Stanley Clements
Benny .... Billy Benedict
Scruno .... Sammy Morrison
Dave .... Bobby Stone

Distributor: Monogram
Director: William Beaudine
Released: June 14, 1943

WINGS OVER THE PACIFIC

Nona .... Inez Cooper

Bobby Stone, Leo Gorcey, Huntz Hall, Sammy Morrison, Billy Benedict, Bill Bates, Bobby Jordan and Stanley Clements in **Ghosts on the Loose** (Monogram).

Allan	Edward Norris
Butler	Montague Love
Pieter	Robert Armstrong
Kurt	Henry Guttman
Harry	Ernie Adams
Chief	Santini Pauiloa
Taro	John Roth
Native	James Lono
2nd Native	George Kamel
3rd Native	Hawksha Paia
Jap Officer	Alex Havier

Distributor: Monogram
Director: Phil Rosen
Released: June 15, 1943

Henry Guttman, Edward Norris, Ernie Adams and Inez Cooper in **Wings Over the Pacific** (Monogram).

Richard Fraser with Brenda Joyce in **Thumbs Up** (Republic).

Grace McDonald, Maureen Cannon, Lois Collier, Frank Faylen and Vera Vague in **Get Going** (Universal).

Emmy Finch	Elsa Lanchester
Bert Lawrence	Arthur Margetson
Sam Keats	J. Pat O'Malley
Janie Brooke	Queenie Leonard
Welfare Supervisor	Molly Lamont
Gertrude Niesen	Gertrude Niesen
Foreman	George Byron
Ray Irwin	Charles Irwin
E. E. Cartwright	Andre Charlot
The Hot Shots	The Hot Shots

Distributor: Republic
Director: Joseph Santley
Released: June 16, 1943

GET GOING

Bob Carlton	Robert Paige
Judy King	Grace McDonald
Matilda Jones	Vera Vague

THUMBS UP

Louise Latimer	Brenda Joyce
Douglas Heath	Richard Fraser

Dr. Hugh Ho Chang, Mary Servoss, Walter Abel, George Reeves and Claudette Colbert in **So Proudly We Hail!** (Paramount).

Jean Parker, Richard Arlen and Bill Henry in **Alaska Highway** (Paramount).

Horace Doblem	Walter Catlett	Lieutenant Joan O'Doul	Paulette Goddard
Doris	Lois Collier	Lieutenant Olivia D'arcy	Veronica Lake
Bonnie	Maureen Cannon	Lieutenant John Summers	George Reeves
Mr. Tuttle	Milburn Stone	Lieutenant Rosemary Larson	Barbara Britton
Vilma Walters	Jennifer Holt	Chaplain	Walter Abel
Mrs. Daugherty	Nana Bryant	Kansas	Sonny Tufts
Hank	Frank Faylen	Captain 'Ma' McGregor	Mary Servoss
		Dr. Jose Bardia	Ted Hecht
		Dr. Harrison	John Litel
		Ling Chee	Dr. Hugh Ho Chang
		Lieutenant Sadie Schwartz	Mary Treen
		Lieutenant Ethel Armstrong	Kitty Kelly
		Lieutenant Elsie Bollenbacher	Helen Lynd
		Lieutenant Toni Dacolli	Lorna Gray
		Lieutenant Irma Emerson	Dorothy Adams
		Lieutenant Betty Peterson	Ann Doran

Distributor: Universal
Director: Jean Yarbrough
Released: June 21, 1943

SO PROUDLY WE HAIL!

Lieutenant Janet Davidson .... Claudette Colbert

Lieutenant Carol Johnson	Jean Willes		First Young Doctor	Damian O'Flynn
Lieutenant Fay Leonard	Lynn Walker		Ship's Captain	Roy Gordon
Lieutenant Margaret Stevenson	Joan Tours		Nurse	Julia Faye
Lieutenant Lynne Hopkins	Jan Wiley		Steward	Jack Luden
Nurse	Mimi Doyle		Major Arthur	Harry Strang
Colonel White	James Bell		Captain Lawrence	Edward Dow
Flight Lt. Archie McGregor	Dick Hogan		Girl	Yvonne DeCarlo
Captain O'Rourke	Bill Goodwin			
Captain O'Brien	James Flavin		*Distributor:* Paramount	
Mr. Larson	Byron Foulger		*Director:* Mark Sandrich	
Mrs. Larson	Elsa Janssen		*Released:* June 22, 1943	
Georgie Larson	Richard Crane			
Colonel Mason	Boyd Davis			
Colonel Clark	Will Wright		**ALASKA HIGHWAY**	
Nurse	Frances Morris			
Young Ensign	James Millican		Woody Ormsby	Richard Arlen

Wendy Barrie and Richard Arlen in **Submarine Alert**
(Paramount).

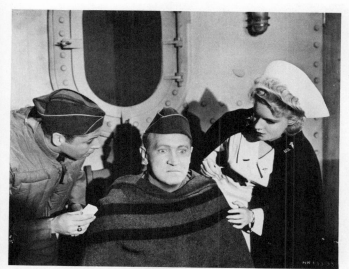

William Tracy, Joe Sawyer and Marjorie Woodworth in **Yanks Ahoy** (United Artists).

Ann Coswell	Jean Parker
Frosty Gimble	Ralph Sanford
Roughhouse	Joe Sawyer
Steve Ormsby	Bill Henry
Sgt. Swithers	John Wegman
Pop Ormsby	Harry Shannon
Blair Caswell	Edward Earle
Hank Lincoln	Keith Richards
Pompadour Jones	Eddie Quillan

Distributor: Paramount
Director: Frank McDonald
Released: June 24, 1943

SUBMARINE ALERT

Lee Deerhold	Richard Arlen
Ann Patterson	Wendy Barrie
Dr. Arthur Huneker	Nils Asther
G. B. Fleming	Roger Pryor
Commander Toyo	Abner Biberman
Vincent Belga	Marc Lawrence
Mr. Bambridge	
	John Miljan
Capt. Hargas	
Tina	Patsy Nash
Freddie Grayson	Ralph Sanford
Henry Haldine	Dwight Frye
Dr. Barclay	Edward Earle
Engineer	William Bakewell

Clerk	Stanley Smith

Distributor: Paramount
Director: Frank McDonald
Released: June 28, 1943

YANKS AHOY

Sgt. Doubleday	William Tracy
Sgt. Ames	Joe Sawyer
Phyllis	Marjorie Woodworth
Capt. Scott	Minor Watson
Capt. Gillis	Walter Woolf King
Lt. Reeves	Robert Kent
Col. Elliott	Romaine Callender
Ensign Crosby	William Bakewell
Jenkins	Frank Faylen
Miss Potter	Marga Ann Deighton
Helmsman	Tom Seidel
Lt. Ransome	John Canady
Dr. Hadley	Irwin Stanley
Jap	Richard Loo
German	Frank Reicher
Second German	Rudolph Lindau
Corp. Quinn	Bud McTaggert
Sailor	Dan Lloyd
Cook Flynn	James Finlayson

Distributor: United Artists
Director: Kurt Neumann
Released: June 29, 1943

Morris Ankrum, Lucille Ball and Henry O'Neill in **Best Foot Forward** (M-G-M).

Grant Withers, Sheila Lynch and Wallace Ford in
The Marines Come Through (Astor).

BEST FOOT FORWARD

Lucille Ball	Lucille Ball
Jack O'Riley	William Gaxton
Helen Schlessenger	Virginia Weidler
Elwood	Tommy Dix
Nancy	Nancy Walker
Minerva	Gloria DeHaven
Dutch	Kenny Bowers
Ethel	June Allyson
Hunk	Jack Jordan
Miss Delaware Water Gap	Beverly Tyler
Cheser Short	Chill Wills
Major Reeber	Henry O'Neill
Miss Talbert	Sara Haden
Harry James and Orchestra	Themselves

Distributor: M-G-M

Director: Edward Buzzell
Released: June 30, 1943

THE MARINES COME THROUGH

Singapore	Wallace Ford
Linda Dale	Toby Wing
Jack	Grant Withers
Maisie	Sheila Lynch
Lt. Landers	Michael Doyle
Dick Weber	Don Lanning
Beckstrom	Frank Rasmussen
Charles	Roy Elkins
Top Sergeant	James Neary
Col. Dale	Thomas McKeon

Distributor: Astor

Alan Baxter, right with German Naval Officers in
Submarine Base (PRC).

Director: Louis Gasnier
Released: July 8, 1943

SUBMARINE BASE

Jim Taggart	John Litel
Joe Morgan	Alan Baxter
Maria	Fifi D'Orsay
Spike	Eric Blore
Dorothy	Iris Adrian
Judy	Jacqueline Dalya
Kroll	Georges Metaxa
Styx	Luis Alberni
Felipo	Rafael Storm
Cavanaugh	George Lee
Angela	Anna Demetrio

Mueller	Lucien Prival

Distributor: PRC
Director: Albert Kelley
Released: July 8, 1943

BOMBER'S MOON

Captain Jeff Dakin	George Montgomery
Alec	Annabella
Captain Paul Husnik	Kent Taylor
Friederich Mueller	Walter Kingsford
Major von Streicher	Martin Kosleck
Major von Grunow	Dennis Hoey
Ernst	Robert Barrat
Karl	Kenneth Brown

Henrik Vanseeler	Victor Kilian	Joan	Evelyn Finney
Priest	Robert Lewis	Slim	Johnny Bond
Kurt	Mike Mazurki	Werner	Budd Buster
Johann	Christian Rub	Fraser	John Merton
Hans	Otto Reichow	Katie	Edna Bennett
Dr. Hartman	Frank Reicher	Barlett	Steve Clark
Elsa	Gretl Dupont	Hans	Bud Osborne

Distributor: 20th Century-Fox   *Distributor:* Monogram
Director: Charles Fuhr   *Director:* S. Roy Luby
Released: July 9, 1943   *Released:* July 12, 1943

COWBOY COMMANDOS   THE SKY'S THE LIMIT

Crash	Ray Corrigan	Fred	Fred Astaire
Denny	Dennis Moore	Joan	Joan Leslie
Alibi	Max Terhune	Harriman	Robert Benchley

George Montgomery and Annabella in **Bomber's Moon** (20th Century-Fox).

Reg	Robert Ryan
Mrs. Fisher	Elizabeth Patterson
Canteen Lady	Marjorie Gateson
Freddie Slack and his Orchestra	Themselves

Distributor: RKO-Radio
Director: Edward H. Griffith
Released: July 13, 1943

Max Terhune, Evelyn Finley, Dennis Moore, Ray Corrigan and Steve Clark in **Cowboy Commandos** (Monogram).

WILD HORSE RUSTLERS

Tom Cameron	Bob Livingston
Fuzzy	Al St. John
Ellen	Linda Johnson
Smoky	Lane Chandler
Collins	Stanley Price
Jake	Frank Ellis
Sheriff	Karl Hackett

Distributor: PRC
Director: Sam Newfield
Released: July 13, 1943

GOOD LUCK, MR. YATES

Ruth Jones	Claire Trevor
Jonesey Jones	Edgar Buchanan
Oliver Yates	Jess Barker

Charlie Edmonds	Tom Neal
Dr. Carl Hesser	Albert Basserman
Johnny Zaloris	Tommy Cook
Jimmy Dixon	Scotty Beckett
Joe Briggs	Frank Sully
Monty King	Douglas Leavitt
Mike Zaloris	Henry Armetta
Katy Zaloris	Rosina Galli
Plunkett	Billy Roy
Bob Coles	Conrad Binyon
Ross	Bobby Larson
Wilson	Rudy Wissler

Distributor: Columbia
Director: Ray Enright
Released: July 15, 1943

FOR WHOM THE BELL TOLLS

Robert Jordan	Gary Cooper
Maria	Ingrid Bergman
Pablo	Akim Tamiroff

Fred Astaire and Joan Leslie in **The Sky's the Limit** (RKO).

Agustin	Arturo de Cordova
Anselmo	Vladimir Sokoloff
Rafael	Mikhail Rasumny
Fernando	Fortunio Bonanova
Andres	Eric Feldary
Primitivo	Victor Varconi

Bob Livingston, Frank Ellis and Al "Fuzzy" St. John
in **Wild Horse Rustlers** (PRC).

Pilar .... Katina Paxinou
El Sordo .... Joseph Calleia
Joaquin .... Lilo Yarson
Paco .... Alexander Granach
Gustavo .... Adia Kuznetzoff
Ignacio .... Leonid Snegoff
General Golz .... Leo Bulgakov
Lieutenant Berrendo .... Duncan Renaldo
Andre .... George Coulouris
Captain Gomez .... Frank Puglia
Colonel Miranda .... Pedro de Cordoba
Staff Officer .... Michael Visaroff
Karkov .... Konstantin Shayne
Captain .... Martin Garralaga
Sniper .... Jean Del Val
Colonel Duval .... Jack Mylong
Kashkin .... Feodor Chaliapin

Claire Trevor and Jess Barker in **Good Luck, Mr. Yates** (Columbia).

Akim Tamiroff, Vladimir Sokoloff, Gary Cooper and
Mikhail Rasumny in **For Whom the Bell Tolls**
(Paramount).

Don Frederico Gonzales .... Pedro de Cordoba
Don Richardo .... Mayo Newhall
Don Benito Garcia .... Michael Dalmatoff
Don Guillermo .... Antonio Vidal
Don Faustino Rivero .... Robert Tafur
Julian .... Armand Roland
Drunkard .... Luis Rojas
Spanish Singer .... Trini Varela
Sergeant .... Dick Botiller
Don Guillermo's Wife .... Soledad Jiminez
Young Cavalry Man .... Yakima Canutt
First Sentry .... Tito Renaldo
Girl in Cafe .... Yvonne DeCarlo

Distributor: Paramount
Director: Sam Wood
Released: July 15, 1943

HERS TO HOLD

Penelope Craig .... Deanna Durbin
Bill Morley .... Joseph Cotten
Judson Craig .... Charles Winninger
Flo .... Evelyn Ankers
Rosey Blake .... Gus Schilling
Dorothy Craig .... Nella Walker
Binns .... Ludwig Stossel
Dr. Crane .... Samuel S. Hinds
Hannah Gordon .... Fay Helm
Arlene .... Iris Adrian
Foreman .... Murray Alper
Mr. Cartwright .... Douglas Wood
Mrs. Cartwright .... Minna Phillips
Nurse Willing .... Nydia Westman
Dr. Bacon .... Irving Bacon

Deanna Durbin, Joseph Cotten, Charles Winninger and Maurice Costello in **Hers to Hold** (Universal).

Distributor: Universal
Director: Frank Ryan
Released: July 16, 1943

BEHIND THE RISING SUN

Tama	Margo
Taro	Tom Neal
Publisher	J. Carrol Naish
Lefty	Robert Ryan
Sara	Gloria Holden
O'Hara	Don Douglas
Boris	George Givot
Grandmother	Adeline Reynolds

Margo, Don Douglas and Gloria Holden in **Behind the Rising Sun** (RKO).

Tama's Father	Leonard Strong
Woman Secretary	Iris Wong
Max	Wolfgang Zilzer
Servant	Shirley Lew
Japanese Officer	Benson Fong
Dinner Guest	Lee Tung Foo
Japanese Wrestler	Mike Mazurki
Japanese Officer	William Yip
Policeman	H. T. Tsiang
Officer	Luke Chan
First Agent	Bruce Wong
Japanese Guard	Leon Lontoc
Geisha Girl	Mei Lee Foo
Capt. Matsuda	Allan Jung
Inspector	Abner Biberman

Onslow Stevens, Steve Geray, Marguerite Chapman and George Sanders in **Appointment in Berlin** (Columbia).

Tama's Mother	Connie Leon
Sister	Nancy Gates
Takahashi	Fred Essler
Japanese Officer	Philip Ahn
Takahashi's Servant	Daisy Lee
Japanese Officer	Richard Loo
Girl Given Dope	Barbara Jean Wong
Japanese Major	Beal Wong
Broker	Charles Lung
Prof. Namachi	Robert Katcher

Distributor: RKO
Director: Edward Dmytryk
Released: July 21, 1943

APPOINTMENT IN BERLIN

Keith Wilson	George Sanders
Ilse Preissing	Marguerite Chapman
Rudolph Preissing	Onslow Stevens
Gretta van Leyden	Gale Sondergaard
Colonel Patterson	Alan Napier
Sir Douglas Wilson	H. P. Sanders
Bill Banning	Don Douglas
Babe Forrester	Jack Lee
Smitty	Alec Craig
MacPhail	Leonard Mudie
Von Ritter	Frederic Worlock
Henri Bader	Steve Geray
Cripple	Wolfgang Zilzer

Distributor: Columbia
Director: Alfred E. Green
Released: July 26, 1943

WATCH ON THE RHINE

Sara Muller	Bette Davis
Kurt Muller	Paul Lukas
Marthe Debrancovis	Geraldine Fitzgerald
Fanny Farrelly	Lucile Watson
Anise	Beulah Bondi
Teck Debrancovis	George Coulouris
David Farrelly	Donald Woods
Phili von Ramme	Henry Daniell
Joshua Miller	Donald Buka
Bodo Muller	Eric Roberts
Babette Muller	Janis Wilson
Young Man	Helmut Dantine
Mrs. Mellie Sewell	Mary Young
Herr Blecher	Kurt Katch
Dr. Klauber	Erwin Kalser
Overdorff	Robert O. Davis
Sam Chandler	Clyde Fillmore

Paul Lukas, Bette Davis and George Coulouris in
Watch on the Rhine (Warner Bros.).

Roland Got, William Frawley and Allen Jung in
We've Never Been Licked (Universal).

Joseph	Frank Wilson
Horace	Clarence Muse
Belle	Violett McDowell
Chauffeur	Creighton Hale
Doc	William Washington
Italian Woman	Elvira Curci
Italian Man	Anthony Caruso
Mr. Chabeuf	Jean de Briac
Miss Drake	Leah Baird
Cyrus Penfield	Howard Hickman
Admiral	Frank Reicher
German Ambassador	Robert O. Fischer
Boy	Alan Hale, Jr.
Trainman	Jack Mower
Taxi Driver	Garry Owen

Distributor: Warner Bros.
Director: Herman Schumlin
Released: July 27, 1943

WE'VE NEVER BEEN LICKED

Brad Craig .... Richard Quine

Irving Berlin in **This is the Army** (Warner Bros.).

Fay Bainter, Wallace Beery and Marilyn Maxwell in
Salute to the Marines (M-G-M).

Cyanide Jenkins .... Noah Beery, Jr.
Nina .... Anne Gwynne
Deedee .... Martha O'Driscoll
Nishikawa .... Edgar Barrier
Fat Man .... William Frawley
'Pop' Lambert .... Harry Davenport

Distributor: Universal
Director: John Rawlins
Released: July 29, 1943

THIS IS THE ARMY

Irving Berlin .... Himself
Jerry Jones .... George Murphy
Eileen Dibble .... Joan Leslie
Maxie Stoloff .... George Tobias

Sergeant McGee .... Alan Hale
Eddie Dibble .... Charles Butterworth
Ethel .... Rosemary De Camp
Mrs. Davidson .... Dolores Costello
Rose Dibble .... Una Merkel
Major Davidson .... Stanley Ridges
Mrs. O'Brien .... Ruth Donnelly
Mrs. Nelson .... Dorothy Peterson
Kate Smith .... Herself
Cafe Singer .... Frances Langford
Singer .... Gertrude Niesen
Johnny Jones .... Ronald Reagan
Joe Louis .... Himself
Soldier .... Allan Anderson
Soldier .... Ezra Stone
Tommy .... Tom D'Andrea
Soldier .... Ross Elliott
Ollie .... Julie Oshins

Billie Burke, Dennis O'Keefe and Martha Scott in **Hi Diddle Diddle** (United Artists).

Ted Nelson	Robert Shanley
Soldier	Philip Truex
Danny Davidson	Herbert Anderson
Mrs. Twardofsky	Ilka Gruning
Soldier On Cot	Doodles Weaver
Waiter	Irving Bacon
Old Timer's Wife	Leah Baird
Sports Announcer	Warner Anderson
Franklin D. Roosevelt	Capt. Jack Young
Camp Cook Soldier	Frank Coghlan, Jr.
Camp Cook Soldier	John Daheim
Father of Soldier	Victor Moore
Father of Soldier	Ernest Truex
Mike Nelson	Jackie Brown
Marie Twardofsky	Patsy Moran
Doorman	James Conlin

Distributor: Warner Bros.
Director: Michael Curtiz
Released: July 29, 1943

SALUTE TO THE MARINES

Sgt. Major William Bailey	Wallace Beery
Jennie Bailey	Fay Bainter
Mr. Caspar	Reginald Owen
'Flashy' Logaz	Keye Luke
Colonel Mason	Ray Collins
Helen Bailey	Marilyn Maxwell
Rufus Cleveland	William Lundigan
Randall James	Donald Curtis
Adjutant	Noah Beery, Sr.

Corporal	Dick Curtis
Private Hanks	Russell Gleason
Mrs. Carson	Rose Hobart

Distributor: M-G-M
Director: Sylvan Simon
Released: August 2, 1943

HI DIDDLE DIDDLE

Col. Hector Phyffe	Adolphe Menjou
Janie Prescott	Martha Scott
Genya Smetana	Pola Negri
Sonny Phyffe	Dennis O'Keefe
Mrs. Prescott	Billy Burke
Leslie Quayle	June Havoc
Senator Simpson	Walter Kingsford
Peter Warrington III	Barton Hepburn
Spinelli	Georges Metaxa
Pianist	Marek Windheim
Croupier	Eddie Marr
Impresario	Paul Porcasi
A Friend	Lorraine Miller
Boughton	Richard Hageman
Fat Man	Bert Roach
Chauffeur	Chick Chandler
Maid	Ellen Lowe
Cashier	Barry McCollum
Bartender	Joe Devlin
Minister	Hal K. Dawson
Doorman	Andrew Toombes

Don Costello, Fred Kelsey, James Flavin, John Loder, Warren Douglas, Joan Winfield and Frank Mayo in **Murder on the Waterfront** (Warner Bros.).

Watson .... Byron Foulger

Distributor: United Artists
Director: Andrew Stone
Released: August 2, 1943

MURDER ON THE WATERFRONT

Joe Davis .... Warren Douglas
Gloria .... Joan Winfield
Lt. Commander Holbrook .... John Loder
Lana Shane .... Ruth Ford
Lt. Dawson .... Bill Crago
1st Officer Barnes .... Bill Kennedy
Capt. David Towne .... William B. Davidson
Gordon Shane .... Don Costello
Commander George Kalin .... James Flavin
Guard .... Bill Edwards

2nd Sentry .... Ross Ford
1st Sentry .... Dewolf Hopper
Daniel Lewis .... John Maxwell
Connors .... Philip Van Zandt
Petty Officer Thomas .... Frank Mayo
Capt. Beal .... Fred Kelsey

Distributor: Warner Bros.
Director: B. Reaves Eason
Released: August 2, 1943

THE MAN FROM DOWN UNDER

Jocko Wilson .... Charles Laughton
Aggie Dawlins .... Binnie Barnes
'Nipper' Wilson .... Richard Carlson
Mary Wilson .... Donna Reed
'Nipper' As A Child .... Christopher Severn

Charles Laughton, Clyde Cook and Binnie Barnes in
The Man from Down Under (M-G-M).

Betty Hutton and the milk maids in **Let's Face It**
(Paramount).

Ginger Gaffney .... Clyde Cook
'Dusty' Rhodes .... Horace McNally
Father Polycarp .... Arthur Shields
Mary, As A Child .... Evelyn Falks
'Boots' .... Hobart Cavanaugh
Father Antoine .... Andre Charlot

Distributor: M-G-M
Director: Robert Z. Leonard
Released: August 4, 1943

LET'S FACE IT

Jerry Walker .... Bob Hope

Robert Stanford, Nick Thompson, Eric Blore, Warren William and Frank Lackteen in **Passport to Suez**
(Columbia).

Winnie Potter	Betty Hutton
Cornelia Pidgeon	Zasu Pitts
Nancy Collister	Phyllis Povah
Barney Hilliard	Dave Willock
Maggie Watson	Eve Arden
Frankie Burns	Cully Richards
Jean	Marjorie Weaver
Muriel	Dona Drake
Julian Watson	Raymond Walburn
Judge H. Clay Pidgeon	Andrew Tombes
George Collister	Arthur Loft
Sergeant Wiggins	Joe Sawyer
Mrs. Wigglesworth	Grace Hayle
Mrs. Taylor	Evelyn Dockson
Milk Maid	Andria Moreland
Canteen Hostess	Kay Linaker
Milk Maid	Brooks Evans
Dance Team	Nicco & Tanya

Distributor: Paramount
Director: Sidney Lanfield
Released: August 5, 1943

PASSPORT TO SUEZ

Michael Lanyard	Warren William
Valerie King	Ann Savage
Jameson	Eric Blore
Donald Jameson	Robert Stanford
Johnny Booth	Sheldon Leonard
Fritz	Lloyd Bridges
Karl	Gavin Muir
Rembrandt	Lou Merrill
Sir Roger Wembley	Frederick Worlock
Cezanne	Jay Novello
Whistler	Sig Arno

Distributor: Columbia
Director: Andre De Toth
Released: August 12, 1943

HOSTAGES

Paula Breda	Arturo de Cordova
Milada Preissinger	Luise Rainer
Janoshik	William Bendix
Jan Pavel	Roland Varno
Lev Preissinger	Oscar Homolka
Maria	Katina Paxinou

Rheinhardt	Paul Lukas
Capt. Patzer	Fred Giermann
Dr. Wallerstein	Felix Basch
Solvik	Michael Visaroff
Peter Lovkowitz	Eric Feldary
Proskosch	John Mylong
Joseph	Mikhail Rasumny
Lieutenant Eisner	Philip Van Zandt

Arturo de Cordova, Luise Rainer and Paul Lukas in
Hostages (Paramount).

Lieutenant Marschmann	Rex Williams
Lieutenant Glasenapp	Hans Conried
Young Nazi Soldier	Louis Adlon
Elderly Nazi Soldier	Richard Ryen
Sergeant	Kurt Neumann

Distributor: Paramount
Director: Frank Tuttle
Released: August 12, 1943

DESTROYER

Steve Boleslavski	Edward G. Robinson
Mickey Donohue	Glenn Ford
Mary Boleslavski	Marguerite Chapman
Kansas Jackson	Edgar Buchanan
Sarecky	Leo Gorcey
Lt. Commander Clark	Regis Toomey
Casey	Ed Brophy
Lt. Morton	Warren Ashe
Bigbee	Craig Woods

Glenn Ford, Edward G. Robinson and Ed Brophy in
Destroyer (Columbia).

Yasha .... Curt Bois

Distributor: Columbia
Director: William A. Seiter
Released: August 16, 1943

THE FALLEN SPARROW

Kit .... John Garfield
Toni Donne .... Maureen O'Hara
Dr. Skaas .... Walter Slezak
Barby Taviton .... Patricia Morison
Whitney Hamilton .... Martha O'Driscoll
Ab Parker .... Bruce Edwards
Anton .... John Banner
Inspector Tobin .... John Miljan
Prince Francois .... Sam Goldenberg
Otto Skaas .... Hugh Beaumont

Maureen O'Hara and John Garfield in **The Fallen Sparrow** (RKO).

Wally Brown, Richard Martin, Claire Carleton and Alan Carney in **Adventures of a Rookie** (RKO).

Distributor: RKO
Director: Richard Wallace
Released: August 17, 1943

ADVENTURES OF A ROOKIE

Jerry Miles .... Wally Brown
Mike Strager .... Alan Carney

Norris Goff as "Abner" and Chester Lauck as "Lum" in **So This is Washington** (RKO).

Bob Prescott .... Richard Martin
Sgt. Burke .... Erford Gage
Peggy Linden .... Margaret Landry
Patsy .... Patti Brill
Ruth .... Rita Corday
Sgt. Wilson .... Robert Andersen
Colonel .... John Hamilton
Mrs. Linden .... Ruth Lee
Eve .... Lorraine Krueger
Margaret .... Ercelle Woods
Betty .... Toddy Peterson
Mr. Linden .... Byron Foulger

Distributor: RKO
Director: Leslie Goodwins
Released: August 20, 1943

SO THIS IS WASHINGTON

Lum .... Chester Lauck
Abner .... Norris Goff
Mr. Marshall .... Alan Mowbray

Robert Blevins .... Roger Clark
Jane Nestor .... Mildred Coles
Aunt Charity .... Sarah Padden
Mrs. Pomeroy .... Minerva Urecal
Grandpappy .... Dan Duncan
Stranger .... Matt McHugh
Taxi Driver .... Barbara Pepper

Distributor: RKO
Director: Raymond McCarey
Released: August 20, 1943

BLACK MARKET RUSTLERS

Crash .... Ray Corrigan
Dennis .... Dennis Moore
Alibi .... Max Terhune
Linda .... Evelyn Finley
Prescott .... Steve Clark
Parry .... John Merton
Corbin .... Glenn Strange
Sheriff .... Carl Sepulveda
Slade .... George Chesebro
Slim .... Hank Worden
Kyper .... Frank Ellis
Ed .... Frosty Royce

Distributor: Monogram
Director: S. Roy Luby
Released: August 31, 1943

Max Terhune and Ray Corrigan in **Black Market Rustlers** (Monogram).

Brian Aherne and Merle Oberon in **First Comes Courage** (Columbia).

FIRST COMES COURAGE

Nicole Larsen .... Merle Oberon
Captain Allan Lowell .... Brian Aherne
Major Paul Dichter .... Carl Esmond
Dr. Aanrud .... Fritz Leiber
Soren .... Erville Alderson
Ole .... Erik Rolf
Col. Kurt von Elser .... Reinhold Schunzel
Rose Linstrom .... Isobel Elsom

Distributor: Columbia
Director: Dorothy Arzner
Released: September 10, 1943

TOP MAN

Don Warren .... Donald O'Connor

Connie .... Susanna Foster
Beth Warren .... Lillian Gish
Tom Warren .... Richard Dix
Jan Warren .... Peggy Ryan
Pat Warren .... Anne Gwynne
Ed Thompson .... Noah Beery, Jr.
Fairchild .... Samuel S. Hinds
Cleo .... Louise Beavers
Tommy .... Dickie Love
Erna .... Marcia Mae Jones
Archie .... David Holt
Count Basie and his Orchestra .... Themselves
Borrah Minnevitch Rascals .... Themselves
Bobby Brooks Quartet .... Themselves

Distributor: Universal
Director: Charles Lamont
Released: September 13, 1943

Anne Gwynne, Lillian Gish, Donald O'Connor, Richard Dix and Peggy Ryan in **Top Man** (Universal).

THOUSANDS CHEER

Kathryn Jones	Kathryn Grayson
Eddie Marsh	Gene Kelly
Hyllary Jones	Mary Astor
Jose	Jose Iturbi
Colonel Jones	John Boles
Captain Avery	Dick Simmons
Chuck	Ben Blue
Sergeant Koslack	Frank Jenks
Alan	Frank Sully
Jack	Wally Cassell
Silent Monk	Ben Lessy
Marie	Frances Rafferty
Helen	Mary Elliott
Mama Corbino	Odette Myrtil
Papa Corbino	Will Kaufman

Ben Lessy, Gene Kelly, Ben Blue, Frank Sully, Wally Cassell, Frank Jenks and Russell Gleason in **Thousands Cheer** (M-G-M).

Kay Kyser Orchestra	....	Themselves
Announcer	....	Lionel Barrymore
Girl At Station	....	Betty Jaynes
Uncle Algy	....	Sig Arno
Taxicab Driver	....	Connie Gilchrist
Woman	....	Bea Nigro
Maid	....	Daisy Buford
Alex	....	Pierre Watkin
Specialty Dancer	....	Paul Speer
Soldier	....	Myron Healey
Soldier	....	Don Taylor
Ringmaster	....	Ray Teal
Sergeant Major	....	Carl Saxe
Lt. Col. Brand	....	Bryant Washburn, Jr.
Capt. Haines	....	Harry Strang
Mother At Station	....	Florence Turner

Also: Donna Reed, Marilyn Maxwell, Margaret O'Brien, June Allyson, Eleanor Powell, Gloria De-Haven, Mickey Rooney, Judy Garland, Red Skelton, Virginia O'Brien, Frank Morgan, Ann Southern, Lucille Ball, Marsha Hunt, Sara Haden, Marta Linden, John Conte, Bob Crosby and his Orchestra, Lena Horne with Benny Carter and his Orchestra, Don Loper and Maxine Barrat.

Distributor: M-G-M
Director: George Sidney
Released: September 15, 1943

PRINCESS O'ROURKE

Princess Maria	....	Olivia de Havilland
Eddie O'Rourke	....	Robert Cummings
Uncle	....	Charles Coburn
Dave	....	Jack Carson

Bob Cummings, Jack Carson and Jane Wyman in
Princess O'Rourke (Warner Bros.).

J. Farrell MacDonald, Arno Frey, Howard Banks and
Frank Buck in **Tiger Fangs** (PRC).

Jean	Jane Wyman
Supreme Court Judge	Harry Davenport
Miss Haskell	Gladys Cooper
Mr. Washburn	Minor Watson
Singer	Nan Wynn
Count Peter de Chandome	Curt Bois
G-Man	Ray Walker
Butler	David Clyde
Mrs. Mulvaney	Nana Bryant
Mrs. Bower	Nydia Westman
Clare Stillwell	Ruth Ford
Stewardess	Julie Bishop
Greek	Frank Puglia
Greek's Wife	Rosina Galli
Mrs. Pulaski	Ferike Boros
Delivery Boy	Dave Willock
Elevator Man	John Dilson

Stranger	Edward Gargan

Distributor: Warner Bros.
Director: Norman Krasna
Released: September 21, 1943

TIGER FANGS

Frank Buck	Frank Buck
Linda MacCardle	June Duprez
Peter Jeremy	Duncan Renaldo
Tom Clayton	Howard Banks
Geoffrey MacCardle	J. Farrell MacDonald
Ali	J. Alex Havier
Doctor Lang	Arno Frey
Henry Gratz	Dan Seymour

Barry Fitzgerald, Thomas Gomez and Robert Mitchum in **Corvette K-225** (Universal).

Takko .... Pedro Regas

Distributor: PRC
Director: Sam Newfield
Released: September 27, 1943

CORVETTE K-225

Lieutenant Commander MacClain
    Randolph Scott
Paul Cartwright .... James Brown
Joyce Cartwright .... Ella Raines
Stooky O'Meara .... Barry Fitzgerald

Warren Douglas, John Loder and Ruth Ford in **Adventures in Iraq** (Warner Bros.).

Walsh .... Andy Devine
Cricket .... Fuzzy Knight
Stone .... Noah Beery, Jr.
Admiral .... Richard Lane
Smithy .... Thomas Gomez
Rawlins .... David Bruce
Jones .... Murray Alper
Gardner .... James Flavin
Evans .... Walter Sande

Distributor: Universal
Director: Richard Rosson
Released: September 27, 1943

Bruce Bennett, Dan Duryea, Humphrey Bogart, Lloyd Bridges and Richard Nugent in **Sahara** (Columbia).

ADVENTURES IN IRAQ

George Torrence .... John Loder
Tess Torrence .... Ruth Ford
Doug Everett .... Warren Douglas
Sheik Ahmid Bel Nor .... Paul Cavanagh
Devins .... Barry Bernard
Timah .... Peggy Carson
Captain Bill Carson .... Bill Crago
High Priest .... Martin Garralaga
Radio Operator .... Bill Edwards
Patroling Guard .... Dick Botiller
Native Officer .... Eugene Borden
Priest .... Manuel Lopez

Distributor: Warner Bros.
Director: D. Ross Lederman
Released: September 27, 1943

SAHARA

Sergeant Joe Gunn	Humphrey Bogart
Waco Hoyt	Bruce Bennett
Giuseppe	J. Carroll Naish
Fred Clarkson	Lloyd Bridges
Tambul	Rex Ingram
Capt. Jason Halliday	Richard Nugent

Brenda Marshall and Philip Dorn in **Paris After Dark** (20th Century-Fox).

Jimmy Doyle	Dan Duryea
Marty Williams	Carl Harbord
Ozzie Bates	Patrick O'Moore
Jean Leroux	Louis Mercier
Peter Stegman	Guy Kingsford
Capt. von Schletow	Kurt Krueger
Major von Falken	John Wengraf
Sergeant Krause	Hans Schumm

Distributor: Columbia
Director: Zoltan Korda
Released: September 29, 1943

PARIS AFTER DARK

Dr. Andre Marbel	George Sanders

Jean Blanchard	Philip Dorn
Yvonne Blanchard	Brenda Marshall
Collette	Madeleine LeBeau
Michel	Marcel Dalio
Col. Pirosh	Robert Lewis
Capt. Franck	Henry Rowland
George Bennoit	Raymond Roe
Victor Durand	Gene Gary
Papa Benoit	Jean Del Val
Max	Curt Bois
Mme. Benoit	Ann Codee
Picard	Louis Borell
Mannheim	John Wengraf
Paul	Michael Visaroff
Nazi Agent	Frank Lyon

Distributor: 20th Century-Fox
Director: Leonide Moguy
Released: October 6, 1943

HI 'YA, SAILOR

Bob Jackson	Donald Woods
Pat Rogers	Elyse Knox
Corky Mills	Eddie Quillan
Deadpan Weaver	Frank Jenks
Nanette	Phyllis Brooks
Lou Asher	Jerome Cowan
Bull Rogan	Matt Willis
Secretary	Florence Lake
Doorman	Charles Coleman
Sam	Mantan Moreland
Police Lieutenant	Jack Mulhall

Also: Ray Eberle and his Orchestra, Wingy Malone and his Orchestra, Delta Rhythm Boys, Leo Diamond Quintet, Mayris Chaney and her Dance Trio, George Beatty, Hacker Duo, Nilsson Sisters

Distributor: Universal
Director: Jean Yarbrough
Released: October 8, 1943

THE NORTH STAR

Marina	Anne Baxter
Kolya	Dana Andrews
Dr. Kurin	Walter Huston
Karp	Walter Brennan

The Delta Rhythm Boys, Hal K. Dawson, Donald Woods, Matt Willis and Eddie Quillan in **Hi' Ya, Sailor** (Universal).

Sophia	Ann Harding	Woman On Hospital Cot	Loudie Claar
Clavdia	Jane Withers	Guerrilla Girl	Lynn Winthrop
Damian	Farley Granger	Petya	Charles Bates
Dr. Von Harden	Erich von Stroheim		
Rodian	Dean Jagger	*Distributor:* RKO	
Grisha	Eric Roberts	*Director:* Lewis Milestone	
Boris	Carl Benton Reid	*Released:* October 13, 1943	
Olga	Ann Carter		
Anna	Esther Dale		
Nadya	Ruth Nelson		
Iakin	Paul Guilfoyle		
Dr. Richter	Martin Kosleck	**NORTHERN PURSUIT**	
German Captain	Tonio Selwart	Steve Wagner	Errol Flynn
German Lieutenant	Peter Pohlenz	Laura McBain	Julie Bishop
Russian Pilot	Robert Lowery	Colonel Hugo von Keller	Helmut Dantine
Russian Gunner	Gene O'Donnell	Jim Austen	John Ridgely
Petrov	Frank Wilcox	Ernst	Gene Lockhart
		Inspector Barnett	Tom Tully

Farley Granger, Anne Baxter, Dana Andrews and
Jane Withers in **The North Star** (RKO).

Dagor	Bernard Nedell
Sergeant	Warren Douglas
Jean	Monte Blue
Angus MsBain	Alec Craig
Hobby	Tom Fadden
Alice	Rose Higgins
Heinzmann	Richard Alden
German Aviator	John Royce
Indian Guide	Joe Herrera
Radio Operator	Carl Harbaugh
Chief Inspector	Russell Hicks
Colonel	Lester Matthews
Soldier	John Forsythe
Nick The Barber	Charles Judels
Army Driver	James Millican
Guard	Robert Hutton

Julie Bishop and Errol Flynn in **Northern Pursuit**
(Warner Bros.).

Lloyd Nolan in **Guadalcanal Diary** (20th Century-Fox).

Distributor: Warner Bros.-First National
Director: Raoul Walsh
Released: October 25, 1943

GUADALCANAL DIARY

Father Donnelly	Preston Foster
Gunner O'Hara	Lloyd Nolan
Taxi Potts	William Bendix
Captain Davis	Richard Conte
Soose	Anthony Quinn
Private Johnny Anderson	Richard Jaeckel
Captain Cross	Roy Roberts
Colonel Grayson	Minor Watson
Ned Rowman	Ralph Byrd
Butch	Lionel Stander
Correspondent	Reed Hadley
Lieutenant Thurmond	John Archer
Tex	Eddie Acuff
Sammy	Robert Rose
Weatherby	Miles Mander
Dispatch Officer	Harry Carter
Major	Jack Luden
Lieutenant	Louis Hart
Captain	Tom Dawson
Colonel Thompson	Selmer Jackson
Japanese Officer	Allen Jung
Japanese Prisoner	Paul Fung

Distributor: 20th Century-Fox
Director: Lewis Seiler
Released: October 27, 1943

Ludwig Donath, John Mylong and Rudolph Anders in **Strange Death of Adolph Hitler** (Universal).

Profe	Hans Schumm
Himmler	Fred Gierman
Palzer	Richard Ryen
Halder	John Mylong
Youth Leader	Kurt Kreuger
Dr. Kaltenbruch	Lester Sharpe
Frau Reitler	Trude Berliner
Judge	Hans von Twardowski
Attorney	Wolfgang Zilzer

Distributor: Universal
Director: James Hogan
Released: October 28, 1943

STRANGE DEATH OF ADOLF HITLER

Franz Huber (Hitler)	Ludwig Donath
Anna Huber	Gale Sondergaard
Herman Marbach	George Dolenz
Bauer	Fritz Kortner
Graub	Ludwig Stossel
Von Zechwitz	William Trenk
Duchess Eugenie	Joan Blair
Hohenberg	Ivan Triesault
Mampe	Rudolph Anders
Godeck	Erno Verebes
Hansl	Merrill Rodin
Viki	Charles Bates
Karl	Kurt Katch

Olivia de Havilland and Sonny Tufts in **Government Girl** (RKO).

Amelita Ward, Margo, James Bell, Charles Arnt, Robert Ryan and John Carradine in **Gangway for Tomorrow** (RKO).

GANGWAY FOR TOMORROW

Lizette	Margo
Wellington	John Carradine
Joe	Robert Ryan
Mary	Amelita Ward
Bob Nolan	William Terry
Fred Taylor	Harry Davenport
Burke	James Bell
Jim Benson	Charles Arnt
Sam	Wally Brown
Swallow	Alan Carney
Dan Barton	Erford Gage
Colonel Mueller	Richard Ryen
Pete	Warren Hymer
Mechanic	Michael St. Angel

Mechanic	Don Dillaway
Hank	Sam McDaniel
Radio Announcer	John Wald

Distributor: RKO
Director: John H. Auer
Released: November 3, 1943

GOVERNMENT GIRL

Smokey	Olivia de Havilland
Browne	Sonny Tufts
May	Anne Shirley
Dana	Jess Barker
Sergeant Joe	James Dunn
Branch	Paul Stewart

Mrs. Wright	Agnes Moorehead
Senator MacVickers	Harry Davenport
Mrs. Harris	Una O'Connor
His Excellency	Sig Rumann
Miss Trask	Jane Darwell
Count Bodinsky	George Givot

Distributor: RKO
Director: Dudley Nichols
Released: November 5, 1943

CRY HAVOC

Lieut. Smith	Margaret Sullavan
Pat	Ann Sothern
Grace	Joan Blondell

Joan Blondell, Heather Angel, Frances Gifford, Dorothy Morris, Julie Bishop, Fely Franquelli, Ella Raines, Gloria Grafton, Ann Sothern, Margaret Sullavan and Marsha Hunt in **Cry Havoc** (M-G-M).

Larry Thompson and Don Ameche in **Happy Land**
(20th Century-Fox).

Capt. Marsh	Fay Bainter
Flo Norris	Marsha Hunt
Connie	Ella Raines
Helen	Frances Gifford
Nydia	Diana Lewis
Andra	Heather Angel
Sue	Dorothy Morris
Sadie	Connie Gilchrist
Steve	Gloria Grafton
Luisita	Fely Granquelli

Distributor: M-G-M
Director: Richard Thorpe
Released: November 9, 1943

HAPPY LAND

Lew Marsh	Don Ameche
Agnes	Frances Dee
Gramp	Harry Carey
Lenore Prentiss	Ann Rutherford
Gretchen Barry	Cara Williams
Rusty	Richard Crane
Tony Cavrek	Henry Morgan
Judge Colvin	Minor Watson
Peter Orcutt	Dickie Moore
Bill Beecher	William Weber
Father Case	Oscar O'Shea
Mrs. Schneider	Adeline Reynolds
Velma	Roseanne Murray

Rusty (Age 12–16)	James West
Rusty (Age 5)	Larry Olsen
Sam Kendall	Bernard Thomas
Arch	Terry Masengale
Bud	Edwin Mills
Everett Moore	James J. Smith
Emmy	Mary Wickes
Jake Hibbs	Walter Baldwin
Mr. MacMurray	Tom Stevenson
Mrs. Prentiss	Eileen Pringle
Mr. Prentiss	Matt Moore
Lenore Prentiss (Age 12)	Darla Hood
Reverend Wood	Richard Abbott
Mattie Dyer	Lillian Bronson
Mayor	Ferris Taylor
Andy	Larry Thompson
Pop Schmidt	Paul Weigel
Jackie	Ned Dobson, Jr.
Ted	Jackie Averill
Clerk	Joe Bernard
Sam Watson	Housley Stevenson
Joe	Elvin Field
Sally Pierce	Juanita Quigley
Shep Wayne	Milton Kibbee
Charles Clayton	John Dilson
Old Ben	Leigh Whipper
Old Man Bowers	Robert Dudley

Distributor: 20th Century-Fox
Director: Irving Pichel
Released: November 10, 1943

Richard Arlen with Jean Parker in **Minesweeper**
(Paramount).

Peter Lorre, Fred Wolff, Richard Ryen, Tonio Selwart, Joseph Calleia, Jean Pierre Aumont, Jack Lambert, Jack Edwards Jr., and Donald Curtis in **The
Cross of Lorraine** (M-G-M).

MINESWEEPER

Jim Smith .... Richard Arlen
Mary Smith .... Jean Parker
Elliot .... Russell Hayden
'Fixit' .... Guinn Williams
Moms .... Emma Dunn
Commander .... Charles D. Brown
Lt. Gilpin .... Frank Fenton
Corney Welch .... Chick Chandler
Lt. Wells .... Douglas Fowley
Cox .... Ralph Sanford
Boatswain Helms .... Billy Nelson

Distributor: Paramount
Director: William Berke
Released: November 10, 1943

THE CROSS OF LORRAINE

Paul .... Jean Pierre Aumont
Victor .... Gene Kelly
Father Sebastian .... Sir Cedric Hardwicke
Francois .... Richard Whorf
Rodriguez .... Joseph Calleia
Sergeant Berger .... Peter Lorre
Duval .... Hume Cronyn
Louis .... Billy Roy
Major Bruhl .... Tonio Selwart
Jacques .... Jack Lambert
Pierre .... Wallace Ford
Marcel .... Donald Curtis
Rene .... Jack Edwards, Jr.
Lieut. Schmidt .... Richard Ryen
Corporal Daxer .... Frederick Giermann

Distributor: M-G-M
Director: Tay Garnett
Released: November 12, 1943

WOMEN IN BONDAGE

Margot Bracken .... Gail Patrick
Toni Hall .... Nancy Kelly
Gertrude Schneider .... Gertrude Michael
Deputy .... Anne Nagel
Ruth Bracken .... Tala Birell
Gladys Bracken .... Mary Forbes
Grete Ziegler .... Maris Wrixon
Herta's Grandmother .... Gisela Werbiseck
Herta Rumann .... Rita Quigley
Litzl .... Francine Bordeaux
Blonde .... Una Franks
Heinz Radike .... Bill Henry
Pastor Renz .... H. B. Warner
Otto Bracken .... Alan Baxter
Dr. Mensch .... Felix Basch
Ernest Bracken .... Roland Varno

Lynn Merrick, Ted Lewis and Michael Duane in **Is Everybody Happy?** (Columbia).

Nancy Kelly and Una Franks in **Women in Bondage** (Monogram).

Corp. Mueller .... Ralph Lynn
Dist. Leader .... Frederic Brunn

Distributor: Monogram
Director: Steve Sekely
Released: November 16, 1943

IS EVERYBODY HAPPY?

Ted Lewis .... Ted Lewis

Tom .... Michael Duane
Kitty .... Nan Wynn
Jerry .... Larry Parks
Ann .... Lynn Merrick
Artie .... Bob Haymes
Joe .... Dick Winslow
Bob .... Harry Barris
Frank .... Frank Stanford
Mrs. Broadbelt .... Fern Emmett
Salbin .... Eddie Kane
Low Merwin .... Ray Walker
Carl Muller .... Anthony Marlowe
Missouri .... George Reed

Distributor: Columbia
Director: Charles Barton
Released: November 18, 1943

JIVE JUNCTION

Peter .... Dickie Moore
Claire .... Tina Thayer

Harry Strang, Dickie Moore and Jan Wiley in **Jive Junction** (PRC).

Gerra	Gerra Young		
Jimmy	Johnny Michaels		
Grant	Jack Wagner		
Miss Forbes	Jan Wiley		
Cubby	Beverly Boyd		
Maglodian	Bill Halligan		
Frank	Johnny Duncan		
Chick	Johnny Clark		
Feher	Frederick Feher		
Mary	Carol Ashley		
Girl	Odessa Laurin		
Sheriff	Bob McKenzie		

Distributor: PRC
Director: Edgar G. Ulmer
Released: November 22, 1943

AROUND THE WORLD

Kay	Kay Kyser
Mischa	Mischa Auer
Joan	Joan Davis
Marcy	Marcy McGuire
Pilot-Clipper	Wally Brown
Joe Gimpus	Alan Carney
Georgia	Georgia Carroll
Harry	Harry Babbitt
Ish	Ish Kabibble
Sully	Sully Mason
Julie	Julie Conway
Diane	Diane Pendleton

Distributor: RKO

Kay Kyser, Marcy McGuire and Mischa Auer in **Around the World** (RKO).

Bobby Larson, Hobo (the dog) and Conrad Binyou in **Underdog** (PRC).

James Ellison and Alice Faye in **The Gang's All Here** (20th Century-Fox).

Director: Alan Dwan
Released: November 24, 1943

THE UNDERDOG

John Tate	Barton MacLane
Henry Tate	Bobby Larson
Amy Tate	Jan Wiley
Mrs. Bailey	Charlotte Wynters
Spike	Conrad Binyon
Mrs. Connors	Elizabeth Valentine
Eddie Mohr	Kenneth Harlan
Kraeger	George Anderson
Officer O'Toole	Jack Kennedy
Hobo, The Dog	Himself

Distributor: PRC
Director: William Nigh
Released: November 24, 1943

THE GANG'S ALL HERE

Eadie	Alice Faye
Rosita	Carmen Miranda
Phil Baker	Phil Baker
Benny Goodman and Band	Themselves
Mr. Mason Sr.	Eugene Pallette
Mrs. Peyton Potter	Charlotte Greenwood
Peyton Potter	Edward E. Horton
Tony De Marco	Tony De Marco
Andy Mason	James Ellison
Vivian	Sheila Ryan
Sergeant Casey	Dave Willock
Specialty Dancer	Miriam Lavelle
Jitterbug Dancer	Charles Saggau
Jitterbug Dancer	Deidre Gale
Benson	George Dobbs
Waiter	Leon Belasco
Maybelle	June Haver
Marine	Frank Faylen
Sailor	Russell Hoyt
Secretary	Virginia Sale
Butler	Leyland Hodgson
Bit Man	Lee Bennett
Girl	Jeanne Crain
Maid	Lillian Yarbo
Doorman	Frank Darien
Stage Manager	Al Murphy
Old Lady	Hallene Hill

Organ Grinder	Gabriel Canzona
Newsboy	Fred Walburn
Dancing Partner	Virginia Wilson

Distributor: 20th Century-Fox
Director: Busby Berkeley
Released: November 29, 1943

Victor Moore and William Gaxton in **The Heat's On** (Columbia).

THE HEAT'S ON

Mae West, Victor Moore, William Gaxton, Lester Allen, Mary Roche, Almira Sessions, Hazel Scott, Alan Dinehart, Lloyd Bridges, Sam Ash, Xavier Cugat and Orchestra, Lina Romay, David Lichine, Leonard Sues, Jack Owens, Joan Thorsen.

Distributor: Columbia
Director: Gregory Ratoff
Released: December 2, 1943

ROOKIES IN BURMA

Wally Brown, Alan Carney, Erford Gage, Joan Barclay, Claire Carleton, Ted Hecht.

Distributor: RKO
Director: Leslie Goodwins
Released: December 16, 1943

Wally Brown and Alan Carney in **Rookies in Burma**
(RKO).

GUNG HO

Col. Thorwald	Randolph Scott
Kathleen Corrigan	Grace McDonald
John Harbison	Alan Curtis
Kurt Richter	Noah Beery, Jr.
Lt. Cristoforos	J. Carrol Naish
Larry O'Ryan	David Bruce
Kozzarowski	Peter Coe
Pigiron	Bob Mitchum
Capt. Dunphy	Richard Lane
Rube Tedrow	Rod Cameron
Transport	Sam Levene
Commander Blade	Milburn Stone
Frankie Montana	Harold Landon
Buddy Andrews	John James
Lt. Roland Browning	Louis Jean Heydt

Distributor: Universal
Director: Ray Enright
Released: December 20, 1943

DESTINATION TOKYO

Captain Cassidy	Cary Grant
Wolf	John Garfield
Cookie	Alan **Hale**
Reserve	John Ridgely
Tin Can	Dane Clark
Executive	Warner Anderson
Pills	William Prince
Tommy	Bob Hutton
Mike	Tom Tully
Mrs. Cassidy	Faye Emerson

Noah Beery Jr., Grace McDonald and David Bruce in **Gung Ho** (Universal).

Dakota	Peter Whitney
English Officer	Warren Douglas
Sparks	John Forsythe
Sound Man	John Alvin
Torpedo Officer	Bill Kennedy
Commanding Officer	John Whitney
Quartermaster	William Challee
Yo Yo	Whit Bissell
Chief Of Boat	George Lloyd
Toscanini	Maurice Murphy
Admiral	Pierre Watkin
Admiral's Aide	Stephen Richards
Hornet's Admiral	Cliff Clark
Debby Cassidy	Deborah Daves
Michael Cassidy	Michael Daves
Admiral's Aide	Jack Mower
Tin Can's Girl	Mary Landa
Man On Phone	Carlyle Blackwell
Captain	Kirby Grant
C. P. O.	Lane Chandler
Wolf's Girl	Joy Barlowe
Market St. Commando	Bill Hunter
Crewmen	George Robotham,
	Dan Borzage,
	William Hudson,
	Duke York,
	Charles Sullivan,
	Harry Bartell,
	Jay Ward,
	Paul Langton

Distributor: Warner Bros.
Director: Delmer Daves
Released: December 21, 1943

A GUY NAMED JOE

Pete Sandidge	Spencer Tracy
Dorinda Durston	Irene Dunne
Ted Randall	Van Johnson
Al Yackey	Ward Bond
'Nails' Kilpatrick	James Gleason
The General	Lionel Barrymore
Dick Rumney	Barry Nelson
Powerhouse O'Rourke	Don De Fore

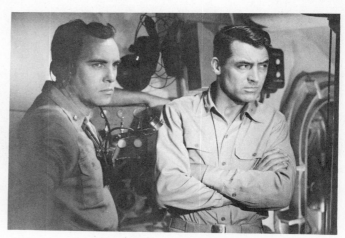

Warner Anderson and Cary Grant in **Destination Tokyo** (Warner Bros.).

Colonel Hendricks	Henry O'Neill
Major Corbett	Addison Richards
Sanderson	Charles Smith
Dance Hall Girl	Mary Elliott
Colonel Sykes	Earl Schenck
Captain Robertson	Maurice Murphy
Old Woman	Gertrude Hoffmann
Lieutenant	Mark Daniels
Ray	William Bishop
Powerhouse Girl	Eve Whitney
Ellen Bright	Esther Williams
Girl At Bar	Kay Williams
Mess Sergeant	Walter Sande
Bartender	Gibson Gowland
Officers In Heaven	John Whitney
	Kirk Alyn
Orderly	James Millican

Ward Bond, Irene Dunne and Spencer Tracy in **A Guy Named Joe** (M-G-M).

Davy .... Ernest Severn
George .... Edward Hardwicke
Cyril .... Raymond Severn

Peter .... Christopher Severn
Lieutenant Ridley .... John Frederick
Majors .... Frank Faylen
Phil Van Zandt
Fliers .... Marshall Reed
Blake Edwards
Corporal .... Irving Bacon
Sergeant Hanson .... Peter Cookson
Lieutenant Hunter .... Matt Willis
Helen .... Jacqueline White

Distributor: M-G-M
Director: Victor Fleming
Released: December 24, 1943

THE SONG OF BERNADETTE

Bernadette .... Jennifer Jones
Antoine .... William Eythe
Peyremaie .... Charles Bickford

Roman Bohnen, Jennifer Jones and Anne Revere in **The Song of Bernadette** (20th Century-Fox).

Dutour	Vincent Price	Convent Mother Superior	Nana Bryant
Dr. Dozous	Lee Cobb	Charles Bouhouhoris	Manart Kippen
Sister Vauzous	Gladys Cooper	Jean Soubirous	Merrill Rodin
Louise Soubirous	Anne Revere	Justin Soubirous	Nino Pepitone, Jr.
Francois Soubirous	Roman Bohnen	Father Pomian	John Maxwell Hayes
Jeanne Abadie	Mary Anderson	Estrade	Jean Del Val
Empress Eugenie	Patricia Morison	Mme. Bruat	Tala Birell
Lacade	Aubrey Mather	Mme. Nicolau	Eula Morgan
Jacomet	Charles Dingle	Dr. St. Cyr	Frank Reicher
Croisine	Edith Barrett	Duran	Charles LaTorre
Louis Bouriette	Sig Rumann	Blessed Virgin	Linda Darnell
Bernarde Casterot	Blanche Yurka	Woman	Mae Marsh
Marie Soubirous	Ermadean Walters	Adolar	Dickie Moore
Callet	Marcel Dalio	Mother Superior	Dorothy Shearer
Lecrampe	Pedro de Cordoba	Bishop	Andre Charlot
Emperor Napoleon	Jerome Cowan	Psychiatrist	Alan Napier
Bishop Of Tarbes	Charles Waldron	Minks	Fritz Leiber
Chaplain	Moroni Olsen		Arthur Hohl

Robert Sully, Hedy Lamarr and Franco Corsaro in
The Heavenly Body (M-G-M).

Robert Ryan and Ginger Rogers in **Tender Comrade** (RKO).

Doctor .... Edward Van Sloan

Distributor: 20th Century-Fox
Director: Henry King
Released: December 27, 1943

THE HEAVENLY BODY

William S. Whitley .... William Powell
Vicky Whitley .... Hedy Lamarr
Lloyd X. Hunter .... James Craig
Margaret Sibyll .... Fay Bainter
Professor Stone .... Henry O'Neill
Nancy Potter .... Spring Byington
Strand .... Robert Sully
Dr. Green .... Morris Ankrum
Sebastian Melas .... Franco Corsaro
Beulah Murphy .... Connie Gilchrist

Distributor: M-G-M
Director: Alexander Hall
Released: December 29, 1943

TENDER COMRADE

Jo .... Ginger Rogers
Chris .... Robert Ryan
Barbara .... Ruth Hussey
Helen Stacey .... Patricia Collinge
Manya .... Mady Christians
Doris .... Kim Hunter

Mrs. Henderson .... Jane Darwell
Jo's Mother .... Mary Forbes
Mike .... Richard Martin

Distributor: RKO
Director: Edward Dmytryk
Released: December 29, 1943

SONG OF RUSSIA

John Meredith .... Robert Taylor
Nadya Stepanova .... Susan Peters
Boris .... John Hodiak
Hank Higgins .... Robert Benchley
Petrov .... Felix Bressart
Stepanov .... Michael Chekhov
Peter .... Darryl Hickman
Anna .... Jacqueline White

Distributor: M-G-M
Director: Gregory Ratoff
Released: December 29, 1943

THREE RUSSIAN GIRLS

Natasha .... Anna Sten
John Hill .... Kent Smith
Tamara .... Mimi Forsythe
Major Braginski .... Alexander Granach
Chijik .... Kathy Frye
Trishin .... Paul Guilfoyle

Susan Peters and Robert Taylor in **Song of Russia** (M-G-M).

Anna Sten with Kent Smith in **Three Russian Girls**
(United Artists).

Sergei	Kane Richmond
Doctor	Manart Kippen
Misha	Jack Gardner
Shoora	Marcia Lenack
Zina	Mary Herriot
Olga	Anna Marie Stewart
Manya	Dorothy Gray
Terkin	Feodor Chaliapin

Distributor: United Artists
Director: Fedor Ozep and Henry Kesler
Released: December 30, 1943

THERE'S SOMETHING ABOUT A SOLDIER

| Wally Williams | Tom Neal |

Carol Harkness	Evelyn Keyes
Frank Mallov	Bruce Bennett
Michael Crocker	John Hubbard
Jean Burton	Jeff Donnell
Alex Grybinski	Frank Sully
Bolivar Jefferson	Lewis Wilson
George Edwards	Robert Stanford
General Sommerton	Jonathan Hale
Lieut. Martin	Hugh Beaumont
Sgt. Cummings	Kane Richmond
Burroughs	Douglass Drake
Jonesy	Craig Woods

Distributor: Columbia
Director: Alfred E. Green
Released: December 31, 1943

James Flavin, Robert Stanford, Bruce Bennett, Lewis Wilson and William Haade in **There's Something About a Soldier** (Columbia).

SWINGTIME JOHNNY

The Andrews Sisters	Themselves
Linda	Harriet Hilliard
Jonathan	Peter Cookson
Sparks	Tim Ryan
Monk	Matt Willis
Steve	William (Bill) Phillips
Gruff Character	Tom Dugan
Mike	Ray Walker
Blonde	Marion Martin
Caldwell	John Hamilton
Raffle Wheel Barker	John Sheehan
Sea Food Barker	Syd Saylor
Bill	Jack Rice
Chairman Of Board	Emmett Vogan
Pop	Herbert Heywood

Charles Hall, Matt Willis, Peter Cookson, Bill Phillips and Harriet Hilliard in **Swingtime Johnny** (Universal).

Allan Jones in **Sing a Jingle** (Universal).

Pierre .... Alphonse Martell	Wiggins .... Billy Newell
Also: Mitch Ayres and his Orchestra	Benny .... Dean Collins
	Also: The King's Men, Four Society Girls
Distributor: Universal	
Director: Edward F. Cline	*Distributor:* Universal
Released: January 3, 1944	*Director:* Edward Lilley
	Released: January 3, 1944

SING A JINGLE

Ray King .... Allan Jones
Muriel Crane .... June Vincent
J. P. Crane .... Samuel S. Hinds
Bucky .... Gus Schilling
Myrtle .... Betty Kean
Andrews .... Jerome Cowan
Abbott .... Edward Norris
Vera Grant .... Joan Castle
Wilbur Crane .... Richard Love
Ann .... Vivian Austin

THE MIRACLE OF MORGAN'S CREEK

Norval Jones .... Eddie Bracken
Trudy Kockenlocker .... Betty Hutton
Emmy Kockenlocker .... Diana Lynn
McGinty .... Brian Donlevy
The Boss .... Akim Tamiroff
Justice Of The Peace .... Porter Hall
Mr. Tuerck .... Emory Parnell
Mr. Johnson .... Alan Bridge
Mr. Rafferty .... Julius Tannen

Frank Moran, Bud Fine, Betty Hutton, Arthur Hoyt,
Eddie Bracken, Diana Lynn, William Demarest and
Porter Hall in **The Miracle of Morgan's Creek** (Paramount).

Fred MacMurray and Paulette Goddard in **Standing
Room Only** (Paramount).

Henry Hull, Tallulah Bankhead, John Hodiak,
Walter Slezak and Canada Lee in **Lifeboat** (20th
Century-Fox).

Newspaper Editor	Victor Potel
Justice's Wife	Almira Sessions
Sally	Esther Howard
Sheriff	J. Farrell MacDonald
Cecilia	Connie Tompkins
Mrs. Johnson	Georgia Caine
Doctor	Torben Meyer
U.S. Marshal	George Melford
The Mayor	Jimmy Conlin
Mr. Schwartz	Harry Rosenthal
Pete	Chester Conklin
First M.P.	Frank Moran
Second M.P.	Budd Fine
McGinty's Secretary	Byron Foulger
McGinty's Secretary	Arthur Hoyt
Head Nurse	Nora Cecil
Man Opening Champagne	Jack Norton
Mussolini	Joe Devlin
Hitler	Bobby Watson

Officer Kockenlocker	William Demarest

Distributor: Paramount
Director: Preston Sturges
Released: January 5, 1944

STANDING ROOM ONLY

Lee Stevens	Fred MacMurray
Jane Rogers	Paulette Goddard
T. J. Todd	Edward Arnold
Alice Todd	Hillary Brooke
Ira Cromwell	Roland Young
Major Cromwell	Anne Revere
Glen Ritchie	Clarence Kolb
Mrs. Ritchie	Isobel Randolph
Hugo Farenhall	Porter Hall
Opal	Marie McDonald

John Wayne in **The Fighting Seabees** (Republic).

Miss Becker	Josephine Whittell
Peggy Fuller	Veda Ann Borg

Distributor: Paramount
Director: Sidney Lanfield
Released: January 7, 1944

LIFEBOAT

Connie Porter	Tallulah Bankhead
Gus	William Bendix
The German	Walter Slezak
Alice	Mary Anderson
Kovak	John Hodiak
Rittenhouse	Henry Hull
Mrs. Higgins	Heather Angel
Stanley Garrett	Hume Cronyn
Joe	Canada Lee
German Sailor	William Yetter, Jr.
Man In Before And After Ad	Alfred Hitchcock

Distributor: 20th Century-Fox
Director: Alfred Hitchcock
Released: January 11, 1944

THE FIGHTING SEABEES

Wedge Donovan	John Wayne
Constance Chesley	Susan Hayward
Lt. Comdr. Robert Yarrow	Dennis O'Keefe
Eddie Powers	William Frawley
Johnny Novasky	Leonid Kinskey
Sawyer Collins	J. M. Kerrigan
Whanger Spreckles	Grant Withers
Ding Jacobs	Paul Fix
Yump Lumkin	Ben Welden
Lt. Kerrick	William Forest
Captain Joyce	Addison Richards
Joe Brick	Jay Norris
Juan	Duncan Renaldo

Distributor: Republic
Director: Edward Ludwig
Released: January 19, 1944

RATIONING

Ben Barton	Wallace Beery
Iris Tuttle	Marjorie Main

Connie Gilchrist, Donald Meek, Sarah Edwards, Wallace Beery and Marjorie Main in **Rationing** (M-G-M).

Wilfred Ball	Donald Meek
Dorothy Tuttle	Dorothy Morris
Cash Riddle	Howard Freeman
Mrs. Porter	Connie Gilchrist
Lance Barton	Tommy Batten
Miss McCue	Gloria Dickson
Senator Edward A. White	Henry O'Neill
Teddy	Richard Hall
Ezra Weeks	Charles Halton
Mr. Morgan	Morris Ankrum
Carol Ann Beery	Herself
Dixie Samson	Douglas Fowley
Roberts	Chester Clute

Distributor: M-G-M
Director: Willis Goldbeck
Released: January 28, 1944

NONE SHALL ESCAPE

Marja Pacierkowski	Marsha Hunt
Wilhelm Grimm	Alexander Knox
Father Warecki	Henry Travers
Karl Grimm	Erik Rolf
Willie Grimm (As A Man)	Richard Crane
Janina	Dorothy Morris
Rabbi Levin	Richard Hale
Alice Grimm	Ruth Nelson
Lt. Gersdorf	Kurt Kreuger
Anna Oremska	Shirley Mills

Elvin Field, Shirley Mills and Alexander Knox in
None Shall Escape (Columbia).

Jan Stys (As A Boy) .... Elvin Field
Jan Stys (As A Man) .... Trevor Bardette
Dr. Matek .... Frank Jaquet
Oremski .... Ray Teal
Stys .... Art Smith
Presiding Judge .... George Lessey

Distributor: Columbia
Director: Andre Detoth
Released: January 28, 1944

PASSPORT TO DESTINY

Ella .... Elsa Lanchester
Franz .... Gordon Oliver
Grete .... Lenore Aubert

Dietrich .... Lionel Royce
Hausmeister .... Fritz Feld
Lieutenant Bosch .... Joseph Vitale
Lord Haw Haw .... Gavin Muir
Professor Walthers .... Lloyd Corrigan
Agnes .... Anita Bolster
Millie .... Lydia Bilbrook
Captain .... Lumsden Hare
Prison Warden .... Hans Schumm

Distributor: RKO
Director: Ray McCarey
Released: January 31, 1944

THE SULLIVANS

Katherine Mary .... Anne Baxter

Leonore Aubert, Elsa Lanchester and Gordon Oliver in **Passport to Destiny** (RKO).

Genevieve	Trudy Marshall
Frank	John Campbell
George	James Cardwell
Matt	John Alvin
Joe	George Offerman, Jr.
Father Francis	Roy Roberts
Lieutenant	Ward Bond
Gladys	Mary McCarty
Al (Child)	Bobby Driscoll
Genevieve (Child)	Nancy June Robinson
Frank (Child)	Marvin Davis
George (Child)	Buddy Swan
Matt (Child)	Billy Cummings
Joe (Child)	Johnny Calkins
Admiral	John Nesbitt
Damage Control Officer	Selmer Jackson
C.P.O.	Harry Shannon
Nurse	Barbara Brown
Yeoman	Larry Thompson
Naval Captain	Addison Richards

Mr. Sullivan	Thomas Mitchell
Mrs. Sullivan	Selena Royle
Al	Edward Ryan

Edward Ryan, George Offerman Jr., James Cardwell, John Alvin and John Campbell in **The Sullivans** (20th Century-Fox).

Distributor: 20th Century-Fox
Director: Lloyd Bacon
Released: February 3, 1944

IN OUR TIME

Jennifer Whittredge	Ida Lupino
Count Stephen Orvid	Paul Henreid
Janina Orvid	Nancy Coleman
Mrs. Bromley	Mary Boland
Count Pavel Orvid	Victor Francen
Zofya Orvid	Nazimova
Uncle Leopold	Michael Chekhov
Antique Dealer	Marek Windheim
Bujanski	Ivan Triesault
Wladek	John Bleiffer
Wanda	Lotta Palfi
Father Josef	Wolfgang Zilzer
Pyotr	Richard Ordynski

Distributor: Warner Bros.
Director: Vincent Sherman
Released: February 4, 1944

UP IN ARMS

Danny Weems	Danny Kaye
Virginia	Dinah Shore
Joe	Dana Andrews
Mary Morgan	Constance Dowling
Colonel Ashley	Louis Calhern
Blackie	George Mathews
Butterball	Benny Baker
Info Jones	Elisha Cook, Jr.
Sgt. Gelsey	Lyle Talbot
Major Brock	Walter Catlett
Ashley's Aide	George Meeker
Ashley's Aide	Richard Powers
Mrs. Willoughby	Margaret Dumont
Singer At Dock	Donald Dickson
Mr. Higginbotham	Charles Arnt
Dr. Freyheisen	Charles Halton
Pitchman	Tom Dugan
Waiter	Sig Arno
Dr. Weavermacher	Harry Hayden
Mr. Campbell	Charles D. Brown
Dr. Jones	Maurice Cass
Head Waiter	Fred Essler
Band Leader	Rudolf Friml, Jr.

Distributor: RKO
Director: Elliott Nugent
Released: February 7, 1944

THE IMPOSTER

Clement	Jean Gabin
Lieutenant Varenne	Richard Whorf

Mary Boland, Ida Lupino and Paul Henreid in **In Our Time** (Warner Bros.).

Bouteau	Allyn Joslyn
Yvonne	Ellen Drew
Hafner	Peter Van Eyck
Colonel de Boivin	Ralph Morgan
Cochery	Eddie Quillan
Monge	John Qualen
Lafarge	Dennis Moore
Clauzel	Milburn Stone
Mortemart	John Philliber
Menessier	Charles McGraw
Matowa	Otho Gaines
Free French Corporal	John Forrest
Priest	Fritz Leiber
Sergeant Clerk	Ian Wolfe
Adjutant	William Davidson
Prosecutor	Frank Wilcox
Officer	Warren Ashe
Soldier	Peter Cookson
Toba	Leigh Whipper
Ekona	Ernest Whitman
Captain	Grandon Rhodes
Prosecutor	George Irving

Danny Kaye and Louis Calhern in **Up in Arms** (RKO).

Distributor: Universal
Director: Julien Duvivier
Released: February 10, 1944

WEEKEND PASS

Barbara	Martha O'Driscoll
Johnny	Noah Beery, Jr.
Bradley	George Barbier
Constable	Andrew Tombes
Sheriff	Irving Bacon
Ray	Dennis Moore
Motor Cop	Edgar Dearing
Kendall	Pierre Watkin
Hilda	Lottie Stein
Wajowsky	Eddie Acuff
Jenkins	Jack Rice
Murphy	Perc Launders

Distributor: Universal

Richard Whorf and John Qualen in **The Imposter** (Universal).

Noah Beery Jr. and Martha O'Driscoll in **Weekend Pass** (Universal).

Peter Lorre, Helmut Dantine, Humphrey Bogart and George Tobias in **Passage to Marseille** (Warner Bros.).

Director: Jean Yarbrough
Released: February 14, 1944

PASSAGE TO MARSEILLE

Matrac	Humphrey Bogart
Capt. Freycinet	Claude Rains
Paula	Michele Morgan
Renault	Philip Dorn
Major Duval	Sydney Greenstreet
Marius	Peter Lorre
Petit	George Tobias
Garou	Helmut Dantine
Manning	John Loder

Capt. Malo	Victor Francen
Grandpere	Vladimir Sokoloff
Chief Engineer	Eduardo Cianelli
Singer	Corinna Mura
First Mate	Konstantin Shayne
Lt. Hastings	Stephen Richards
Lt. Lenoir	Charles La Torre
Jourdain	Hans Conried
Second Mate	Monte Blue
Mess Boy	Billy Roy
Bijou	Frederick Brunn
Second Engineer	Louis Mercier

Distributor: Warner Bros.-First National
Director: Michael Curtiz
Released: February 17, 1944

Robert Walker in **See Here, Private Hargrove** (M-G-M).

ACTION IN ARABIA

Gordon	George Sanders
Yvonne	Virginia Bruce
Mouniran	Lenore Aubert
Danesco	Gene Lockhart
Reed	Robert Armstrong
Rashid	H. B. Warner
Latimer	Alan Napier
Leroux	Andre Charlot
Chakka	Marcel Dalio
Chalmers	Robert Anderson
Kareem	Jamiel Hasson
Hamilton	John Hamilton
Hotel Clerk	Rafael Storm

Gene Lockhart and George Sanders in **Action in Arabia** (RKO).

226

Hamid .... Mike Ansara

Distributor: RKO
Director: Leonide Moguy
Released: February 18, 1944

SEE HERE, PRIVATE HARGROVE

Marion Hargrove	Robert Walker
Carol Halliday	Donna Reed
Mr. Halliday	Robert Benchley
Private Mulvehill	Keenan Wynn
Bob	Bob Crosby
Brody S. Griffith	Ray Collins
Sergt. Cramp	Chill Wills
Mrs. Halliday	Marta Linden
Uncle George	Grant Mitchell
Private Orrin Esty	George Offerman, Jr.

General Dillon	Edward Fielding
Sgt. Heldon	Donald Curtis
Private Bill Burk	William Phillips
Captain Manville	Douglas Fowley
Colonel Forbes	Morris Ankrum
Sergeant	Mickey Rentschler
M.P.	Frank Faylen
Doctor	Jack Luden
Lieutenant	Maurice Murphy
Capt. Hamilton	Clarence Straight
Mr. Smith	William Newell
Captain	Louis Jean Heydt
Corporal	Ken Scott
Officer Of Day	Michael Owen
Corporal	Stephen Barclay
Exercise Sgt.	John Kelly
Mess Sgt.	Joe Devlin
Executive Officer	Dennis Moore
Field Operator	Rod Bacon

Richard Loo with Dana Andrews in **The Purple Heart**
(20th Century-Fox).

Farmer	Louis Mason
Farmer's Wife	Connie Gilchrist
Captain	Harry Strang
Old Man	Harry Tyler
Porter	Mantan Moreland
Lieutenant	Myron Healey
Girl Clerk	Mary McLeod
Captain Hammond	Eddie Acuff
Lieutenant	Fred Kohler, Jr.

Jean Parker and Bill Henry in **The Navy Way** (Paramount).

Executive Officer	James Warren
Field Operator	Blake Edward

Distributor: M-G-M
Director: Wesley Ruggles
Released: February 18, 1944

THE PURPLE HEART

Capt. Harvey Ross	Dana Andrews
Lieut. Angelo Canelli	Richard Conte
Sergt. Howard Clinton	Farley Granger
Sergt. Jan Skvoznik	Kevin O'Shea
Lieut. Peter Vincent	Donald Barry
Mrs. Ross	Trudy Marshall
Lieut. Wayne Greenbaum	Sam Levene
Lieut. Kenneth Bayforth	Charles Russell
Sergt. Martin Stoner	John Craven
Johana Hartwig	Tala Birell
General Ito Mitsubi	Richard Loo
Mitsuru Toyama	Peter Chong
Peter Voroshevski	Gregory Gaye

Karl Keppel	Torben Meyer
Ludwig Kruger	Kurt Katch
Manuel Siva	Martin Garralaga
Karl Schleswig	Erwin Kalser
Boris Evenik	Igor Dolgaruki
Francisco De Los Santos	Nestor Paiva
Paul Ludovescu	Alex Papana
Yuen Chiu Ling	H. T. Tsiang
Moy Ling	Benson Fong
Admiral Kentara Yamagichi	Key Chang
Itsubi Sakai	Allen Jung
Police Captain	Wing Foo
Court Clerk	Paul Fung
Prosecutor	Joseph Kim
Court Stenographer	Luke Chan
Toma Nagota	Beal Wong
Hank Morrison	Marshall Thompson

Distributor: 20th Century-Fox
Director: Lewis Milestone
Released: February 23, 1944

THE NAVY WAY

Johnny Jersey	Robert Lowery
Ellen Sayre	Jean Parker
Mal Randall	Bill Henry
Frankie Gimball	Roscoe Karns
Trudy	Sharon Douglas
C.P.O. Harper	Robert Armstrong
Steve Appleby	Richard Powers
Billy Jamison	Larry Nunn
Agnes	Mary Treen

Distributor: Paramount
Director: William Berke
Released: February 25, 1944

SWEETHEARTS OF THE U. S. A.

Patsy	Una Merkel
Parky	Parkyarkarkus
Don Clark	Donald Novis
Helen Grant	Lillian Cornell
Loretta	Judith Gibson
Bill Craige	Joel Friend
Mrs. Carver	Cobina Wright, Sr.
Josephine	Marion Martin
Clipper	Vince Barnett

A scene from **Sweethearts of the U.S.A.** (Monogram).

Gilhooley	Ralph Sanford	Kewpie	Johnnie 'Scat' Davis
Napoleon	Joseph Kirk	Miss Hawks	Mabel Paige

Also: Georgann Smith, Joe Devlin, Edmund Cobb, Dorothy Bradshaw, Charles Williams, Jan Garber Orchestra, Henry King Orchestra, Phil Ohman Orchestra.

Madge .... Jean Wallace
Pickles .... Roland Dupree
Christine .... Christine Forsythe
Band .... D'Artega All-Girl Orch.

Distributor: Monogram
Director: Lew Collins
Released: February 25, 1944

Distributor: Paramount
Director: Lester Fuller
Released: February 28, 1944

YOU CAN'T RATION LOVE

Betty .... Betty Rhodes
John .... Johnnie Johnston
Pete .... Bill Edwards
Marian .... Marjorie Weaver
Bubbles .... Marie Wilson

HOUR BEFORE THE DAWN

Jim Hetherton .... Franchot Tone
Dora Bruchmann .... Veronica Lake
May Hetherton .... Binnie Barnes
Roger Hetherton .... John Sutton
General Hetherton .... Henry Stephenson

Johnny Johnston, Betty Rhodes, Bill Edwards and Marjorie Weaver in **You Can't Ration Love** (Paramount).

Sir Leslie Buchanan	Philip Merivale
Capt. Atterley	Leslie Dennison
Kurt Bruchmann	Nils Asther
Tommy Hetherton	David Leland
Freddy Merritt	Edmond Breon
Farmer Searle	Donald Stuart
Maid	Viola Moore
Mrs. Parkins	Aminta Dyne
Sam	Harry Cording

Distributor: Paramount
Director: Frank Tuttle
Released: February 28, 1944

VOICE IN THE WIND

Jan Volny
.... Francis Lederer

El Hombre

Marya	Sigrid Gurie
Dr. Hoffman	J. Edward Bromberg
Luigi	J. Carrol Naish
Angelo	Alexander Granach
Marco	David Cota
Anna	Olga Fabian
Captain von Neubach	Howard Johnson
Piesecke	Hans Schumm
Bartender	Luis Alberni
Detective	George Sorel
Policeman	Martin Garralaga
Portuguese Girl	Jacqueline Dalya
Novak	Rudolph Nyzet
Vasek	Fred Nurney
Guard No. 1	Bob Stevenson
Guard No. 2	Otto Reichow
Refugee	Martin Berliner

Distributor: United Artists

Veronica Lake in **The Hour Before the Dawn** (Paramount).

Francis Lederer and Sigrid Gurie in **Voice in the Wind** (United Artists).

Peter Lawford and Irene Dunne in **The White Cliffs of Dover** (M-G-M).

Director: Arthur Ripley
Released: March 3, 1944

THE WHITE CLIFFS OF DOVER

Susan Ashwood	Irene Dunne
Sir John Ashwood	Alan Marshal
Hiram Porter Dunn	Frank Morgan
John Ashwood II As A Boy	Roddy McDowall
Nanny	Dame May Whitty
Colonel	C. Aubrey Smith
Lady Jean Ashwood	Gladys Cooper
John Ashwood II (Age 24)	Peter Lawford
Sam Bennett	Van Johnson
Reggie	John Warburton
Rosamund	Jill Esmond
Gwennie	Brenda Forbes
Mrs. Bland	Norma Varden
Betsy (10 Years)	Elizabeth Taylor
Betsy (18 Years)	June Lockhart
Farmer Kenney	Charles Irwin
Mrs. Kenney	Jean Prescott
American Soldier	Tom Drake
Mrs. Bancroft	Isobel Elsom
Major Bancroft	Edmund Breon
Major Loring	Miles Mander
Miss Lambert	Ann Curzon
Gerhard	Steven Muller
Dietrich	Norbert Multer
Helen	Molly Lamont
The Vicar	Lumsden Hare
Benson	Arthur Shields
Plump Lady	Doris Lloyd
Immigration Officer	Matthew Boulton
Woman On Train	Ethel Griffies
Footman	Herbert Evans
Duke Of Waverly	Keith Hitchcock
Duchess	Vera Graaff
Miller	Anita Bolster
Skipper	Ian Wolfe
Billings	Alec Craig
Jennings	Clyde Cook

Distributor: M-G-M
Director: Clarence Brown
Released: March 13, 1944

FOUR JILLS IN A JEEP

Kay Francis	Herself
Carole Landis	Herself
Martha Raye	Herself
Mitzi Mayfair	Herself
Jimmy Dorsey and Orchestra	Themselves
Alice Faye	Herself
Betty Grable	Herself

John Harvey with Carole Landis in **Four Jills in a Jeep** (20th Century-Fox).

Carmen Miranda	Herself
George Jessel	Himself
Ted Warren	John Harvey
Eddie	Phil Silvers
Lieutenant Dick Ryan	Dick Haymes
Captain Lloyd	Lester Matthews
Captain Stewart	Glen Langan
General	Paul Harvey
Colonel Hartley	Miles Mander
Lady Carlton Smith	Winifred Harris
Nurse Captain	Mary Servoss
Soldier	B. S. Pully

Distributor: 20th Century-Fox
Director: William A. Seiter
Released: March 17, 1944

LADIES COURAGEOUS

Roberta Harper	Loretta Young
Virgie Alford	Geraldine Fitzgerald
Nadine	Diana Barrymore
Gerry Vail	Anne Gwynne
Wilhelmina	Evelyn Ankers

232

David Bruce and Geraldine Fitzgerald in **Ladies Courageous** (Universal).

Tommy Harper	Phillip Terry	Gloria Vance	Vera Zorina
Frank Garrison	David Bruce	Nick West	Charles Grapewin
Jill	Lois Collier	Kitty	Grace MacDonald
Mary Frances	June Vincent	Louie West	Charles Butterworth
Brig. General Wade	Samuel S. Hinds	Bruce	George Macready
Colonel Brennan	Richard Fraser	Annie	Elizabeth Patterson
Snapper	Frank Jenks	Barrett	Theodor von Eltz
Bee Jay	Janet Shaw	Doctor Henderson	Regis Toomey
Alex Anderson	Kane Richmond	Laura	Ramsey Ames
		Junior	Spooks

Distributor: Universal
Director: John Rawlins
Released: March 24, 1944

FOLLOW THE BOYS

Tony West	George Raft

Also: Mack Gray, Molly Lamont, John Meredith, John Estes, Ralph Gardner, Doris Lloyd, Charles D. Brown, Nelson Leigh, Lane Chandler, Cyril Ring, Emmett Vogan, Addison Richards, Frank Larue, Tony Marsh, Stanley Andrews, Leslie Denison, Leyland Hodgson, Bill Healy, Frank Jenks, Ralph Dunn, Billy Benedict, Grandon Rhodes, Howard Hickman, Edwin Stanley, Roy Darmour,

233

Grace McDonald, Charles Grapewin, Charles Butterworth and Sophie Tucker in **Follow the Boys** (Universal).

Carl Vernell, Tony Hughes, Wallis Clark, Richard Crane, Frank Wilcox, Jimmy Carpenter, Bernard Thomas, Carey Harrison, George Riley, Steve Brodie, Jack Wegman, Billy Wayne, Clyde Cook, Bobby Barber, Dick Nelson, Jack Whitney, Walter Tetley, Anthony Warde, William Forrest, Tom Hanlon, Don McGill, Franklin Parker, Dennis Moore, Odessa Lauren, Nancy Brinckman, Bill Dyer, Janet Shaw, Jan Wiley, Martin Ashe, Duke York, Joel Allen, Carlyle Blackwell, Lennie Smith, Michael Kirk, Bob Ashley, Jackie Lou Harding, Genevieve Bell, Mel Schubert, Stephen Wayne, Edwin Stanley, Charles King, Don Kramer, Allan Cooke, Luis Torres, Nicnolai, John Duane, Ed Browne, Clair Freeman, Bill Meador, Eddie Kover. And: Jeanette MacDonald, Orson Welles' Mercury Wonder Show, Marlene Dietrich, Dinah Shore,

Abner Biberman, Ann Savage, George Lynn and Tom Neal in **Two-Man Submarine** (Columbia).

Donald O'Connor, Peggy Ryan, W. C. Fields, The Andrews Sisters, Arturo Rubenstein, Carman Amaya and her Company, Sophie Tucker, Delta Rhythm Boys, Leonard Gautier's Bricklayers, Ted Lewis and his Band, Freddie Slack and his Orchestra, Charlie Spivak and his Orchestra, Louis Jordan and his Orchestra, Louise Beavers, Clarence Muse, Maxie Rosenbloom, Maria Montez, Susanna Foster, Louise Allbritton, Robert Paige, Alan Curtis, Lon Chaney, Gloria Jean, Andy Devine, Turhan Bey, Evelyn Ankers, Noah Beery, Jr., Gale Sondergaard, Peter Coe, Nigel Bruce, Thomas Gomez and Samuel S. Hinds.

Distributor: Universal
Director: Eddie Sutherland
Released: March 27, 1944

Pat O'Malley, Bob Haymes, Lewis Wilson and Jane Lawrence in **Sailor's Holiday** (Columbia).

Jane Frazee in **Rosie the Riveter** (Republic).

TWO-MAN SUBMARINE

Jerry Evans	Tom Neal
Pat Benson	Ann Savage
Dr. Augustus Hadley	J. Carrol Naish
Walt Hedges	Robert Williams
Gabe Fabian	Abner Biberman
Norman Fosmer	George Lynn
Fuzzytop	J. Alex Havier

Distributor: Columbia
Director: Lew Landers
Released: March 29, 1944

SAILOR'S HOLIDAY

Marble Head Tomkins	Arthur Lake
Clementine Brown	Jane Lawrence
Bill Hayes	Bob Haymes
Gloria Flynn	Shelley Winter
Iron Man Collins	Lewis Wilson
Ferd Baxter	Edmund Mac Donald
Studio Guide	Pat O'Malley
Director	Herbert Rawlinson
Assistant Director	Buddy Yarus
Maid	Vi Athens
Ronald Blair	George Ford

Distributor: Columbia
Director: William Berke
Released: March 29, 1944

Larry Parks and Ann Miller in **Hey, Rookie** (Columbia).

ROSIE THE RIVETER

Rosie Warren	Jane Frazee
Charlie Doran	Frank Albertson
Vera Watson	Vera Vague
Kelly Kennedy	Frank Jenks
Clem Prouty	Lloyd Corrigan
Wayne Calhoun	Frank Fenton
Grandma Quill	Maude Eburne
Buzz	Carl 'Alfalfa' Switzer
Mabel	Louise Erickson
Stella Prouty	Ellen Lowe
Sgt. Mulvaney	Arthur Loft
Piano Mover	Tom Kennedy

Distributor: Republic
Director: Joseph Santley
Released: April 5, 1944

Lynn Bari with Edward G. Robinson in **Tampico** (20th Century-Fox).

TAMPICO

Captain Bart Manson	Edward G. Robinson
Kathie Hall	Lynn Bari
Fred Adamson	Victor McLaglen
Watson	Robert Bailey
Valdez	Marc Lawrence
Silhouette Man	E. J. Ballentine
Dolores	Mona Maris
Druger	Tonio Selwart
Mueller	Carl Ekberg
Crawford	Roy Roberts
Stranger	George Sorel
Naval Officer	Charles Lang

Quartermaster	Ralph Byrd	Captain	Peter Helmers
Crew-Members	Paul Kruger	Second Lieutenant	Otto Reichow
	Martin Cinchy	Commander	Ludwig Donath
	Constantin Romanoff	Radio Operator	Rudolph Lindau
	Oscar Hendrian	Port Pilot	Jean Del Val
	Louis Hart	Second Officer	Hans von Morhart
Justice Of The Peace	Antonio Moreno		
Naval Commander	Nestor Paiva		
Rodriguez	Muni Seroff		
Photographer	Juan Varro		
Dr. Brown	Ben Erway		
Mrs. Kelly	Helen Brown		
Serra	Martin Garralaga		
Proprietor	Margaret Martin		
Messenger Boy	David Cote		
Navigator	Arno Frey		
Waiter	Chris-Pin Martin		
Waiter	Trevor Bardette		

Distributor: 20th Century-Fox
Director: Lothar Mendes
Released: April 5, 1944

HEY, ROOKIE

Judge Pfeiffer	Joe Besser
Winnie Clark	Ann Miller
Jim Lighter	Larry Parks
Sergeant	Joe Sawyer

Gordon Oliver, Elaine Shepard, Wally Brown and
Alan Carney in **Seven Days Ashore** (RKO).

237

Bert Pfeiffer	Jimmy Little
Colonel Robbins	Selmer Jackson
Captain Jessop	Larry Thompson
Mrs. Clark	Barbara Brown
General Willis	Charles Trowbridge
Sam Jonas	Charles Wilson
Corporal Trupp	Syd Saylor
Maxon	Doodles Weaver

Also: Hi, Lo, Jack and a Dame, Condos Brothers, The Vagabonds, Johnson Brothers, Jack Gilford, Judy Clark and the Solid Senders, Bob Evans with Jerry O'Leary and the Hal McIntyre Orchestra.

Distributor: Columbia
Director: Charles Barton
Released: April 6, 1944

SEVEN DAYS ASHORE

Monty	Wally Brown
Orval	Alan Carney
Dot	Marcy McGuire
Dan Arland	Gordon Oliver
Carol	Virginia Mayo
Lucy	Amelita Ward
Annabelle	Elaine Shepard
Jason	Dooley Wilson
Mrs. Arland	Marjorie Gateson
Mr. Arland	Alan Dinehart
Hazel	Miriam Levelle
Mrs. Croxton-Lynch	Margaret Dumont
Captain Harvey	Emory Parnell
Process Server	Ian Wolfe

And: Freddie Slack and Orchestra
Freddie Fisher Band

Distributor: RKO
Director: John H. Auer
Released: April 21, 1944

MEET THE PEOPLE

Julie Hampton	Lucille Ball
William 'Swanee' Swanson	Dick Powell
'Woodpecker' Peg	Virginia O'Brien
The Commander	Bert Lahr
Mr. Smith	Rags Ragland
Annie	June Allyson

Uncle Felix	Steve Geray
'Buck'	Paul Regan
Mr. Peetwick	Howard Freeman
Steffi	Betty Jaynes
John Swanson	John Craven
Monte Rowland	Morris Ankrum
Miriam	Mariam Lavelle
Ziggie	Ziggie Talent
Oriental Dancers	Mata & Hari

Distributor: M-G-M
Director: Charles Reisner
Released: April 21, 1944

ADDRESS UNKNOWN

Martin Schulz	Paul Lukas
Baron von Friesche	Carl Esmond
Heinrich Schulz	Peter Van Eyck
Elsa	Mady Christians
Max Eisenstein	Morris Carnovsky
Griselle	K. T. Stevens
Postman	Emory Parnell
Mrs. Delancey	Mary Young
Jimmie Blake	Frank Faylen

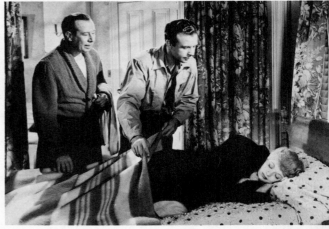

Bert Lahr, Dick Powell and Lucille Ball in **Meet the People** (M-G-M).

Pip-Squeak	Charles Halton
Stage Director	Erwin Kalser
Professor Schmidt	Frank Reicher
Carl	Dale Cornell
Wilhelm	Peter Newmeyer

Mady Christians, Carl Esmond and Paul Lukas in
Address Unknown (Columbia).

Youngest .... Larry Joe Olsen
Hugo .... Gary Gray

Distributor: Columbia
Director: William Cameron Menzies
Released: April 24, 1944

UNCERTAIN GLORY

Jean Picard .... Errol Flynn
Marcel Bonet .... Paul Lukas
Marianne .... Jean Sullivan
Mme. Maret .... Lucile Watson
Louise .... Faye Emerson
Captain, Mobile Guard .... James Flavin
Police Commissioner .... Douglass Dumbrille

Father Le Clerc .... Dennis Hoey
Henri Duval .... Sheldon Leonard
Mme. Bonet .... Odette Myrtil
Prison Priest .... Francis Pierlot
Razeau .... Wallis Clark
Latour .... Victor Kilian
Saboteur .... Ivan Triesault
Vitrac .... Albert Van Antwerp
Warden .... Art Smith
Innkeeper .... Carl Harbaugh
Drover's Wife .... Mary Servoss
Restaurant Keeper .... Charles La Torre
Executioner .... Pedro de Cordoba
Pierre Bonet .... Bobby Walberg
Drover .... Erskine Sanford
German Officer .... Felix Basch
Veterinary .... Joel Friedkin

Faye Emerson and Errol Flynn in **Uncertain Glory** (Warner Bros.).

Distributor: Warner Bros.-First National
Director: Raoul Walsh
Released: April 24, 1944

PIN UP GIRL

Lorry Jones	Betty Grable
Tommy Dooley	John Harvey
Marian	Martha Raye
Eddie	Joe E. Brown
Barney Briggs	Eugene Pallette
Skating Vanities	Themselves
Kay	Dorothea Kent
Dud Miller	Dave Willock
Specialty Dancers	Condos Brothers
Charlie Spivak and Orchestra	Themselves
Stage Doorman	Robert Homans
Headwaiter	Marcel Dalio
George	Roger Clark
Captain Of Waiters	Leon Belasco
Window Cleaner	Irving Bacon
Messenger Boy	Walter Tetley
Scrubwoman	Ruth Warren
Waiter	Max Willenz
Red Cap	Mantan Moreland
Red Cap	Charles Moore

Distributor: 20th Century-Fox
Director: Bruce Humberstone
Released: April 25, 1944

THE HITLER GANG

Adolf Hitler	Robert Watson
Captain Ernst Roehm	Roman Bohnen
Joseph Goebbels	Martin Kosleck
Rudolph Hess	Victor Varconi
Heinrich Himmler	Luis Van Rooten
Hermann Goering	Alexander Pope
Pastor Niemoeller	Ivan Triesault
'Geli' Raubal	Poldy Dur

Dave Willock and Dorothea Kent in **Pin Up Girl** (20th Century-Fox).

Angela Raubal	Helen Thimig
General Ludendorff	Reinhold Schunzel
Gen. von Hindenburg	Sig Ruman
Julius Streicher	Alexander Granach
Gregor Strasser	Fritz Kortner
Alfred Rosenberg	Tonio Selwart
Adolf Wagner	Richard Ryen
Cardinal von Faulhaber	Ray Collins
Gustav von Kahr	Ludwig Donath
Anton Drexler	Erno Verebes
Franz von Papen	Walter Kingsford

General von Epp	Fred Nurney	Johnny	Renny McEvoy
Col. von Reichenau	Arthur Loft	Alabam	Oliver Thorndike
Fritz Thyssen	Lionel Royce	Ping	Philip Ahn
		Ruth	Barbara Britton
Distributor: Paramount		Francis	Melvin Francis
Director: John Farrow		Kraus	Joel Allen
Released: April 26, 1944		Whaley	James Millican
		Borghetti	Mike Kilian
		Hunter	Doodles Weaver

THE STORY OF DR. WASSELL

Dr. Corydon M. Wassell	Gary Cooper	Dr. Ralph Wayne	Lester Matthews
Madeline	Laraine Day	Dr. Vranken	Ludwig Donath
Bettina	Signe Hasso	Dr. Wei	Richard Loo
Hopkins	Dennis O'Keefe	Dr. Holmes	Davison Clark
Tremartini	Carol Thurston	Captain Carruthers	Richard Nugent
Lieutenant Dirk Van Daal	Carl Esmond	Lieutenant Bainbridge	Morton Lowry
Murdock	Paul Kelly	Captain Balen	George Macready
Anderson	Elliott Reid	Captain Ryk	Victor Varconi
Commander Bill Goggins	Stanley Ridges	Admiral Hart	Edward Fielding
		Captain	Harvey Stephens
		Rear Admiral	Minor Watson

Bobby Watson, Victor Varconi, Poldy Dur and Helen
Thimig in **The Hitler Gang** (Paramount).

Gary Cooper and Laraine Day in **The Story of Dr. Wassell** (Paramount).

Little English Boy	William Severn
Mother Of Little Boy	Edith Barrett
Mrs. Wayne	Catherine Craig
Japanese Temple Guide	Frank Puglia
Missionary	Irving Bacon
Missionary's Wife	Ottola Nesmith
Admiral Hart's Aide	Hugh Beaumont
Lieutenant Smith	George Lynn
Fashta	Linda Brent
Praying Woman	Ann Doran
Anne, Dutch Nurse	Julia Faye
Girl	Yvonne DeCarlo

Distributor: Paramount
Director: Cecil B. De Mille
Released: April 26, 1944

Van Johnson and June Allyson in **Two Girls and a Sailor** (M-G-M).

Gregory Peck and Tamara Toumanova in **Days of Glory** (RKO).

TWO GIRLS AND A SAILOR

John Dyckman Brown III	Van Johnson
Patsy Deyo	June Allyson
Jean Deyo	Gloria De Haven
Jose Iturbi	Himself
Billy Kipp	Jimmy Durante
Concerto Number	Gracie Allen
Specialty	Lena Horne
Frank Miller	Tom Drake
John Dyckman Brown I	Henry Stephenson
John Dyckman Brown II	Henry O'Neill
Ben	Ben Blue
Carlos	Carlos Ramirez
Private Adams	Frank Sully
Albert Coates	Himself
Mr. Nizby	Donald Meek
Amparo Novarro	Herself
Virginia O'Brien	Herself
The Wilde Twins	Themselves
Dick Deyo	Frank Jenks
Harry James Orchestra	Themselves
Xavier Cugat and Orchestra	Themselves

Distributor: M-G-M
Director: Richard Thorpe
Released: April 27, 1944

DAYS OF GLORY

Nina	Tamara Toumanova

Paul Henreid, Eleanor Parker and George Tobias in **Between Two Worlds** (Warner Bros.).

Semyon	Lowell Gilmore
Fedor	Hugo Haas
Olga	Dena Penn
Mitya	Glenn Vernon
Dimitri	Igor Dolgoruki
Petrov	Edward L. Durst
Johann Staub	Lou Crosby
Ducrenko	William Challee
Seminov	Joseph Vitale
Colonel Prilenko	Erford Gage
German Lieutenant	Ivan Triesault
Vera	Maria Bibikov
Anton	Edgar Licho
Mariya	Gretl Dupont
Von Rundhol	Peter Helmers

Vladimir	Gregory Peck
Sasha	Alan Reed
Yelena	Maria Palmer

Distributor: RKO
Director: Jacques Tourneur
Released: April 27, 1944

Louise Allbritton, Patric Knowles, Donald O'Connor
and Susanna Foster in **This is the Life** (Universal).

James Ellison, Simone Simon and Chick Chandler in **Johnny Doesn't Live Here Any More** (Monogram).

Michael O'Shea, Vincent Price, Stanley Prager, William Eythe, John Archer, Bob Bailey and Harry Morgan in **The Eve of St. Mark** (20th Century-Fox).

BETWEEN TWO WORLDS

Tom Prior	John Garfield
Henry	Paul Henreid
Thompson	Sydney Greenstreet
Ann	Eleanor Parker
Scrubby	Edmund Gwenn
Pete Musick	George Tobias
Lingley	George Coulouris
Maxine	Faye Emerson
Mrs. Midget	Sara Allgood
Rev. William Duke	Dennis King
Mrs. Cliveden-Banks	Isobel Elsom
Cliveden-Banks	Gilbert Emery
Dispatcher	Lester Matthews
Clerk	Pat O'Moore

Distributor: Warner Bros.
Director: Edward A. Blatt
Released: May 5, 1944

Jack Carson and Jane Wyman in **Make Your Own Bed** (Warner Bros.).

THIS IS THE LIFE

Jimmy	Donald O'Connor
Angela	Susanna Foster
Sally McGuire	Peggy Ryan
Harriet	Louise Allbritton
Hilary Jarret	Patric Knowles
Aunt Betsy	Dorothy Peterson
Doctor Plum	Jonathan Hale
Gus	Eddie Quillan
Eddie	Frank Jenks

Music Teacher	Frank Puglia
Leon	Maurice Marsac
Mrs. Tiggett	Virginia Brissac

Also: Ray Eberle and his Orchestra, Bobby Brooks Quartet

Distributor: Universal
Director: Felix Feist
Released: May 10, 1944

Robert Young, Margaret O'Brien and Charles Laughton in **The Canterville Ghost** (M-G-M).

JOHNNY DOESN'T LIVE HERE ANYMORE

Kathie	Simone Simon
Mike	James Ellison
Johnny	William Terry
Mrs. Collins	Minna Gombell
Jack	Chick Chandler
Judge	Alan Dinehart
Sally	Gladys Blake
Jeff	Robert Mitchum
Irene	Dorothy Granger
George	Grady Sutton
Mr. Collins	Chester Clute
Shrew	Fern Emmett
Gremlin	Jerry Maren
Gladys	Janet Shaw

Distributor: Monogram
Director: Joe May
Released: May 15, 1944

Robert Bailey, Trudy Marshall and Ronald Graham in
Ladies of Washington (20th Century-Fox).

THE EVE OF ST. MARK

Janet Feller	Anne Baxter
Private Quizz West	William Eythe
Private Thomas Mulveray	Michael O'Shea
Private Francis Marion	Vincent Price
Nell West	Ruth Nelson
Deckman West	Ray Collins
Private Glinka	Stanley Prager
Private Shevlin	Henry Morgan
Corporal Tate	Robert Bailey
Lill Bird	Joann Dolan
Sal Bird	Toni Favor
Sergeant Ruby	George Matthews
Private Carter	John Archer
Sergeant Kriven	Murray Alper
Zip West	Dickie Moore
Pepita	Jovan E. Rola
Chaplain	Harry Shannon
Guide	David Essex
Sheep Wagon Driver	Arthur Hohl
The Captain	Roger Clark
Neil West	Jimmy Clark

Distributor: 20th Century-Fox
Director: John M. Stahl
Released: May 22, 1944

MAKE YOUR OWN BED

Jerry Curtis	Jack Carson
Susan Courtney	Jane Wyman
Walter Whirtle	Alan Hale

Vivian Whirtle	Irene Manning
Boris Murphy	George Tobias
Lester Knight	Robert Shayne
Marie Gruber	Tala Birell
Fritz Alten	Ricardo Cortez
Elsa Wehmer	Marjorie Hoshelle
Paul Hassen	Kurt Katch
Mr. Brooking	Harry Bradley
F.B.I. Man	William Kennedy

Distributor: Warner Bros.
Director: Peter Godfrey
Released: May 22, 1944

THE CANTERVILLE GHOST

Sir Simon de Canterville	
	Charles Laughton
The Ghost	
Cuffy Williams	Margaret O'Brien
Sergeant Benson	William Gargan
Lord Canterville	Reginald Owen
Big Harry	Rags Ragland
Mrs. Umney	Una O'Connor
Sir Valentine Williams	Donald Stuart
Mrs. Polverdine	Elisabeth Risdon
Lieutenant Kane	Frank Faylen
Mr. Potts	Lumsden Hare
Metropolus	Mike Mazurki
Hector	William Moss
Eddie	Bobby Readick
Bugsy McDougle	Marc Cramer
Jordan	William Tannen
Anthony de Canterville	Peter Lawford

Distributor: M-G-M
Director: Jules Dassin
Released: May 22, 1944

LADIES OF WASHINGTON

Carol	Trudy Marshall
Dr. Mayberry	Ronald Graham
Michael	Anthony Quinn
Jerry	Sheila Ryan
Stephen	Robert Bailey
Helen	Beverly Whitney
Adelaide	Jackie Paley
Investigator	Carleton Young

Mother Henry	John Philliber
Vicky	Robin Raymond
Amy	Doris Merrick
Betty	Barbara Booth
Frieda	Jo-Carroll Dennison
Marjorie	Lillian Porter
Lieutenant Lake	Harry Shannon
Nellie	Ruby Dandridge
Inspector Saunders	Charles D. Brown
Dr. Crane	Pierre Watkin
Mrs. Crane	Nella Walker
Dorothy	Inna Gest
Nurse	Rosalind Keith
Susan	Edna Mae Jones

Distributor: 20th Century-Fox
Director: Louis King
Released: May 25, 1944

Marten Lamont, John Carradine, Claire Rochelle and Billy Nelson in **Waterfront** (PRC).

WATERFRONT

Victor Marlowe	John Carradine
Dr. Carl Decker	J. Carrol Naish
Freda Hauser	Maris Wrixon
Max Kramer	Edwin Maxwell
Jerry Donovan	Terry Frost
Zimmerman	John Bleifer
Mike Gorman	Marten Lamont
Mrs. Hauser	Olga Fabian
Maisie	Claire Rochelle
Butch	Billy Nelson

Distributor: PRC
Director: Steve Sekely
Released: May 25, 1944

THE BLACK PARACHUTE

General von Bodenbach	John Carradine
Marya Orloff	Osa Massen
Michael Lindley	Larry Parks
Olga	Jeanne Bates
King Stephen	Jonathan Hale
Col. Pavlec	Ivan Triesault
Nicholas	Trevor Bardette
Joseph	Art Smith
Pilot	Robert Lowell
Kur Vandan	Charles Wagenheim

Erik Dundeen	Charles Waldron
Cobbler	Ernie Adams

Distributor: Columbia
Director: Lew Landers
Released: June 5, 1944

SECRET COMMAND

Sam Gallagher	Pat O'Brien
Jill McCann	Carole Landis
Jeff Gallagher	Chester Morris
Lea Damaron	Ruth Warrick
Red Kelly	Barton MacLane
Brownell	Tom Tully
Miller	Wallace Ford
Max Lessing	Howard Freeman

Jeanne Bates, Art Smith and Larry Parks in **The Black Parachute** (Columbia).

Chester Morris and Pat O'Brien in **Secret Command** (Columbia).

Ben Royall	Erik Rolf
Curly	Matt McHugh
Shawn	Frank Sully
Simms	Frank Fenton
James Thane	Charles D. Brown
Joan	Carol Nugent

Distributor: Columbia
Director: Eddie Sutherland
Released: June 5, 1944

HAIL THE CONQUERING HERO

Woodrow	Eddie Bracken
Libby	Ella Raines
Mr. Noble	Raymond Walburn
Sergeant	William Demarest

Eddie Bracken and William Demarest in **Hail the Conquering Hero** (Paramount).

Deanna Durbin and Gene Kelly in **Christmas Holiday** (Universal).

Gabriel Dell and Leo Gorcey in **Follow the Leader**
(Monogram).

Chairman	Franklin Pangborn	American Legion Bandleader	Johnny Sinclair
Libby's Aunt	Elizabeth Patterson	Mr. Schultz	Torben Meyer
Mrs. Truesmith	Georgia Caine	Western Union Man	Chester Conklin
Bugsy	Freddie Steele	Reverend Upperman	Arthur Hoyt
Forrest Noble	Bill Edwards	Sheriff	George Melford
Doc Bissell	Harry Hayden	Town Painter	Frank Moran
Judge Dennis	Jimmy Conlin	Town Councilmen	Tom McGuire
Corporal	Jimmy Dundee		Philo McCullough
Political Boss	Alan Bridge		Franklyn Farnum
Mrs. Noble	Esther Howard		Kenneth Gibson
Marine Colonel	Robert Warwick	Manager Of Cafe	Paul Porcasi
Juke	Len Hendry	Bartender	George Anderson
Jonesy	James Damore	Singer	Julie Gibson
Bill	Stephen Gregory	Marine Colonel's Wife	Mildred Harris
Progressive Bandleader	Victor Potel	Mamie's Mother	Dot Farley
Alfie, Junior Bandleader	Merrill Rodin	Mamie	Marjean Neville
Regular Band Leader	Jack Norton	Colonel's Daughter	Maxine Fife

Telephone Operator .... Pauline Drake

Distributor: Paramount
Director: Preston Sturges
Released: June 7, 1944

CHRISTMAS HOLIDAY

Jackie Lamont
.... Deanna Durbin

Abigail Martin
Robert Manette .... Gene Kelly
Simon Fenimore .... Richard Whorf
Charles Mason .... Dean Harens
Valerie de Merode .... Gladys George
Mrs. Manette .... Gale Sondergaard
Gerald Tyler .... David Bruce

Distributor: Universal
Director: Robert Siodmak
Released: June 7, 1944

FOLLOW THE LEADER

Muggs .... Leo Gorcey
Glimpy .... Huntz Hall
Fingers .... Gabriel Dell
Spider .... Billy Benedict
Milly .... Joan Marsh
Larry .... Jack LaRue
Mrs. McGinnis .... Mary Gordon
Cop .... J. Farrell MacDonald
Danny .... Dave Durand
Speed .... Bobby Stone
Dave .... Jimmy Strand
Skinny .... Bud Gorman
Also: Gene Austin and the Sherrill Sisters

Distributor: Monogram
Director: William Beaudine
Released: June 8, 1944

THE MASK OF DIMITRIOS

Mr. Peters .... Sydney Greenstreet
Dimitrios .... Zachary Scott
Irana .... Faye Emerson
Leyden .... Peter Lorre
Grodek .... Victor Francen

Bulic .... Steven Geray
Mme. Chavez .... Florence Bates
Marukakis .... Eduardo Ciannelli
Col. Haki .... Kurt Katch
Mrs. Bulic .... Marjorie Hoshelle
Werner .... Georges Metaxa
Pappas .... John Abbott
Abdul .... Monte Blue
Konrad .... David Hoffman

Distributor: Warner Bros.
Director: Jean Negulesco
Released: June 8, 1944

Peter Lorre and Kurt Katch in **The Mask of Dimitrios** (Warner Bros.).

SECRETS OF SCOTLAND YARD

John Usher
.... Edgar Barrier

Robert Usher
Sudan Ainger .... Stephanie Bachelor
Sir Christopher Belt .... C. Aubrey Smith
Waterlow .... Lionel Atwill
Sir Reginald Meade .... Henry Stephenson
Mortimer Cope .... John Abbott
Roylott Bevan .... Walter Kingsford
Josef .... Martin Kosleck
Alfred Morgan .... Forrester Harvey
Mason .... Frederic Worlock
Col. Hedley .... Matthew Boulton
David Usher .... Bobby Cooper

Distributor: Republic

Louis V. Arco in **Secrets of Scotland Yard** (Republic).

Director: George Blair
Released: June 9, 1944

I LOVE A SOLDIER

Eva Morgan	Paulette Goddard
Dan Gilgore	Sonny Tufts
Cissy Grant	Mary Treen
Stiff Banks	Walter Sande
Jenny	Ann Doran
Etta Lane	Beulah Bondi
Gracie	Marie McDonald
Murph	Barry Fitzgerald
Williams	James Bell
John	Hugh Beaumont
Little Soldier	Frank Albertson
Doctor	Roy Gordon

Distributor: Paramount
Director: Mark Sandrich
Released: June 14, 1944

MARINE RAIDERS

Major Steve Lockhard	Pat O'Brien
Capt. Dan Craig	Robert Ryan
Ellen Foster	Ruth Hussey
Sergeant Louis Leary	Frank McHugh
Sergeant Maguire	Barton MacLane
Jimmy	Richard Martin
Miller	Edmund Glover
Tony Hewitt	Russell Wade
Lt. Harrigan	Robert Anderson
Lt. Sherwood	Michael St. Angel
Sally	Martha MacVicar

Cook .... Harry Brown

Distributor: RKO
Director: Harold Schuster
Released: July 11, 1944

TAKE IT OR LEAVE IT

Phil Baker .... Himself
Phil Silvers .... Himself
Eddie .... Edward Ryan
Kate Collins .... Marjorie Massow
Herb Gordon .... Stanley Prager
Dr. Edward Preston .... Roy Gordon
Miss Burke .... Nana Bryant

Robert Ryan, Russell Wade, Selmer Jackson and Pat O'Brien in **Marine Raiders** (RKO).

Paulette Goddard with Sonny Tufts in **I Love a Soldier** (Paramount).

Ling Tan .... Walter Huston
Mrs. Ling Tan .... Aline MacMahon
Wu Lien .... Akim Tamiroff
Lao Er .... Turhan Bey
Lao San .... Hurd Hatfield
Orchid .... Frances Rafferty
Third Cousin's Wife .... Agnes Moorehead
Third Cousin .... Henry Travers
Captain Sato .... Robert Lewis
Japanese Kitchen Overseer .... J. Carrol Naish
Lao Ta .... Robert Bice
Mrs. Wu Lien .... Jacqueline De Wit
Fourth Cousin .... Clarence Lung
Neighbor Shen .... Paul E. Burns
Wu Soo .... Anna Demetrio

Program Director .... Carleton Young
Secretary .... Ann Corcoran
Mrs. Preston .... Nella Walker
Mrs. Bramble .... Renie Riano
Taxi Driver .... Frank Jenks
Truck Driver .... B. S. Pully

Distributor: 20th Century-Fox
Director: Benjamin Stoloff
Released: July 17, 1944

DRAGON SEED

Jade .... Katharine Hepburn

Edward Ryan with Marjorie Massow in **Take It or Leave It** (20th Century-Fox).

255

Major Yohagi	Ted Hecht	Japanese Official	Leonard Strong
Captain Yasuda	Abner Biberman	Narrator	Lionel Barrymore
Old Peddler	Leonard Mudie		
Japanese Diplomat	Charles Lung		
Student	Benson Fong		
Japanese Guard	Philip Van Zandt		

Distributor: M-G-M
Directors: Jack Conway, Harold S. Bucquet
Released: July 18, 1944

Japanese Officer	Al Hill
Japanese Soldier	J. Alex Havier
Leader Of City People	Philip Ahn
Speaker With Movies	Roland Got
Young Farmer	Robert Lee
Old Clerk	Frank Puglia
Hysterical Woman	Claire DuBrey
Innkeeper	Lee Tung Foo
Japanese Soldier	Jay Novello

MR. WINKLE GOES TO WAR

Wilbert Winkle	Edward G. Robinson
Amy Winkle	Ruth Warrick
Barry	Ted Donaldson
Jack Pettigrew	Bob Haymes
Sgt. 'Alphabet'	Richard Lane
Joe Tinker	Robert Armstrong

Frances Rafferty in **Dragon Seed** (M-G-M).

Don Ameche and Charles Bickford in **Wing and a Prayer** (20th Century-Fox).

Also: George Mathews, B. S. Pully, Dave Willock, Murray Alper, Charles Lang, Irving Bacon, John Miles, Joe Haworth, Charles Smith, Ray Teal, Matt McHugh, Charles Trowbridge, John Kelly, Larry Thompson, Billy Lechner.

Distributor: 20th Century-Fox
Director: Henry Hathaway
Released: July 24, 1944

THE SEVENTH CROSS

George Heisler	Spencer Tracy
Toni	Signe Hasso
Paul Roeder	Hume Cronyn
Liesel Roeder	Jessica Tandy
Mme. Marelli	Agnes Moorehead
Franz Marnet	Herbert Rudley
Poldi Schlamm	Felix Bressart
Wallau	Ray Collins
Zillach	Alexander Granach
Mrs. Sauer	Katherine Locke
Bruno Sauer	George Macready
Fiedler	Paul Guilfoyle
Dr. Lowenstein	Steven Geray
Leo Herman	Kurt Katch
Leni	Kaaren Verne
Fuellgrabe	Konstantin Shayne
Bellani	George Suzanne
Overkamp	John Wengraf
Fahrenburg	George Zucco
Hellwig	Steven Muller
Fraulein Bachmann	Eily Malyon

Hume Cronyn, Spencer Tracy and Paul Guilfoyle in
The Seventh Cross (M-G-M).

Richard Erdman, Robert Hutton and Joyce Reynolds
in **Janie** (Warner Bros.).

Laraine Day and Alan Marshal in **Bride by Mistake**
(RKO).

Distributor: M-G-M
Director: Fred Zinneman
Released: July 24, 1944

JANIE

Pvt. Dick Lawrence	Robert Hutton
Charles Conway	Edward Arnold
Lucille Conway	Ann Harding
John van Brunt	Robert Benchley
Reardon	Alan Hale
Elsbeth Conway	Clare Foley
Mrs. Thelma Lawrence	Barbara Brown
April	Hattie McDaniel
Wilber 'Scooper' Nolan	Dick Erdman
Mickey	Jackie Moran
Paula Rainey	Ann Gillis
Bernadine Dodd	Ruth Tobey
Carrie Lou Trivett	Virginia Patton
Hortense Bennett	Colleen Townsend
'Dead Pan' Hackett	William Frambes
Susan Wiley	George Lee Settle
Photographer	Peter Stackpole
Sgt. Carl	Michael Harrison
Colonel Lucas	Russell Hicks
Janie	Joyce Reynolds

Distributor: Warner Bros.
Director: Michael Curtiz
Released: July 25, 1944

BRIDE BY MISTAKE

Tony	Alan Marshal

Mary Lee, William Terry, Cheryl Walker, Charles Arnt, Milton Kibbee, Addison Richards and Jackie Moran in **Three Little Sisters** (Republic).

Stanley Ridges, Charles Halton, Alexander Knox,
Geraldine Fitzgerald and Charles Coburn in **Wilson**
(20th Century-Fox).

Norah	Laraine Day
Sylvia	Marsha Hunt
Phil Vernon	Allyn Joslyn
Connors	Edgar Buchanan
Corey	Michael St. Angel
Ross	Marc Cramer
Donald	William Post, Jr.
Chaplain	Bruce Edwards
Jane	Nancy Gates
Samuel	Slim Summerville
Major Harvey	John Miljan
Lieutenant Wilson	Robert Anderson

Distributor: RKO
Director: Richard Wallace
Released: July 27, 1944

THREE LITTLE SISTERS

Sue Scott	Mary Lee
Hallie Scott	Ruth Terry
Lily Scott	Cheryl Walker
Pvt. Robert Mason	William Terry
Chad Jones	Jackie Moran
Ezra Larkin	Charles Arnt
Pvt. 'Rosey' Rownan	Frank Jenks
Pvt. Ferguson	William Shirley
Ambrose Pepperdine	Tom Fadden
Twitchell	Tom London
Tom Scott	Milt Kibbee
Col. Flemming	Addison Richards
Mabel	Lillian Randolph
Benjy	Sam 'Deacon' McDaniel

Mayor Thatcher .... Forrest Taylor

Distributor: Republic
Director: Joseph Santley
Released: July 28, 1944

WILSON

Woodrow Wilson .... Alexander Knox
Prof. Henry Holmes .... Charles Coburn
Edith Wilson .... Geraldine Fitzgerald
Joseph Tumulty .... Thomas Mitchell
Ellen Wilson .... Ruth Nelson
Senator Henry Cabot Lodge
.... Sir Cedric Hardwicke
Williams Gibbs McAdoo .... Vincent Price
George Felton .... William Eythe
Eleanor Wilson .... Mary Anderson
Margaret Wilson .... Ruth Ford
Josephus Daniels .... Sidney Blackmer
Jessie Wilson .... Madeleine Forbes
Admiral Grayson .... Stanley Ridges
Eddie Foy .... Eddie Foy, Jr.
Colonel House .... Charles Halton
Senator B. H. Jones .... Thurston Hall
Edward Sullivan .... J. M. Kerrigan
Jim Beeker .... James Rennie
Helen Bones .... Katherine Locke
Secretary Lansing .... Stanley Logan
Clemenceau .... Marcel Dalio
William Jennings Bryan .... Edwin Maxwell
Lloyd George .... Clifford Brooke

Chick Chandler and George Meeker in **Seven Doors to Death** (PRC).

Anne Gillis, Richard Lane and Elyse Knox in **A Wave, a Wac and a Marine** (Monogram).

Von Bernstorff .... Tonio Selwart
Senator Watson .... John Ince
Senator Bromfield .... Charles Miller
Barney Baruch .... Francis X. Bushman
McCoombs .... George Macready
Granddaughter .... Phyllis Brooks
Charles F. Murphy .... Cy Kendall
Ike Hoover .... Roy Roberts
Jennie, The Maid .... Anne O'Neal
Secretary Lane .... Arthur Loft
Secretary Colby .... Russell Gaige
Secretary Payne .... Jamesson Shade
Secretary Baker .... Reginald Sheffield
Secretary Garrison .... Robert Middlemass
Secretary Burleson .... Matt Moore
Secretary Houston .... George Anderson
Chief Justice White .... Joseph J. Greene
Secretary William B. Wilson .... Larry McGrath
Senator .... Gilson Gowland
Champ Clark .... Davison Clark
Jeannette Rankin .... Hilda Plowright
Usher .... Reed Hadley
La Follette .... Ralph Dunn
General Bliss .... Major Sam Harris

Distributor: 20th Century-Fox
Director: Henry King
Released: August 2, 1944

SEVEN DOORS TO DEATH

June Clyde, Chick Chandler, George Meeker,

Ann Sothern and Tom Drake in **Maisie Goes to Reno** (M-G-M).

Michael Raffetto, Gregory Gaye, Edgar Dearing, Rebel Randall, Milton Wallace, Casey MacGregor.

Distributor: PRC
Director: Elmer Clifton
Released: August 5, 1944

A WAVE, A WAC AND A MARINE

Marian	Elyse Knox
Margaret Ames	Sally Eilers
Betty	Ramsay Ames
Judy	Ann Gillis
Producer R. J.	Alan Dinehart
Eileen	Marjorie Woodworth
Henny	Henny Youngman
Red	Charles 'Red' Marshall

Singer	Connie Haines
Marty Allen	Richard Lane
Mike	Cy Kendall
Newswoman	Aileen Pringle
Freddie Rich and Orchestra	Themselves

Distributor: Monogram
Director: Phil Karlstein
Released: August 12, 1944

MAISIE GOES TO RENO

Maisie Revier	Ann Sothern
'Flip' Hennahan	John Hodiak
Bill Fullerton	Tom Drake
Winifred Ashbourne	Marta Linden
Roger Pelham	Paul Cavanagh

Gloria Fullerton	Ava Gardner
J. E. Clave	Bernard Nedell
Jerry	Roland Dupree
Tommy Cutter	Chick Chandler
Elaine	Bunny Waters
Parsons	Donald Meek

Distributor: M-G-M
Director: Harry Beaumont
Released: August 15, 1944

ENEMY OF WOMEN

Maria Brandt	Claudia Drake
Paul Joseph Boebbels	Paul Andor

Frederick Giermann with Bruce Bennett in **U-Boat Prisoner** (Columbia).

Released: August 21, 1944

U-BOAT PRISONER

Archie Gibbs	Bruce Bennett
Kapitan Ganz	Erik Rolf
Alfonse Lamont	John Abbott
Rudehoff	John Wengraf
Commander Bristol	Robert Williams
Clyde Hamilton	Kenneth MacDonald
Biencawicz	Erwin Kalser
Sigo van Der Brek	Egon Brecher
First Officer Kerck	Frederick Giermann
Hagemann	Arno Frey
Dorner	Sven-Hugo Borg

H. B. Warner and Claudia Drake in **Enemy of Women** (Monogram).

Dr. Hans Traeger	Donald Woods
Colonel Brandt	H. B. Warner
Madga Quandt	Sigrid Gurie
Mr. Quandt	Ralph Morgan
Bertha	Gloria Stuart
Wallburg	Robert Barrat
Jenny Hartmann	Beryl Wallace
Krause	Byron Foulger
Hanussen	Lester Dorr
Hanke	Craig Whitley
Uncle Hugo	Charles Halton
Mrs. Bendler	Marin Sais

Distributor: Monogram
Director: Alfred Zeisler

Lana Turner with James Craig in **Marriage Is a Private Affair** (M-G-M).

Craig Stevens, Alexis Smith, John Ridgely, Ann Sheridan, Jack Carson, Jane Wyman and Eve Arden in **The Doughgirls** (Warner Bros.).

Lt. Hagen	Nelson Leigh	Joseph I. Murdock	Hugh Marlowe
Lt. Blake	Fred Graff	Mrs. Selworth	Natalie Schafer
Commander Prentiss	Trevor Bardette	Major Bob Wilton	Keenan Wynn
Lt. Nolan	Paul Conrad	Ted Mortimer	Herbert Rudley
Braustig	Eric Feldary	Mr. Selworth	Paul Cavanagh
		Mr. Scofield	Morris Ankrum
		Martha	Jane Green
		Bill Rice	Tom Drake
		Mary Saunders	Shirley Patterson
		Minister	Rev. Neal Dodd
		Nurse	Nana Bryant
		Senora Guizman	Cecilia Callejo
		Mrs. Courtland West	Virginia Brissac
		Ned Bolton	Byron Foulger
		Col. Ryder	Addison Richards

Distributor: Columbia
Director: Lew Landers
Released: August 22, 1944

MARRIAGE IS A PRIVATE AFFAIR

Theo West	Lana Turner
Captain Miles Lancing	James Craig
Lieutenant Tom West	John Hodiak
Sissy Mortimer	Frances Gifford

Distributor: M-G-M

Director: Robert Z. Leonard
Released: August 23, 1944

THE DOUGHGIRLS

Edna	Ann Sheridan
Nan	Alexis Smith
Arthur	Jack Carson
Vivian	Jane Wyman
Mrs. Cadman	Irene Manning
Slade	Charles Ruggles
Natalia	Eve Arden
Julian	John Ridgely
Breckenridge Drake	Alan Mowbray
Buckley	John Alexander
Tom	Craig Stevens
Mrs. Cartwright	Barbara Brown
Lieutenant Keary	Stephen Richards
Mr. Jordan	Francis Pierlot
Judge Franklin	Donald MacBride
Timothy Walsh	Regis Toomey
The Stranger	Joe de Rita

Distributor: Warner Bros.
Director: James V. Kern
Released: August 30, 1944

TILL WE MEET AGAIN

John	Ray Milland
Sister Clothilde	Barbara Britton

Ray Milland and Barbara Britton in **Till We Meet Again** (Paramount).

Vitrey (Mayor)	Walter Slezak
Mother Superior	Lucile Watson
Major Krupp	Konstantin Shayne
Cabeau	Vladimir Sokoloff
Madame Sarroux	Marguerite D'Alvarez
Elise	Mona Freeman
Henri Maret	William Edmunds
Waiter-Gaston	George Davis
Examiner	Peter Helmers
Gestapo Chief	John Wengraf
Portress	Mira McKinney
Mme. Bouchard	Tala Birell

Distributor: Paramount
Director: Frank Borzage
Released: August 30, 1944

STORM OVER LISBON

Maritza	Vera Hruba Ralston
John Craig	Richard Arlen
Deresco	Erich von Stroheim
Alexis Vanderlyn	Otto Kruger
Blanco	Eduardo Ciannelli
Bill Flanagan	Robert Livingston
Evelyn	Mona Barrie
Murgatroyd	Frank Orth
Maude	Sarah Edwards
Agatha	Alice Fleming
Street Singer	Leon Belasco
Henchman	Kenne Duncan

Distributor: Republic
Director: George Sherman
Released: September 5, 1944

SAN DIEGO, I LOVE YOU

John Caldwell	Jon Hall
Virginia McCooley	Louise Allbritton
Philip McCooley	Edward Everett Horton
Nelson	Eric Blore
Bus Driver	Buster Keaton
Miss Jones	Irene Ryan
Walter McCooley	Rudy Wissler
Joey McCooley	Gerald Perreau
Larry McCooley	Charles Bates
Pete McCooley	Don Davis
Miss Lake	Florence Lake

Richard Arlen, Erich von Stroheim and Eduardo Ciannelli in **Storm Over Lisbon** (Republic).

Charles Bates, Rudy Wissler, Edward Everett Horton, Louise Allbritton and Don Davis in **San Diego, I Love You** (Universal).

Percy	Chester Clute
Mrs. Lovelace	Sarah Selby
Mrs. Callope	Fern Emmett

Distributor: Universal
Director: Reginald Le Borg
Released: September 5, 1944

RAINBOW ISLAND

Lona	Dorothy Lamour
Toby Smith	Eddie Bracken
Pete Jenkins	Gil Lamb
Ken Masters	Barry Sullivan
Dr. Curtis	Forrest Orr
Queen Okalana	Anne Revere
High Priest Kahuna	Reed Hadley

Barry Sullivan, Dorothy Lamour, Eddie Bracken, Gil Lamb and Forrest Orr in **Rainbow Island** (Paramount).

Alcoa	Marc Lawrence
Executioner	Adia Kuznetzoff
Miki	Olga San Juan
Moana	Elena Verdugo

Distributor: Paramount
Director: Ralph Murphy
Released: September 5, 1944

WHEN THE LIGHTS GO ON AGAIN

Ted Benson	Jimmy Lydon
Arline Cary	Barbara Belden
Mr. Benson	Grant Mitchell
Mrs. Benson	Dorothy Peterson
Bill Regan	Regis Toomey
Pat Benson	George Cleveland
Tom Cary	Harry Shannon
Joey Benson	Warren Mills
First Marine	Williard Jielson
Second Marine	Jac Turrell
Third Marine	Bill Nelson
Medical Officer	Larry Thompson
Middle Aged Woman	Myrtle Ferguson
Old Panhandler	Emmett Lynn
Peggy	Jill Browning
Barbara	Roberta Carlin
Jim Bagby	Guy Blake
First Farmer	Al Stewart
Second Farmer	Elmo Lincoln
Engineer	Joseph Crehan

Distributor: PRC
Director: William K. Howard
Released: September 14, 1944

IN THE MEANTIME, DARLING

Maggie	Jeanne Crain
Lieut. Daniel Ferguson	Frank Latimore
H. B. Preston	Eugene Pallette
Mrs. Preston	Mary Nash
Lieut. Red Pianatowski	Stanley Prager
Shirley	Gale Robbins
Jerry Armstrong	Jane Randolph
Mrs. MacAndrews	Doris Merrick
Mrs. Sayre	Cara Williams
Mrs. Bennett	Ann Corcoran
Major Phillips	Reed Hadley
Mrs. Nelson	Heather Angel

Jeanne Crain and Frank Latimore in **In the Meantime, Darling** (20th Century-Fox).

Harry Shannon, Barbara Belden and Jimmy Lydon in **When the Lights Go On Again** (PRC).

Evelyn	Doris Merrick
Hartley	Arthur Space
Mayme	Veda Ann Borg
Egbert	Bobby Blake
Charlton	Frank Fenton
Hartman	James Bush
Dutchy	Phil Van Zandt
Aunt Sophie	Esther Howard
Grandpa	Robert Dudley
Motor Policeman	Edgar Dearing
Manning	Selmer Jackson
Butler	Harry Hayden
Station Attendant	Francis Ford
Drunk	Jack Norton

Mrs. Farnum	Bonnie Bannon
Lieut. Farnum	William Colby
Colonel Corkery	Cliff Clark
Mrs. Corkery	Elisabeth Risdon
Mrs. Cook	Majorie Massow
Lieut. Sayre	Lee Bennett
Lieut. Sullivan	Roger Clark

Distributor: 20th Century-Fox
Director: Otto Preminger
Released: September 22, 1944

THE BIG NOISE

Laurel and Hardy	Themselves

Oliver Hardy, Esther Howard and Stan Laurel in **The Big Noise** (20th Century-Fox).

Conductor	Charles Wilson	Old Man Bartoc	Morris Carnovsky
Speaker	Ken Christy	Frank	Lloyd Bridges
Jap Officer	Beal Wong	Altmeter	Eric Feldary
German Officer	Louis Arco	Mrs. Varin	Helen Beverly

Distributor: 20th Century-Fox
Director: Mal St. Clair
Released: September 22, 1944

THE MASTER RACE

Von Beck	George Coulouris
Phil Carson	Stanley Ridges
Helena	Osa Massen
Andrei	Carl Esmond
Nina	Nancy Gates

William Forsythe	Gavin Muir
Katry	Paul Guilfoyle
Sgt. O'Farrell	Richard Nugent
Schmidt	Louis Donath
John	Herbert Rudley
Baby	Ghislaine Perreau
Jacob Weiner	Jason Robards
George Rudan	Merrill Roden

Distributor: RKO
Director: Herbert J. Biberman
Released: September 22, 1944

George Coulouris and others in **The Master Race** (RKO).

Grey Shadow, Sharyn Moffett, Jill Esmond, Jerry Mickelson, Larry Olsen and Bobby Larson in **My Pal, Wolf** (RKO).

MY PAL, WOLF

Gretchen	Sharyn Moffett
Miss Munn	Jill Esmond
Mrs. Blevin	Una O'Connor
Wilson	George Cleveland
Papa Eisdaar	Charles Arnt
Ruby	Claire Carleton
Mrs. Anstey	Leona Maricle
Mr. Anstey	Bruce Edwards
Secretary Of War	Edward Fielding
Mama Eisdaar	Alga Fabian
Fred	Larry Olsen
Alf	Jerry Michelson
Karl	Bobby Larson
Sergeant Blake	Marc Cramer
Wolf	Grey Shadow

Distributor: RKO
Director: Alfred Werker
Released: September 25, 1944

THE IMPATIENT YEARS

Janie Anderson	Jean Arthur
Andy Anderson	Lee Bowman
William Smith	Charles Coburn
Judge	Edgar Buchanan
Bell 'Boy'	Charley Grapewin
Henry Fairchild	Phil Brown
Minister	Harry Davenport

Minister's Wife	Jane Darwell
Hotel Clerk	Grant Mitchell
Top Sergeant	Frank Jenks
Counter Man	Frank Orth
Marriage Clerk	Charles Arnt
Attorney	Robert Emmett Keane

Distributor: Columbia
Director: Irving Cummings
Released: September 25, 1944

THE CONSPIRATORS

Irene	Hedy Lamarr
Vincent	Paul Henreid

Lee Bowman and Jean Arthur in **The Impatient Years** (Columbia).

Quintanilla	Sydney Greenstreet
Bernazsky	Peter Lorre
Von Mohr	Victor Francen
Capt. Pereira	Joseph Calleia
Rosa	Carol Thurston
Miguel	Vladimir Sokoloff
Almeida	Eduardo Ciannelli
Dr. Schmitt	Steven Geray
Lutzke	Kurt Katch
Wynat	Gregory Gay
Croupier	Marcel Dalio
The Con Man	George Macready
Mrs. Benson	Doris Lloyd
Leiris	Louis Mercier

Jennings	Monte Blue
Page Boy	Billy Roy
Antonio	David Hoffman
The Slugger	Otto Reichow
Waiter	Leon Belasco
Casino Attendant	Frank Reicher

Distributor: Warner Bros.
Director: Jean Negulesco
Released: October 17, 1944

TO HAVE AND HAVE NOT

Harry Morgan	Humphrey Bogart
Eddie	Walter Brennan
Marie Browning	Lauren Bacall
Hellene de Bursac	Dolores Moran
Cricket	Hoagy Carmichael
Paul de Bursac	Walter Molnar
Lieut. Coyo	Sheldon Leonard
Gerard	Marcel Dalio
Johnson	Walter Sande
Capt. Renard	Dan Seymour
Bodyguard	Aldo Nadi

Victor Francen and Hedy Lamarr in **The Conspirators** (Warner Bros.).

Beauclerc	Paul Marion
Mrs. Beauclerc	Patricia Shay
Rosalie	Janette Grae
Bartender	Pat West
Horatio	Sir Lancelot

Walter Sande, Humphrey Bogart and Lauren Bacall
in **To Have and Have Not** (Warner Bros.).

Quartermaster	Eugene Borden
Negro Urchins	Elzie Emanuel
	Harold Garrison
Civilian	Pedro Regas
Headwaiter	Major Fred Farrell
Cashier	Adrienne D'Ambricourt
Emil	Emmett Smith
Degaullists	Maurice Marsac
	Fred Dosch
	George Suzanne
	Louis Mercier
	Crane Whitley
Detective	Hall Kelly
Chef	Joseph Milani
Naval Ensign	Ron Randell
Dancer	Audrey Armstrong
Cashier	Marguerita Sylva

Distributor: Warner Bros.
Director: Howard Hawks
Released: October 18, 1944

MINISTRY OF FEAR

Stephen Neale	Ray Milland
Carla Hilfe	Marjorie Reynolds
Willi Hilfe	Carl Esmond
Mrs. Bellane No. 2	Hillary Brooks
Prentise	Percy Waram
Cost (Travers)	Dan Duryea
Dr. Forrester	Alan Napier
Mr. Rennit	Erskine Sanford
Mr. Newland	Thomas Louden
Mrs. Bellane No. 1	Aminta Dyne

Ray Milland and Marjorie Reynolds in **Ministry of Fear** (Paramount).

Blind Man	Eustace Wyatt
Miss Penteel	Mary Field
Mr. Newboy	Byron Foulger
Dr. Morton	Lester Mathews

Distributor: Paramount
Director: Fritz Lang
Released: October 19, 1944

THE VERY THOUGHT OF YOU

Dave	Dennis Morgan
Janet	Eleanor Parker
'Fixit'	Dane Clark

Faye Emerson, Eleanor Parker, Dennis Morgan and Dane Clark in **The Very Thought of You** (Warner Bros.).

Cora	Faye Emerson
Mrs. Wheeler	Beulah Bondi
Pop Wheeler	Henry Travers
Fred	William Prince
Molly	Andrea King
Cal	John Alvin
Bernice	Marianne O'Brien
Ellie	Georgia Lee Settle
Soda Jerk	Dick Erdman
Minister	Francis Pierlot

Distributor: Warner Bros.
Director: Delmar Daves
Released: October 20, 1944

SOMETHING FOR THE BOYS

Chiquita Hart	Carmen Miranda

Michael O'Shea with Vivian Blaine in **Something for the Boys** (20th Century-Fox).

Sgt. Rocky Fulton	Michael O'Shea
Blossom Hart	Vivian Blaine
Harry Hart	Phil Silvers
Melanie Walker	Sheila Ryan
Sgt. Laddie Green	Perry Como
Lieut. Ashley Crothers	Glenn Langan
Lieutenant	Roger Clark
Secretary	Cara Williams
Col. Jeff L. Calhoun	Thurston Hall
Col. Grubbs	Clarence Kolb
Supervisor	Paul Hurst

Robert Walker, Van Johnson and Spencer Tracy in
Thirty Seconds Over Tokyo (M-G-M).

Jane Ball and Mark Daniels in **Winged Victory**
(20th Century-Fox).

Eddie Cantor in **Hollywood Canteen** (Warner
Bros.).

Southern Colonel .... Andrew Tombes

Distributor: 20th Century-Fox
Director: Lewis Seiler
Released: November 1, 1944

Dorothea Kent, Elyse Knox, Rick Vallin and Murray Alper in **Army Wives** (Monogram).

THIRTY SECONDS OVER TOKYO

Lt. Col. James H. Doolittle	Spencer Tracy
Ted Lawson	Van Johnson
David Thatcher	Robert Walker
Ellen Jones Lawson	Phyllis Thaxter
Dean Davenport	Tim Murdock
Davey Jones	Scott McKay
Bob Clever	Gordon McDonald
Charles McClure	Don De Fore
Bob Gray	Robert Mitchum
Shorty Manch	John R. Reilly
Doc White	Horace McNally
Lieutenant Randall	Donald Curtis
Lieutenant Miller	Louis Jean Heydt
Don Smith	William Phillips
Brick Holstrom	Douglas Cowan
Captain Ski York	Paul Langton
Lieutenant Jurika	Leon Ames
General	Moroni Olsen
Young Chung	Benson Fong
Old Chung	Dr. Hsin Chi
Girls In Officer's Club	Myrna Dell, Peggy Maley, Hazel Brooks, Elaine Shepard, Kay Williams

Jane	Dorothy Morris
Mrs. Parker	Ann Shoemaker
Mr. Parker	Alan Napier
Foo Ling	Wah Lee
Guerrilla Charlie	Ching Wah Lee
Emmy York	Jacqueline White
Dick Joyce	Jack McClendon
Pilot	John Kellogg
Spike Henderson	Peter Varney
M.P.	Steve Brodie
Captain Halsey	Morris Ankrum
Mrs. Jones	Selena Royle
Judge	Harry Hayden
Second Officer	Blake Edwards
Hoss Wyler	Will Walls
Hallmark	Jay Norris

Distributor: M-G-M
Director: Mervyn Leroy
Released: November 15, 1944

WINGED VICTORY

Frankie Davis	Lon McCallister
Helen	Jeanne Crain
Irving Miller	Edmond O'Brien
Jane Preston	Jane Ball
Alan Ross	Mark Daniels
Dorothy Ross	Jo-Carroll Dennison
Danny 'Pinky' Scariano	Don Taylor
Doctor	Lee J. Cobb

Dan Duryea and soldiers in **Main Street After Dark** (M-G-M).

Jane Frazee, Ruth Warren, Eddie Bruce and Pat
Lane in **She's a Sweetheart** (Columbia).

Ruth Miller	Judy Holliday	Cadet Peter Clark	Harry Lewis
O'Brian	Peter Lind Hayes	Officer	Ray Bidwell
Major Halper	Alan Baxter	Flight Surgeon	Henry Rowland
Mrs. Ross	Geraldine Wall	Captain Speer	Carroll Riddle
Whitey	Red Buttons	Carmen Miranda	Sascha Branstoff
Mr. Scariano	George Humbert	Master Of Ceremonies	Archie Robbins
Bobby Crills	Barry Nelson	Irving Jr.	Timmy Hawkins
Dave Anderson	Rune Hultman	Mrs. Gardner	Moyna MacGill
Jimmy Gardner	Richard Hogan	Man	Don Beddoe
Colonel Gibney	Phillip Bourneuf	Wac	Frances Gladwin
Captain McIntyre	Gary Merrill	Cigarette Girl	Sally Yarnell
Colonel Ross	Damian O'Flynn		
Lieutenant Thompson	George Reeves		
Barker	George Petrie		
Milhauser	Alfred Ryder		
Adams	Karl Malden		
Gleason	Martin Ritt		

Distributor: 20th Century-Fox
Director: George Cukor
Released: November 22, 1944

HOLLYWOOD CANTEEN

Slim	Robert Hutton
Sergeant	Dane Clark
Angela	Janis Paige
Mr. Brodel	Jonathan Hale
Mrs. Brodel	Barbara Brown
Soldiers On Deck	Steve Richards
	Dick Erdman
Marine Sergeant	James Flavin
Dance Director	Eddie Marr
Director	Theodore von Eltz
Captain	Ray Teal
Orchestra Leader	Rudolph Friml, Jr.
Tough Marine	George Turner
Stan	Jimmy Conlin
Burke	Ralph Langford
Mrs. Lowry	Dorothy Christy
Benson	Phil Warren
Kirby	Ralph Lewis

Themselves: Joan Leslie, Andrews Sisters, Jack Benny, Joe E. Brown, Eddie Cantor, Kitty Carlisle, Jack Carson, Joan Crawford, Helmut Dantine, Bette Davis, Faye Emerson, Victor Francen, John Garfield, Sydney Greenstreet, Alan Hale, Paul Henreid, Andrea King, Peter Lorre, Ida Lupino, Irene Manning, Nora Martin, Joan McCracken, Dolores Moran, Dennis Morgan, Eleanor Parker, William Prince, Joyce Reynolds, John Ridgely, Roy Rogers and Trigger, S. Z. Sakall, Alexis Smith, Zachary Scott, Barbara Stanwyck, Craig Stevens, Joseph Szigeti, Donald Woods, Jane Wyman, Jimmy Dorsey and his Band, Carmen Cavallaro and his Orchestra, Golden Gate Quartet, Rosario and Antonio, Sons of the Pioneers, Virginia Patton, Lynne Shayne, Johnny Mitchell, John Sheridan, Colleen Townsend, Angela Green, Paul Brooke, Marianne O'Brien, Dorothy Malone, Bill Kennedy, Mary Gordon, Chef Joseph Milani, Betty Brodel.

Distributor: Warner Bros.
Director: Delmar Daves
Released: December 5, 1944

ARMY WIVES

Jerry	Elyse Knox
Mrs. Shannahan	Marjorie Rambeau
Barney	Rick Vallin
Louise	Dorothea Kent
Mike	Murray Alper
Verne	Hardie Albright
Pat Shannahan	Kenneth Brown
Billy Shannahan	Billy Lenhart
Sgt. Shannahan	Eddie Dunn

Anne Baxter, John Hodiak, Billy Cummings, Bobby Driscoll and Charles Winninger in **Sunday Dinner for a Soldier** (20th Century-Fox).

Distributor: Monogram
Director: Phil Rosen
Released: December 6, 1944

MAIN STREET AFTER DARK

Lieut. Lorrigan	Edward Arnold
Ma Dibson	Selena Royle
Lefty	Tom Trout
Jessie Belle	Audrey Totter
Posey	Dan Duryea
Keller	Hume Cronyn
Rosalie	Dorothy Ruth Morris

Distributor: M-G-M
Director: Edward Cahn
Released: December 6, 1944

SHE'S A SWEETHEART

Maxine Lecour	Jane Frazee
Rocky Hill	Larry Parks

Martha O'Driscoll and Noah Beery Jr. in **Hi Beautiful** (Universal)

Mom	Jane Darwell
Jeanne	Nina Foch
Paul	Ross Hunter
Pete Ryan	Jimmy Lloyd
Jimmy Loomis	Loren Tindall
Frances	Carole Mathews
Fred Tilly	Eddie Bruce
Matt	Pat Lane
Poker	Danny Desmond
Edith	Ruth Warren
Wes	Dave Willock

Distributor: Columbia
Director: Del Lord
Released: December 7, 1944

SUNDAY DINNER FOR A SOLDIER

Tessa	Anne Baxter

Eric Moore	John Hodiak
Grandfather	Charles Winninger
Agatha	Anne Revere
Mary	Connie Marshall
Mr. York	Chill Wills
Kenneth Normand	Robert Bailey
Jeep	Bobby Driscoll
Mrs. Dobson	Jane Darwell
Michael	Billy Cummings
Samanthy	Marietta Canty
Wac Lieutenant	Barbara Sears
M.P.	Larry Thompson
M.P.	Bernie Sell
Photographer	Chester Conklin

Distributor: 20th Century-Fox
Director: Lloyd Bacon
Released: December 8, 1944

HI BEAUTIFUL

Patty Callahan	Martha O'Driscoll
Jeff	Noah Beery, Jr.
Millie	Hattie McDaniel
Bisbee	Walter Catlett
Babcock	Tim Ryan
Mrs. Bisbee	Florence Lake
Attendant	Grady Sutton
Husband	Lou Lubin
Wife	Virginia Sale
Bus Driver	Tom Dugan
Passenger	Dick Elliott
Soldier Specialty	James Dodd

Distributor: Universal
Director: Leslie Goodwins
Released: December 18, 1944

MUSIC FOR MILLIONS

'Mike'	Margaret O'Brien
Jose Iturbi	Himself
Andrews	Jimmy Durante
Barbara Ainsworth	June Allyson
Rosalind	Marsha Hunt
Uncle Ferdinand	Hugh Herbert
Doctor	Harry Davenport
Marie	Marie Wilson
Larry	Larry Adler
Kickebush	Ben Lessy
Traveler's Aid Woman	Connie Gilchrist
Elsa	Katharine Balfour
Helen	Helen Gilbert
Anita	Mary Parker
Jane	Madeleine LeBeau

Margaret O'Brien in **Music for Millions** (M-G-M).

Distributor: M-G-M
Director: Henry Koster
Released: December 18, 1944

DANGEROUS PASSAGE

Joe Beck .... Robert Lowery

Robert Lowery and Alec Craig in **Dangerous Passage** (Paramount).

Nita Paxton	Phyllis Brooks
Daniel Bergstrom	Charles Arnt
Mike Zomano	Jack LaRue
Buck Harris	Victor Kilian
Captain Saul	William Edmunds
Dawson	Alec Craig
Vaughn	John Eldredge

Distributor: Paramount
Director: William Berke
Released: December 18, 1944

TOMORROW THE WORLD

Mike Frame	Fredric March
Leona Richards	Betty Field
Jessie	Agnes Moorehead
Emil Bruckner	Skippy Homeier
Pat Frame	Joan Carroll
Frieda	Edit Angold
Stan	Rudy Wissler
Ray	Boots Brown

Dennis	Marvin Davis
Millie	Patsy Ann Thompson
School Principal	Mary Newton
Mailman	Tom Fadden

Distributor: United Artists
Director: Leslie Fenton
Released: December 18, 1944

HERE COME THE WAVES

Johnny Cabot	Bing Crosby
Susie Allison	Betty Hutton
Rosemary Allison	Betty Hutton
Windy	Sonny Tufts
Ruth	Ann Doran
Tex	Gwen Crawford
Dorothy	Noel Neill
Lieutenant Townsend	Catherine Craig
Isabel	Marjorie Henshaw
Bandleader	Harry Barris
Ensign Kirk	Mae Clarke
High-Ranking Officer	Minor Watson
Specialty Dancers	Dorothy Jarnac
	Joel Friend
The Commodore	Oscar O'Shea
Miles and Kover Trio	Don Kramer
	Eddie Kover
	Ruth Miles
Specialty Dancers	Roberta Jonay
	Guy Zanett
First Fainting Girl	Mona Freeman

Joan Carroll with Skippy Homeier in **Tomorrow the World** (United Artists).

Sonny Tufts and Betty Hutton in **Here Come the Waves** (Paramount).

Victor Moore, Ann Miller and Kay Kyser in **Carolina Blues** (Columbia).

Bobby Larson, Tom Neal and Teddy Infuhr in **The Unwritten Code** (Columbia).

Joseph Cotten, Ginger Rogers and Tom Tully in **I'll Be Seeing You** (United Artists).

C.P.O.	William Haade
Lieutenant Commander	William Forrest
Lieutenant Colonel	Cyril Ring
Captain Johnson	Charles D. Brown

Distributor: Paramount
Director: Mark Sandrich
Released: December 18, 1944

CAROLINA BLUES

Kay Kyser	Himself
Julie Carver	Ann Miller
Phineas J. Carver	Victor Moore
Elliott Carver	Victor Moore
Hiram Carver	Victor Moore
Horatio Carver	Victor Moore
Aunt Martha Carver	Victor Moore
Aunt Minerva Carver	Victor Moore
Charlotte Barton	Jeff Donnell
Tom Gordon	Howard Freeman
Georgia Carroll	Herself
Ish Kabibble	M. A. Bogue
Harry Babbitt	Himself
Sully Mason	Himself
Diana	Diana Pendleton
Roland Frisby	Robert Williams
Skinny	Doodles Weaver
Maisie	Dorothea Kent
Cab Driver	Frank Orth
Eddie	Eddie Acuff

Distributor: Columbia
Director: Leigh Jason
Released: December 20, 1944

THE UNWRITTEN CODE

Mary Lee Norris	Ann Savage
Sergeant Terry Hunter	Tom Neal

Corporal Karl Richter	Roland Varno
Mr. Norris	Howard Freeman
Mrs. Norris	Mary Currier
Willie Norris	Bobby Larson
Dutchy Schultz	Teddy Infuhr
Heinrich Krause	Otto Reichow
Schultz	Fred Essler
Luedtke	Frederick Giermann
Kunze	Tom Holland
Ulrich	Phil Van Zandt
Schroeder	Carl Ekberg
Sheriff	Alan Bridge

Distributor: Columbia
Director: Herman Rotsten
Released: December 20, 1944

Allyn Joslyn, Evelyn Keyes, Ivan Triesault, Marguerite Chapman, Nina Foch and John Wengraf in **Strange Affair** (Columbia).

Mikhail Rasumny, Fred MacMurray and Claudette Colbert in **Practically Yours** (Paramount).

PRACTICALLY YOURS

Peggy Martin	Claudette Colbert
Lt. (S.G.) Daniel Bellamy	Fred MacMurray
Albert Beagell	Gil Lamb
Marvin P. Meglin	Cecil Kellaway
Judge Simpson	Robert Benchley
Commander Harpe	Tom Powers
Musical Comedy Star	Jane Frazee
Elen Macy	Rosemary De Camp
Mrs. Meglin	Isabel Randolph
La Crosse	Mikhail Rasumny

Distributor: Paramount

I'LL BE SEEING YOU

Mary Marshall	Ginger Rogers
Zachary Morgan	Joseph Cotten
Barbara Marshall	Shirley Temple
Mrs. Marshall	Spring Byington
Mr. Marshall	Tom Tully
Swanson	Chill Wills
Lieutenant Bruce	Dare Harris
Sailor On Train	Kenny Bowers

Distributor: United Artists
Director: William Dieterle
Released: December 20, 1944

Robert Livingston with Vera Hruba Ralston in **Lake Placid Serenade** (Republic).

Director: Mitchell Leisen
Released: December 20, 1944

STRANGE AFFAIR

Bill Harrison .... Allyn Joslyn
Jacqueline Harrison .... Evelyn Keyes
Marie Dumont .... Marguerite Chapman
Lt. Washburn .... Edgar Buchanan
Freda Brenner .... Nina Foch
Domino .... Hugo Haas
Laundry Truck Driver .... Shemp Howard
Sergeant Erwin .... Frank Jenks
Dr. Brenner .... Erwin Kalser
Leslie Carlson .... Tonio Selwart
Rudolph Kruger .... John Wengraf
Johansen .... Erik Rolf

Gloria .... Carole Mathews
Motor Cop .... Edgar Dearing
Truck Driver .... Ray Teal

Distributor: Columbia
Director: Alfred E. Green
Released: December 21, 1944

LAKE PLACID SERENADE

Vera Haschek .... Vera Rhuba Ralston
Carl Cermak .... Eugene Pallette
Countess .... Vera Vague
Paul Jordan .... Robert Livingston
Irene .... Stephanie Bachelor
Webb .... Walter Catlett
Haschek .... Lloyd Corrigan

Wallace Beery and Frank Fenton in **This Man's Navy**
(M-G-M).

287

Susan	Ruth Terry
Jiggers	William Frawley
Walter Benda	John Litel
Mayor	Ludwig Stossel
Club President	Andrew Tombes

Also: Ray Noble and Orchestra, Harry Owens Royal Hawaiians, Mcgowan and Mac, Twinkle Watts, The Merry Meisters, Roy Rogers

Distributor: Republic
Director: Steve Sekely
Released: December 21, 1944

THIS MAN'S NAVY

Ned Trumpet	Wallace Beery
Jess Weaver	Tom Drake

Michael St. Angel in **What a Blonde** (RKO).

Jimmy Shannon	James Gleason
Cathey Cortland	Jan Clayton
Maude Weaver	Selena Royle
Joe Hodum	Noah Beery, Sr.
Lieut. Cmdr. Graystone	Henry O'Neill
Tim Shannon	Steve Brodie
Bert Bland	George Chandler
Operations Officer	Donald Curtis
Cadet Rayshek	Arthur Walsh
David	Will Fowler
Sparks	Richard Crockett

Distributor: M-G-M

Director: William A. Wellman
Released: January 4, 1945

WHAT A BLONDE

Fowler	Leon Errol
Pomeroy	Richard Lane
Andrew	Michael St. Angel
Cynthia	Elaine Riley
Pat	Veda Ann Borg
Mrs. Fowler	Lydia Bilbrook
Mr. Dafoe	Clarence Kolb
Mrs. Dafoe	Ann Shoemaker
Gugliemi	Chef Milani
McPherson	Emory Parnell
Watson	Larry Wheat
Annie	Dorothy Vaughan
Redmond	Jason Robards

Distributor: RKO
Director: Leslie Goodwins
Released: February 1, 1945

THEY SHALL HAVE FAITH

Joan Randall	Gale Storm
Grandfather	C. Aubrey Smith
Tex	Johnny Mack Brown
Uncle Charles	Frank Craven
Dr. Randall	Conrad Nagel
1st Soldier	Billy Wilkerson
Aunt Mary	Mary Boland
Ricky	Johnny Downs
Martha	Catherine McLeod
Williams	Selmer Jackson
Alabam	Matt Willis
2nd Soldier	Russ Whitman

Distributor: Monogram
Director: William Nigh
Released: February 2, 1945

THE ENCHANTED COTTAGE

Laura	Dorothy McGuire
Oliver	Robert Young
Hillgrove	Herbert Marshall
Mrs. Minnett	Mildred Natwick
Volet Price	Spring Byington

Johnny Downs and Conrad Nagel in **They Shall Have Faith** (Monogram).

Beatrice	Hillary Brooke	Capt. Bill Barclay	Bill Johnson
Frederick	Richard Gaines	Harriet Corwin	Natalie Schafer
Danny	Alec Englander	Gladys Hopkins	Lee Patrick
Mrs. Stanton	Mary Worth	Junior Vanderheusen	Jess Barker
Canteen Manager	Josephine Whittell	Sarah Swanson	June Lockhart
Marine	Robert Clarke	Capt. Sanders	Marta Linden
Soldier	Edin Nicholas	Capt. Joseph Mannering	Tim Murdock

Distributor: RKO
Director: John Cromwell
Released: February 15, 1945

Distributor: M-G-M
Director: Edward Buzzell
Released: February 15, 1945

KEEP YOUR POWDER DRY

Valerie Parks	Lana Turner
Leigh Rand	Laraine Day
Ann Darrison	Susan Peters
Lieut. Col. Spottiswoode	Agnes Moorehead

OBJECTIVE, BURMA!

Major Nelson	Errol Flynn
Sergeant Treacy	James Brown
Lieutenant Jacobs	William Prince
Gabby Gordon	George Tobias

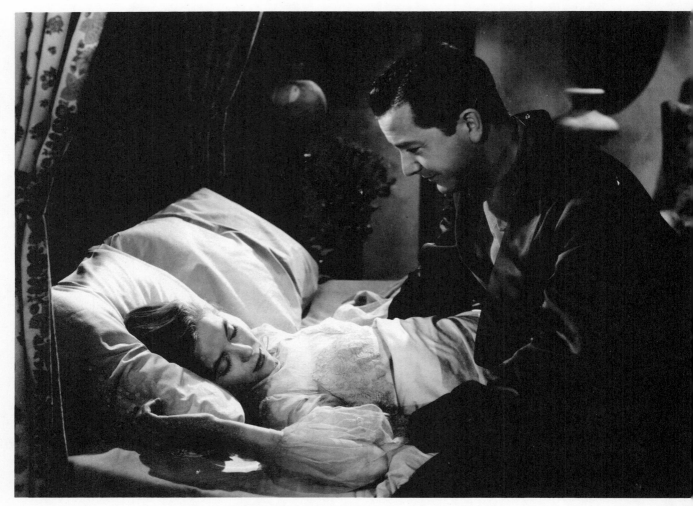

Dorothy McGuire and Robert Young in **The Enchanted Cottage** (RKO).

Jess Barker and Lana Turner in **Keep Your Powder Dry** (M-G-M).

William Prince, Warner Anderson, Erroll Flynn and Frank Tang in **Objective, Burma!** (Warner Bros.).

Mark Williams	Henry Hull
Colonel Carter	Warner Anderson
Hogan	John Alvin
Lieutenant Barker	Stephen Richards
Nebraska Hooper	Richard Erdman
Miggleori	Anthony Caruso
Captain Hennessey	Hugh Beaumont
Negulesco	John Whitney
Brophy	Joel Allen
Soapy Higgins	Buddy Yarus
Captain Li	Frank Tang
Fred Hollis	William Hudson
Sergeant Chettu	Rodd Redwing
Ghurka	Asit Koomar
Co-Pilot	John Sheridan
Major Fitzpatrick	Lester Matthews
General Stilwell	Erville Anderson

Distributor: Warner Bros—First National
Director: Raoul Walsh
Released: February 17, 1945

GOD IS MY CO-PILOT

Colonel Robert L. Scott	Dennis Morgan
Johnny Petach	Dane Clark
Major General Chennault	Raymond Massey
'Big Mike' Harrigan	Alan Hale
Catherine Scott	Andrea King
Tex Hill	John Ridgely
Colonel Meriam Cooper	Stanley Ridges
Ed Rector	Craig Stevens
Bob Neale	Warren Douglas
Sergeant Baldridge	Stephen Richards

Raymond Massey, Stephen Richards, Craig Stevens, John Ridgely, Bernie Sell, Minor Watson and Dennis Morgan in **God is My Co-Pilot** (Warner Bros.).

Private Motley	Charles Smith
Colonel Caleb V. Haynes	Minor Watson
Tokyo Joe	Richard Loo
Sergeant Aaltonen	Murray Alper
Gil Bright	Bernie Sell
Lieutenant Doug Sharp	Joel Allen

Hugh Hoo, Roland Varno and Nancy Kelly in **Betrayal from the East** (RKO).

Lieutenant 'Alabama' Wilson	John Miles
Lieutenant Jack Horner	Paul Brooke
'Prank'	Clarence Muse
Doctor Reynolds	William Forrest
Chinese Captain	Frank Tang
Japanese Announcer	Philip Ahn
Frank Schiel	Dan Dowling
General Kitcheburo	Paul Fung
Specialty Dancer	Frances Chan
British Officer-Prisoner	Sanders Clark
American Girl Prisoner	Phyllis Adair
American Pilot	Dale Van Sickle
American Pilot	Tom Steele
American Pilot	Art Foster
Scott As A Boy	Buddy Burroughs
Catherine's Father	George Cleveland
Robin Lee	Gigi Perreau
A.V.G. Groundman	Don McGuire
A.V.G. Groundman	William Challee
Newspaper Editor	Joel Friedkin
Major	James Flavin

Distributor: Warner Bros.
Director: Robert Florey
Released: February 21, 1945

BETRAYAL FROM THE EAST

Eddie	Lee Tracy
Peggy	Nancy Kelly
Tanni	Richard Loo
Yamato	Abner Biberman
Scott	Regis Toomey
Kato	Philip Ahn
Capt. Bates	Addison Richards
Purdy	Bruce Edwards
Araki	Hugh Hoo
Omaya	Sen Yung
Kurt	Roland Varno
Marsden	Louis Jean Heydt
Hildebrand	Jason Robards

Distributor: RKO
Director: William Berke
Released: February 25, 1945

G.I. HONEYMOON

Ann	Gale Storm
Bob	Peter Cookson

Gale Storm, Peter Cookson and Ralph Lewis in **G. I. Honeymoon** (Monogram).

Flo	Arline Judge
Blubber	Frank Jenks
Ace	Jerome Cowan
Lavinia	Virginia Brissac
Lieut. Randall	Ralph Lewis

Jonas	Earl Hodgins
Mrs. Barton	Ruth Lee
Rev. Horace	Andrew Tombes
Col. Smith	Jonathan Hale
Mrs. Smith	Lois Austin
Major Brown	John Valentine
Mrs. Brown	Claire Whitney
Capt. Stein	Frank Stevens
Sergt. Harrigan	Jack Overman

Distributor: Monogram
Director: Phil Karlstein
Released: February 26, 1945

HOTEL BERLIN

Martin Richter	Helmut Dantine
Lisa Dorn	Andrea King

Henry Victor, Frederick Giermann and Andrea King in **Hotel Berlin** (Warner Bros.).

Arnim Von Dahnwitz	Raymond Massey
Tillie Weiler	Faye Emerson
Johannes Koenig	Peter Lorre
Hermann Koenig	Alan Hale
Joachim Helm	George Coulouris
Von Stetten	Henry Daniell
Heinrichs	Peter Whitney
Frau Sarah Baruch	Helene Thimig
Kliebert	Steven Geray
Maj. Otto Kauders	Kurt Krueger
Walter	Paul Andor

Larry Parks, Jeanne Bates and Loren Tindall in **Sergeant Mike** (Columbia).

Dr. Dorf	Erwin Kalser
Bellboy No. 6	Dickie Tyler
Woman Tele, Msgr.	Elsa Heiis
Fritz	Frank Reicher
Kurt	Paul Panzer
Von Buelow	John Mylong
Gretchen	Ruth Albu
Gomez	Jay Novello
Frau Plottke	Lotte Stein
Franz (Barber)	Torben Meyer

Distributor: Warner Bros.
Director: Peter Godfrey
Released: March 2, 1945

SERGEANT MIKE

Allen	Larry Parks
Terry	Jeanne Bates
Simms	Loren Tindall
Patrick Henry	Jim Bannon
Sgt. Rankin	Robert Williams
Reed	Richard Powers
S. K. Arno	Larry Joe Olsen
Monohan	Eddie Acuff
Rogers	John Tyrrell
Hall	Charles Wagenheim
Mike	Himself
Pearl	Herself

Distributor: Columbia

Shelley Winters, Lee Bowman, Rita Hayworth and Florence Bates in **Tonight and Every Night** (Columbia).

Director: Harry Levin
Released: March 13, 1945

TONIGHT AND EVERY NIGHT

Rosalind Bruce .... Rita Hayworth
Paul Lundy .... Lee Bowman
Judy Kane .... Janet Blair
Tommy Lawson .... Marc Platt
Angela .... Leslie Brooks
The Great Waldo .... Professor Lamberti
Toni .... Dusty Anderson
Leslie Wiggins .... Stephen Crane
Life Photographer .... Jim Bannon

May Tolliver .... Florence Bates
Sam Royce .... Ernest Cossart
Rev. Gerald Lundy .... Philip Merivale
David Long .... Patrick O'Moore
Group Captain .... Gavin Muir
Bubbles .... Shelley Winters
Pamela .... Marilyn Johnson
Frenchie .... Mildred Law
Joan .... Elizabeth Inglise
Mrs. Peabody .... Aminta Dyne
Mrs. Good .... Joy Harrington
Annette .... Ann Codee

Distributor: Columbia
Director: Victor Saville
Released: March 16, 1945

THE MAN WHO WALKED ALONE

Corporal Marion Scott	David O'Brien
Wilhelmina Hammond	Kay Aldridge
Wiggins	Walter Catlett
Champ	Big Boy Williams
Mrs. Hammond	Isabel Randolph
Alvin Baily	Smith Ballew
Patricia Hammond	Nancy June Robinson
Aunt Harriet	Ruth Lee
Mr. Monroe	Chester Clute
Mrs. Monroe	Vivian Oakland

Distributor: PRC
Director: Christy Cabanne
Released: March 17, 1945

A scene from **The Man Who Walked Alone** (PRC).

Judy Garland and Robert Walker in **The Clock** (M-G-M).

Richard Arlen and Lola Lane in **Identity Unknown** (Republic).

IDENTITY UNKNOWN

Johnny March	Richard Arlen
Sally MacGregor	Cheryl Walker
Rocks Donnelly	Roger Pryor
Toddy Loring	Bobby Driscoll
Wanda	Lola Lane
Major Williams	Ian Keith
Joe Granowski	John Forrest
Mrs. Anderson	Sarah Padden
Mr. Anderson	Forrest Taylor
Frankie	Frank Marlowe
Harry	Harry Tyler

THE CLOCK

Alice Mayberry	Judy Garland
Corporal Joe Allen	Robert Walker
Al Henry	James Gleason
The Drunk	Keenan Wynn
Bill	Marshall Thompson
Mrs. Al Henry	Lucile Gleason
Helen	Ruth Brady

Distributor: M-G-M
Director: Vincente Minelli
Released: March 22, 1945

Marguerite Chapman and Paul Muni in **Counter-Attack** (Columbia).

Victor McLaglen, Chester Morris and Veda Ann Borg in **Rough, Tough and Ready** (Columbia).

Colonel Marlin	Nelson Leigh
Auctioneer	Charles Williams
Needles	Charles Jordan
Spike	Dick Scott
Nurse	Marjorie Manners
Motor Cop	Eddie Baker

Distributor: Republic
Director: Walter Colmes
Released: April 2, 1945

ROUGH, TOUGH AND READY

Brad Crowder	Chester Morris
Owen McCarey	Victor McLaglen

Jo Matheson	Jean Rogers		
Lorine Gray	Veda Ann Borg		
Kitty Duval	Amelita Ward	Alexei Kulkov	Paul Muni
Paul	Robert Williams	Lisa Elenko	Marguerite Chapman
Herbie	John Tyrrell	Kirichenko	Larry Parks
Tony	Fred Graff	Galkronye	Philip Van Zandt
Capt. Murray	Addison Richards	Colonel Semenov	George Macready
Lieut. Freitas	William Forrest	Kostyuk	Roman Bohnen
Brille	Tex Harding	Ernemann	Harro Meller
Peterson	Loren Tindall	Vassilev	Erik Rolf
Sparks	Bob Meredith	Stillman	Rudolph Anders
Nana	Ida Moore	Ostrovski	Ian Wolfe
O'Toole	Blackie Whiteford	Weiler	Frederick Giermann
		Krafft	Paul Andor
		Grillparzer	Ivan Triesault
		Mueller	Ludwig Donath
		Huebsch	Louis Adlon

Distributor: Columbia
Director: Del Lord
Released: April 2, 1945

J. Carrol Naish, Arturo de Cordova, Dorothy Lamour and Fernando Alvarado in **A Medal for Benny** (Paramount).

Petrov .... Trevor Bardette
General Kalinev .... Richard Hale

Distributor: Columbia
Director: Zoltan Korda
Released: April 3, 1945

A MEDAL FOR BENNY

Lolita Sierra .... Dorothy Lamour
Joe Morales .... Arturo de Cordova
Charley Martin .... J. Carrol Naish
Raphael Catalina .... Mikhail Rasumny
Chito Sierra .... Fernando Alvarado
Zack Mibbs .... Charles Dingle
Edgar Lovekin .... Frank McHugh
Toodles Castro .... Rosita Moreno
Pantara's Mayor .... Grant Mitchell
The General .... Douglas Dumbrille

Distributor: Paramount
Director: Irving Pichel
Released: April 16, 1945

Laraine Day, Ann Harding and Bill Williams in
Those Endearing Young Charms (RKO).

THOSE ENDEARING YOUNG CHARMS

Hank .... Robert Young
Helen .... Laraine Day
Mrs. Brandt .... Ann Harding
Captain Larry Stowe .... Marc Cramer
Suzanne .... Anne Jeffreys
Young Sailor .... Glenn Vernon

Haughty Floor Lady .... Norma Varden
Ted .... Lawrence Tierney
Dot .... Vera Marshe
Jerry .... Bill Williams

Distributor: RKO
Director: Lewis Allen
Released: April 27, 1945

SON OF LASSIE

Joe Curraclough .... Peter Lawford
Sam Carraclough .... Donald Crisp
Priscilla .... June Lockhart
Duke of Rudling .... Nigel Bruce
Henrik .... Billy Severn
Anton .... Leon Ames
Sergeant Eddie Brown .... Donald Curtis
Olav .... Nils Asther
Sergeant Schmidt .... Robert Lewis
Joanna .... Fay Helm
Willi .... Peter Helmers
Karl .... Otto Reichow
Hedda .... Patricia Prest
Thea .... Helen Koford
Arne .... Leon Tyler
Old Woman .... Lotta Palfi
Washwoman .... Eily Malyon
Also: Lassie and Laddie

Distributor: M-G-M
Director: S. Sylvan Simon
Released: April 20, 1945

BLOOD ON THE SUN

Nick Condon .... James Cagney
Iris Hilliard .... Sylvia Sidney
Ollie Miller .... Wallace Ford
Edith Miller .... Rosemary De Camp
Col. Tojo .... Robert Armstrong
Premiere Tanaka .... John Emery
Hijikata .... Leonard Strong
Prince Tatsugi .... Frank Puglia
Capt. Oshima .... Jack Halloran
Kajioka .... Hugh Ho
Yamamoto .... Philip Ahn
Hayashi .... Joseph Kim

Tamada	Marvin Mueller	Mrs. Lora Tedder	Irene Manning
Joseph Cassell	Rhys Williams	Captain Becker	Helmut Dantine
Arthur Bickett	Porter Hall	Dr. Orville Tedder	Alan Hale
Charley Sprague	James Bell	Gramp	Samuel S. Hinds
Amah	Grace Lem	Hank Albright	Bill Kennedy
Chinese Servant	Oy Chan	Lieut. von Kleist	Kurt Kreuger
Hotel Manager	George Paris	Hoffman	Rudolph Anders
Johnny Clarke	Hugh Beaumont	Klaus	Hans Schumm
		Danny (10 Years Old)	Blayney Lewis

Distributor: United Artists
Director: Frank Lloyd
Released: April 26, 1945

Distributor: Warner Bros.
Director: Edward A. Blatt
Released: May 1, 1945

ESCAPE IN THE DESERT

Jane	Jean Sullivan
Philip Artveld	Philip Dorn

A GUY, A GAL AND A PAL

Jimmy Jones	Ross Hunter

Peter Lawford and June Lockhart in **Son of Lassie**
(M-G-M).

Peter Chong and James Cagney in **Blood on the Sun** (United Artists).

Helen Carter	Lynn Merrick
Butch	Ted Donaldson
Granville Breckenridge	George Meeker
Norton	Jack Norton
Barclay	Will Stanton
Porter	Sam McDaniel
Mayor	Alan Bridge
Annette Perry	Mary McLeod
Mrs. Breckenridge	Mary Forbes
General	Russell Hicks
General's Wife	Nella Walker

Distributor: Columbia
Director: Oscar Boetticher, Jr.
Released: May 11, 1945

Hans Schumm and Helmut Dantine in **Escape in the Desert** (Warner Bros.).

CHINA SKY

Thompson	Randolph Scott
Sara	Ruth Warrick
Louise	Ellen Drew
Chen Ta	Anthony Quinn
Siu Mei	Carol Thurston
Col. Yasuda	Richard Loo
'Little Goat'	'Ducky' Louie
Dr. Kim	Philip Ahn
Chung	Benson Fong
Magistrate	H. T. Tsiang
Charlie	Chin Kuang Chow

Ross Hunter, Lynn Merrick and Ted Donaldson in **A Guy, a Gal and a Pal** (Columbia).

Distributor: RKO
Director: Ray Enright
Released: May 16, 1945

PILLOW TO POST

Jean Howard	Ida Lupino
Col. Otley	Sydney Greenstreet
Don Mallory	William Prince
Capt. Jack Ross	Stuart Erwin
Slim Clark	Johnny Mitchell
Mrs. Wingate	Ruth Donnelly
Mrs. Kate Otley	Barbara Brown
Taxi Driver	Frank Orth
Mrs. Mallory	Regina Wallace
Lucille	Willie Best

Ruth Warrick, Randolph Scott and Anthony Quinn
in **China Sky** (RKO).

Mr. Howard	Paul Harvey
Loolie	Carol Hughes
Wilbur	Bobby Blake
Mrs. Bromley	Anne O'Neal
Wilbur's Mother	Marie Blake
Charlotte Mills	Victoria Horne
Jerry Martin	Lelah Tyler
Doris Wilson	Sue Moore
Archie	Don McGuire
Gertrude Wilson	Joyce Compton

Distributor: Warner Bros.
Director: Vincent Sherman
Released: May 17, 1945

WHERE DO WE GO FROM HERE?

Bill	Fred MacMurray
Sally	Joan Leslie
Lucilla	June Haver
Genie (Ali)	Gene Sheldon
Indian Chief	Anthony Quinn
Benito	Carlos Ramirez
General George Washington	Alan Mowbray
Christopher Columbus	Fortunio Bonanova
Hessian Colonel	Herman Bing
Kreiger	Howard Freeman
Benedict Arnold	John Davison
Old Lady	Rosina Galli
Attorney	Fred Essler

Ida Lupino with William Prince in **Pillow to Post**
(Warner Bros.).

Gene Sheldon, Joan Leslie and Fred MacMurray in
Where Do We Go From Here? (20th Century-Fox).

Lauritz Melchior, Esther Williams, Van Johnson and
Ethel Griffies in **Thrill of a Romance** (M-G-M).

John Wayne with Beulah Bondi in **Back to Bataan**
(RKO).

Distributor: 20th Century-Fox
Director: Gregory Ratoff
Released: May 23, 1945

THRILL OF A ROMANCE

Cynthia Glenn	Esther Williams
Major Thomas Milvaine	Van Johnson
Maude Bancroft	Frances Gifford
Hobart Glenn	Henry Travers
Nona Glenn	Spring Byington
Nils Knudsen	Lauritz Melchior
Orchestra Leader	Tommy Dorsey
Robert G. Delbar	Carleton Young
Susan	Helene Stanley
K. O. Karny	Donald Curtis
Lyonel	Jerry Scott
Dr. Tove	Billy House
Mrs. Fenway	Ethel Griffies
Oscar	Vince Barnett
Julio	Fernando Alvarado
Betty	Joan Fay Macoboy
Gypsy Orchestra Leader	Carli Elinor
J. P. Bancroft	Thurston Hall
Specialty	King Sisters
Chess Player	Alex Novinsky
	Stuart Holmes
Tycoon	Pierre Watkins
Hotel Clerk	Frank Ferguson
Naval Ensign	Tim Murdock
Ga-Ga Bride	Jean Porter

Joan Woodbury, Robert Scott and Jimmy Lloyd in **Ten Cents a Dance** (Columbia).

Canadian Fliers	Douglas Cowan
	Henry Daniels, Jr.
Hotel Clerk	Selmer Jackson
Mr. Vemmering	Robert E. O'Connor
Guest At Reception	Dagmar Oakland
Johnny	Tom Brannigan
Headwaiter	Arno Frey
Mr. Carter	Dick Earle
Secretary	Virginia Brissac
Detective	Jack Baxley
Dance Extra	Ray Goulding

Distributor: M-G-M
Director: Richard Thorpe
Released: May 23, 1945

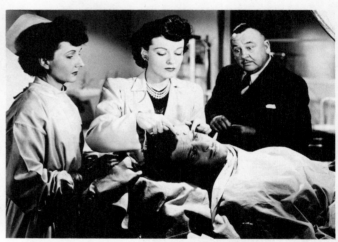

Mary Currier, Ruth Hussey, Bert Roach and John Carroll in **Bedside Manner** (United Artists).

BACK TO BATAAN

Colonel Madden	John Wayne
Captain Bonifacio	Anthony Quinn
Miss Barnes	Beulah Bondi
Dalisay	Fely Franquelli
Major Hasko	Richard Loo
Colonel Kuroki	Philip Ahn
Sgt. Biernesa	J. Alex Havier
Maximo	'Ducky' Louie
Lt. Commander Waite	Lawrence Tierney
General Homma	Leonard Strong
Jackson	Paul Fix

Ernie Pyle with Burgess Meredith in **The Story of
G. I. Joe** (United Artists).

Jap Captain	Abner Biberman
Senor Bello	Vladimir Sokoloff

Distributor: RKO
Director: Edward Dmytryk
Released: May 31, 1945

TEN CENTS A DANCE

Jeanne Hollis	Jane Frazee
Billy Sparks	Jimmy Lloyd
Ted Kimball III	Robert Scott
Babe	Joan Woodbury
Breezy Walker	John Calvert
Bits	George McKay
Joey	Edward Hyans
Sadie	Dorothea Kent
Marge	Carole Mathews
Glad	Muriel Morris

Vi	Pattie Robbins
Mae	Marilyn Johnson
Pat	Jewel McGowan
Rocky	Billy Nelson

Distributor: Columbia
Director: Will Jason
Released: June 7, 1945

BEDSIDE MANNER

Morgan Hale	John Carroll
Hedy Fredericks	Ruth Hussey
Doc Fredericks	Charles Ruggles
Lola	Ann Rutherford
Tanya	Claudia Drake
Stella	Renee Godfrey
Gravitt	Esther Dale
Mr. Pope	Grant Mitchell

Fred MacMurray in **Captain Eddie** (20th Century-Fox).

Tommy Smith	Joel McGinnis
Dick Smith	John James
Harry Smith	Frank Jenks
George	Bert Roach
Mary	Vera Marsh
Elmer Jones	Sid Saylor
Mr. Perkins	Earl Hodgins
Mrs. Livingston	Mary Currier
Mrs. Moriarity	Constance Purdy
Mrs. Pringle	Mrs. Gardner Crane
Head Waiter	Joe Devlin
Waiter	Dimitrios Alexis
Good-Looking Stranger	Don Brody

Distributor: United Artists
Director: Andrew Stone
Released: June 14, 1945

THE STORY OF G. I. JOE

Ernie Pyle	Burgess Meredith
Lieutenant Walker	Robert Mitchum
Sergeant Warnicki	Freddie Steele
Private Dondaro	Wally Cassell
Private Spencer	Jimmy Lloyd
Private Murphy	Jack Reilly
Private Mew	Bill Murphy
Cookie	William Self
Sergeant At Showers	Dick Rich
Whitey	Billy Benedict

Distributor: United Artists
Director: William A. Wellman
Released: June 18, 1945

CAPTAIN EDDIE

Edward Rickenbacker	Fred MacMurray
Adelaide	Lynn Bari
William Rickenbacker	Charles Bickford
Ike Howard	Thomas Mitchell
Lieut. Whittaker	Lloyd Nolan
Tom Clark	James Gleason
Elise Rickenbacker	Mary Philips
Eddie Rickenbacker (Boy)	Darryl Hickman
Mrs. Frost	Spring Byington
Private Bartek	Richard Conte
Sgt. Reynolds	Charles Russell
Capt. Cherry	Richard Crane
Col. Adamson	Stanley Ridges
Jabez	Clem Bevans
Lester Thomas	Grady Sutton
Lacey	Chick Chandler
Louis Rickenbacker	Swayne Hickman
Mary Rickenbacker	Mary June Robinson
Emma Rickenbacker	Winifred Glyn
Dewey Rickenbacker	Gregory Muradian
Albert Rickenbacker	David Spencer
Bill Rickenbacker	Elvin Field
Lieut. de Angelis	George Mitchell
Mr. Frost	Boyd Davis
Sgt. Alex	Lon Carner
Mrs. Westrom	Mary Gordon
Dinkenspiel	Joseph J. Greene
Census Taker	Olin Howlin
Mr. Foley	Robert Malcolm
Mrs. Foley	Leila McIntyre
Simmons	Harry Shannon
Flo Clark	Virginia Brissac
Charlie	Peter Michael
Freddie	Peter Garcy
Professor Montagne	Fred Essler
Mme. Montagne	Lotta Stein

Distributor: 20th Century-Fox
Director: Lloyd Bacon
Released: June 19, 1945

A BELL FOR ADANO

Tina	Gene Tierney
Major Joppolo	John Hodiak
Sergeant Borth	William Bendix
Lieutenant Livingstone	Glenn Langan
Nicolo	Richard Conte
Sergeant Trampani	Stanley Prager
Captain Purvis	Henry Morgan
Guiseppe	Montague Banks
Commander Robertson	Reed Hadley
Colonel Middleton	Roy Roberts
Father Pensovecchio	Hugo Haas
Zito	Marcel Dalio
Gargano	Fortunio Bonanova
Errante	Henry Armetta
Erba	Roman Bohnen

William Bendix and Eduardo Ciannelli in **A Bell for Adano** (20th Century-Fox).

Cacopardo	Luis Alberni
Mayor Nasta	Eduardo Ciannelli
Tomasino	William Edmunds
Francisca	Yvonne Vautrot
Captain Anderson	John Russell
Rosa	Anna Demetrio
Lt. Col. Sartorius	James Rennie
Mercurio Salvatore	Charles La Torre
Alfronti	Charles Judels
Basile	Frank Jaquet
Zapulla	Gino Corrado
Craxi	Peter Cusanelli
General McKay	Minor Watson
Edward	Grady Sutton
Capello	Joseph Milani
M.P.	Edward Hyans

Distributor: 20th Century-Fox
Director: Henry King
Released: June 21, 1945

Charles Drake, Lizabeth Scott, Bob Cummings and
Don DeFore in **You Came Along** (Paramount).

YOU CAME ALONG

Bob Collins	Robert Cummings
Ivy Hotchkiss	Lizabeth Scott
Shakespeare	Don De Fore
Handsome	Charles Drake
Joyce Heath	Julie Bishop
Frances Hotchkiss	Kim Hunter
Bill Allen	Robert Sully
Helen Forrest	Herself
Col. Stubbs	Rhys Williams
Hotel Clerk	Franklin Pangborn
Uncle Jack	Minor Watson
Middle-Aged Man	Howard Freeman
Second Man	Andrew Tombes
Chairman	Lewis L. Russell
Bellboy	Frank Faylen
Col. Armstrong	Will Wright
Gertrude	Cindy Garner
Carol Dix	Marjorie Woodworth
Gloria Revere	Ruth Roman
Capt. Taylor	Crane Whitley

Distributor: Paramount
Director: John Farrow
Released: July 5, 1945

ANCHORS AWEIGH

Clarence Doolittle	Frank Sinatra
Joseph Brady	Gene Kelly
Susan Abbott	Kathryn Grayson
Jose Iturbi	Himself
Donald Martin	Dean Stockwell
Carlos	Carlos Ramirez

Admiral Hammond	Henry O'Neill	Waitress	Renie Riano
Commander	Leon Ames	Commander	Alex Callam
Police Sergeant	Rags Ragland	Sailor	Harry Barris
Police Captain	Edgar Kennedy	Sailor	John James
Girl From Brooklyn	Pamela Britton	Sailor	Wally Cassell
Hamburger Man	Henry Armetta	Sailor	Douglas Cowan
Cafe Manager	Billy Gilbert	Sailor	Henry Daniels, Jr.
Little Girl Beggar	Sharon McManus	Sailor	Phil Hanna
Studio Cop	James Burke	Sailor	William 'Bill' Phillips
Radio Cop	James Flavin	Sailor	Tom Trout
Iturbi's Assistant	Chester Clute	Hamburger Woman	Esther Michelson
Bertram Kramer	Grady Sutton	Movie Director	William Forrest
Lana Turner Double	Peggy Maley	Asst. Movie Director	Ray Teal
Iturbi Secretary	Sondra Rodgers	Bartender	Milton Kibbee
Soldier	Garry Owen		
Soldier	Steve Brodie		
Butler	Charles Coleman		
Bearded Man	Milton Parsons		

Distributor: M-G-M
Director: George Sidney
Released: July 14, 1945

Frank Sinatra and Gene Kelly in **Anchors Aweigh** (M-G-M).

CHRISTMAS IN CONNECTICUT

Elisabeth Lane	Barbara Stanwyck
Jefferson Jones	Dennis Morgan
Alexander Yardley	Sydney Greenstreet
John Sloan	Reginald Gardiner
Felix Bassenak	S. Z. Sakall
Dudley Beecham	Robert Shayne
Norah	Una O'Connor
Sinkewicz	Frank Jenks
Mary Lee	Joyce Compton
Judge Crothers	Dick Elliott
Nurse Smith	Betty Alexander
Postman	Allen Fox

Irving Bacon, Leon Ames and Ginger Rogers in **Weekend at the Waldorf** (M-G-M).

Sydney Greenstreet, Dennis Morgan, S. Z. Sakall and Reginald Gardiner in **Christmas in Connecticut** (Warner Bros.).

WEEKEND AT THE WALDORF

Irene Malvern	Ginger Rogers
Chip Collyer	Walter Pidgeon
Captain James Hollis	Van Johnson
Bunny Smith	Lana Turner
Randy Morton	Robert Benchley
Martin X. Edley	Edward Arnold
Mme. Jaleska	Constance Collier
Henry Burton	Leon Ames
Dr. Campbell	Warner Anderson
Cynthia Drew	Phyllis Thaxter
Oliver Webson	Keenan Wynn
Stevens	Porter Hall

Prim Secretary	Lillian Bronson
Bartender	Charles Sherlock
Sam	Emmett Smith
Sleigh Driver	Arthur Aylesworth
Mrs. Gerseg	Jody Gilbert
Mr. Higgenbottom	Charles Arnt
Harper	Fred Kelsey
Potter	Walter Baldwin
First State Trooper	Jack Mower
Second State Trooper	John Dehner
Mrs. Wright	Marie Blake
Elkins	Olaf Hytten

Distributor: Warner Bros.
Director: Peter Godfrey
Released: July 20, 1945

Irene Dunne and Charles Coburn in **Over 21** (Columbia).

Karen Morley and John Loder in **Jealousy** (Republic).

Mr. Jessup	Samuel S. Hinds	Alix	John Wengraf
Bey Of Aribajan	George Zucco	The Woman	Ruth Lee
Xavier Cugat	Himself	Cassidy	William Hall
Juanita	Lina Romay	Pianist	Rex Evans
Singer	Bob Graham	Literary Type	Wyndham Standing
Lieutenant John Rand	Michael Kirby	Anna's Boy Friend	Harry Barris
Jane Rand	Cora Sue Collins	Barber	Byron Foulger
Anna	Rosemary De Camp	Assistant Manager	Gladden James
Kate Douglas	Jacqueline DeWit	Orchestra Leader	Carli Elinor
Emile	Frank Puglia	Bell Captain	Dick Crockett
Hi Johns	Charles Wilson		
Same Skelly	Irving Bacon		
British Secretary	Miles Mander		
Mrs. H. Davenport Drew	Nana Bryant		
McPherson	Russell Hicks		
Irma	Ludmilla Pitoeff		
Night Maid	Naomi Childers		
House Detective Blake	Moroni Olsen		
Chief Jennings	William Halligan		

Distributor: M-G-M
Director: Robert Z. Leonard
Released: July 23, 1945

OVER 21

Paula Wharton .... Irene Dunne

Don McGuire, Mark Stevens, Charles Sherlock,
Warren Douglas, John Garfield, Rosemary DeCamp
and Dane Clark in **Pride of the Marines** (Warner
Bros.).

Max Wharton	Alexander Knox
Robert Gow	Charles Coburn
Jan Lupton	Jeff Donnell
Roy Lupton	Loren Tindall
Mrs. Foley	Lee Patrick
Frank MacDougal	Phil Brown
Mrs. Gates	Cora Witherspoon
Colonel Foley	Charles Evans
Joel I. Nixon	Pierre Watkin
Mrs. Dumbrowski	Anne Loos
Mrs. Clark	Nanette Parks
Mrs. Collins	Adelle Roberts
Mrs. Greenberg	Jean Stevens

Distributor: Columbia
Director: Charles Vidor
Released: July 25, 1945

JEALOUSY

Dr. David Brent	John Loder
Janet Urban	Jane Randolph
Dr. Monica Anderson	Karen Morley
Peter Urban	Nils Asther
Hugo Kral	Hugo Haas
Melvyn Russell	Holmes Herbert
Shop Owner	Michael Mark
Bob	Mauritz Hugo
Secretary	Peggy Leon
Nurse	Mary Arden
Expressman	Noble 'Kid' Chissell

Distributor: Republic
Director: Gustav Machaty
Released: July 26, 1945

PRIDE OF THE MARINES

Al Schmid	John Garfield
Ruth Hartley	Eleanor Parker
Lee Diamond	Dane Clark
Jim Merchant	John Ridgely
Virginia Pfeiffer	Rosemary De Camp
Ella Merchant	Ann Doran
Lucy Merchant	Ann Todd
Kebabian	Warren Douglas
Irish	Don McGuire
Tom	Tom D'Andrea
Doctor	Rory Mallinson
Ainslee	Stephen Richards
Johnny Rivers	Anthony Caruso
Capt. Burroughs	Moroni Olsen
Red	Dave Willock
Second Marine	John Sheridan
Lieutenant	John Miles
Corporal	John Compton
Lenny	Lennie Bremen
Corpsman	Michael Brown

Distributor: Warner Bros.
Director: Delmar Daves
Released: August 7, 1945

DANGEROUS PARTNERS

Jeff Caighn	James Craig
Carola Ballister	Signe Hasso
Albert Richard Kingby	Edmund Gwenn
Lili Roegan	Audrey Totter
Marie Drumman	Mabel Paige
Clyde Ballister	John Warburton
Duffy	Henry O'Neill
Jonathan	Grant Withers

Distributor: M-G-M
Director: Edward L. Cahn
Released: August 7, 1945

LOVE LETTERS

Singleton	Jennifer Jones
Alan Quinton	Joseph Cotten
Dilly Carson	Ann Richards
Helen Wentworth	Anita Louise
Mack	Cecil Kellaway
Beatrice Remington	Gladys Cooper
Derek Quinton	Byron Barr
Roger Morland	Robert Sully
Defense Attorney	Reginald Denny
Bishop	Ernest Cossart
Jim Connings	James Millican
Mr. Quinton	Lumsden Hare
Mrs. Quinton	Winifred Harris
Bishop's Wife	Ethel May Halls
Judge	Matthew Boulton
Postman	David Clyde
Vicar	Ian Wolfe
Dodd	Alec Craig
Jupp	Arthur Hohl

Distributor: Paramount
Director: William Dieterle
Released: August 17, 1945

FIRST YANK INTO TOKYO

Major Ross	Tom Neal
Abby Drake	Barbara Hale

Signe Hasso with James Craig in **Dangerous Partners** (M-G-M).

Jardine	Marc Cramer
Colonel Okanura	Richard Loo
Haan-Soo	Keye Luke
Major Nogira	Leonard Strong
Captain Tanabo	Benson Fong
Major Ichibo	Clarence Lang

Joseph Cotten and Anita Louise in **Love Letters** (Paramount).

Barbara Hale with Marc Cramer in **First Yank Into Tokyo** (RKO).

Captain Sato .... Keye Chang
Captain Andrew Kent .... Michael St. Angel

Distributor: RKO
Director: Gordon Douglas
Released: September 5, 1945

THE HOUSE ON 92ND STREET

Bill Dietrich .... William Eythe
Inspector George A. Briggs .... Lloyd Nolan
Elsa Gebhardt .... Signe Hasso
Charles Ogden Roper .... Gene Lockhart
Colonel Hammersohn .... Leo G. Carroll
Johanna Scmedt .... Lydia St. Clair
Walker .... William Post, Jr.

Lt. Commander Stowe .... Roland Varno
Sergeant McNair .... Andrew McLaglen

Distributor: United Artists
Director: Gregory Ratoff
Released: September 14, 1945

KISS AND TELL

Corliss Archer .... Shirley Temple
Dexter Franklin .... Jerome Courtland
Mr. Archer .... Walter Abel
Mrs. Archer .... Katharine Alexander
Uncle George .... Robert Benchley
Mr. Franklin .... Porter Hall
Mrs. Franklin .... Edna Holland
Mildred Pringle .... Virginia Welles
Mr. Pringle .... Tom Tully
Mrs. Pringle .... Mary Philips
Raymond Pringle .... Darryl Hickman
Pvt. Jimmy Earhart .... Scott Mc Kay
Lenny Archer .... Scott Elliott
Louise .... Kathryn Card

Distributor: Columbia
Director: Richard Wallace
Released: October 3, 1945

STRANGE HOLIDAY

John Stephenson .... Claude Rains

Martin Kosleck, Claude Rains and Paul Dubov in
Strange Holiday (Elite Pictures).

Robert Walker, Jean Porter and Keenan Wynn in
What Next, Corporal Hargrove? (M-G-M).

John, Jr. .... Bobbie Stebbins
Peggy Lee .... Barbara Bates
Woodrow .... Paul Hilton
Mrs. Jean Stephenson .... Gloria Holden
Sam Morgan .... Milton Kibbee
Farmer .... Walter White
Truck Driver .... Wally Maher
Examiner .... Martin Kosleck
Betty .... Priscilla Lyon
Boyfriend .... David Bradford

Distributor: Elite Pictures
Director: Arch Oboler
Released: October 19, 1945

WHAT NEXT, CORPORAL HARGROVE?

Corporal Marion Hargrove .... Robert Walker
Pvt. Thomas Mulvehill .... Keenan Wynn
Jeanne Ouidoc .... Jean Porter
Sergeant Cramp .... Chill Wills
Mayor Ouidoc .... Hugh Haas
Bill Burk .... William 'Bill' Phillips
Marcel Vivin .... Fred Essler
Joe Lupot .... Cameron Mitchell
Curtis .... Tom Landigan
Neilson .... Dick Hirbe
Ellerton .... Arthur Walsh
Gilly .... Maurice Marks
Captain Drake .... Paul Langton
Sergeant Hill .... James Davis

John Wayne, Donna Reed and Robert Montgomery
in **They Were Expendable** (M-G-M).

Lieutenant Morley	John Carlyle		'Boats' Mulcahey	Ward Bond
Major Kingby	Walter Sande		Ensign Snake Gardner	Marshall Thompson
Captain Parkson	Theodore Newton		Ensign 'Andy' Andrews	Paul Langton
Lieutenant Dillon	Robert Kent		Major James Morton	Leon Ames
Sergeant Staple	Matt Willis		Seaman Jones	Arthur Walsh
Chaplain Mallowy	Richard Bailey		Lieutenant 'Shorty' Long	Donald Curtis

Distributor: M-G-M
Director: Richard Thorpe
Released: November 21, 1945

THEY WERE EXPENDABLE

Lieutenant John Brickley	Robert Montgomery		Ensign George Cross	Cameron Mitchell
Lieutenant 'Rusty' Ryan	John Wayne		Ensign Tony Aiken	Jeff York
Lieutenant Sandy Davyss	Donna Reed		'Slug' Mahan	Murray Alper
General Martin	Jack Holt		'Squarehead' Larsen	Harry Tenbrook
			'Doc' The Storekeeper	Jack Pennick
			Benny Lecoco	Alex Havier
			Admiral Blackwell	Charles Trowbridge
			The General	Robert Barrat
			Elder Tompkins	Bruce Kellogg
			Ensign Brown	Tim Murdock
			Ohio	Louis Jean Heydt
			Dad Knowland	Russell Simpson